T0234575

Lecture Notes in Computer Science 9578

Commenced Publication in 1973
Founding and Former Series Editors:
Gerhard Goos, Juris Hartmanis, and Jan van Leeuwen

More information about this series at http://www.springer.com/series/7410

Erich Rome · Marianthi Theocharidou
Stephen Wolthusen (Eds.)

Critical Information Infrastructures Security

10th International Conference, CRITIS 2015
Berlin, Germany, October 5–7, 2015
Revised Selected Papers

 Springer

Editors
Erich Rome
Autonomus Intelligent Systems
Fraunhofer Institute
Sankt Augustin
Germany

Stephen Wolthusen
University of London
London
UK

Marianthi Theocharidou
Institute for the Protection and Security
  of the Citizen
European Commission - Joint Research
  Centre
Ispra
Italy

ISSN 0302-9743   ISSN 1611-3349   (electronic)
Lecture Notes in Computer Science
ISBN 978-3-319-33330-4   ISBN 978-3-319-33331-1   (eBook)
DOI 10.1007/978-3-319-33331-1

Library of Congress Control Number: 2016934196

LNCS Sublibrary: SL4 – Security and Cryptology

Printed on acid-free paper

This Springer imprint is published by Springer Nature
The registered company is Springer International Publishing AG Switzerland

Preface

The 2015 International Conference on Critical Information Infrastructures Security (CRITIS 2015) was the tenth conference in the series, which has accompanied and in many cases anticipated the developments in information infrastructure security and the increasingly tight integration of information systems with the physical infrastructure and cyber-physical systems in general. The conference not only provides a forum for the research community from academia but also offers links to the application domains, government, and supranational entities.

The present volume contains the carefully reviewed proceedings of the 10th CRITIS, held October 5–7 at the Fraunhofer Forum in Berlin, Germany. As the field expands, the conference still retains its concentrated single-track character to ensure that discussion and analysis are possible. As a result of this, we were able to accept 18 papers out of a total of 53 submissions, each of which was carefully peer reviewed anonymously by at least three expert reviewers, resulting in an acceptance rate of approximately 34 %. In addition, six short papers with work in progress were also selected for oral presentation.

The topics covered by the research papers range from the abstract analysis of resilience and robustness in individual and interconnected infrastructure networks employing a number of distinct approaches to analyses of cyber-physical and particularly control systems security with an emphasis on the energy sector. Another area of continued interest to the community also reflected in the papers is the construction and validation of models or exercises, which are accompanied by case studies allowing the validation and sharing of experiences.

As in previous years, while CRITIS is proudly international in its scope, it also serves as an informal forum for the European research community in the critical infrastructures area. By offering a space for poster presentations and discussions, researchers are made aware of on-going developments that are perhaps not yet or not fully reflected in publications and are given an opportunity to exchange views on them and not only on the oral presentations of finalized research.

This continuation of the series of successful CRITIS workshops has once again allowed the research and stakeholder community from academia, research institutions, industry, and government entities to meet and exchange views covering the key areas facing critical infrastructure protection. This was reflected in the carefully selected full research papers as well as in discussions and the poster talks.

The research papers in this volume further reflect the feedback and discussions at the workshop. Similar care was also applied to demonstrations and poster presentations. ENEA demonstrated a decision support system for CI operators that is in use by CI operators in Italy, showing that it is possible to transfer CIP research results into practical application. The posters displayed a representative sample of current C(I)IP research.

In continuation of an initiative first taken up at the 2014 CRITIS, the conference also included an award for young researchers in the area (the 2nd CIPRNet Young CRITIS Award), seeking to recognize and encourage the integration of talented younger researchers into the community. The three candidate papers are featured in a dedicated section of this volume. This year's CYCA award was bestowed to Varun Badrinath Krishna for the paper titled "ARIMA-Based Modeling and Validation of Consumption Readings in Power Grids."

A number of keynote talks rounded off the conference program, covering government, academia, industry, and supranational entities. Cyrill Brunschwiler (Compass Security, Germany) spoke on "Urgency and Key Success Factors of Security Audits in Critical Energy Infrastructure," continuing the informal emphasis on energy infrastructure security. The cyber aspect was presented by Andy Mühlheim (SwissGrid, Switzerland) in his keynote "Critical Systems Protection in a Connected World." Resilience was the main theme of the keynote talks by Evangelos Ouzounis (ENISA, Greece; "Enhancing the Security of Critical Infrastructures — ENISA's Approach") and Margot Weijnen (TU Delft, The Netherlands; "Shaping Resilient Critical Infrastructures in a Fragmented World"), while the keynote by Timo Hauschild (Federal Office for Information Security, Germany) investigated the balance between government–industry cooperation and regulation in his talk ("Cooperative and Regulation Approaches in a Changing IT Threat Landscape"). We would like to use this preface to once again express our gratitude to these keynote speakers.

A year that has seen the security of control systems and particularly their use in cyber-warfare move from a somewhat theoretical approach only recently to a commonplace aspect of conflict that is also reflected in mainstream media and the national security strategies of many nations continues to emphasize the importance of the CRITIS conference while a number of related, specialized events pick up on some of the themes originating over the past decade at CRITIS. As the research community as a whole grows it may no longer be possible to have a single integrating event, but we believe that the role of CRITIS will continue to evolve as a nucleus for such lines of enquiry.

As always, the realization of a conference does not happen in a vacuum, and it is first and foremost the authors and conference participants with their original research contributions and interactions with speakers and panelists that shape the character and success of the CRITIS conference. We would also like to thank the Technical Program Committee members whose timely and thorough reviews helped ensure not only the high quality of the research contributions, but also provided valuable insights to authors. We look forward to the second decade of the CRITIS conference.

February 2015   Erich Rome

                                                  Marianthi Theocharidou

                                                  Stephen Wolthusen

Organization

CRITIS 2015 was organized by Fraunhofer Institute for Intelligent Analysis and Information Systems (IAIS) and hosted by the Fraunhofer Forum Berlin, Germany.

Executive Committee

General and Local Chair

Erich Rome   Fraunhofer IAIS, Germany

Program Co-chairs

Marianthi Theocharidou   European Commission Joint Research Centre, Italy
Stephen Wolthusen   Royal Holloway, University of London, UK and Gjøvik
                            University College, Norway

Publicity Chair

Cristina Alcaraz   University of Málaga, Spain

Conference Series Chairs

Bernhard Hämmerli   ACRIS and HSLU, Switzerland
Javier Lopez   University of Málaga, Spain

Steering Committee

Bernhard Hämmerli   ACRIS and HSLU, Switzerland
Javier Lopez   University of Málaga, Spain
Stephen Wolthusen   Royal Holloway, University of London, UK and Gjøvik
                            University College, Norway
Erich Rome   Fraunhofer IAIS, Germany
Marianthi Theocharidou   European Commission Joint Research Centre, Italy
Eric Luiijf   TNO, The Netherlands
Sandro Bologna   AIIC, Italy
Cristina Alcaraz   University of Málaga, Spain

International Program Committee

Cristina Alcaraz   University of Málaga, Spain
Fabrizio Baiardi   Università di Pisa, Italy
Yohan Barbarin   CEA, France
Robin Bloomfield   City University London, UK
Sandro Bologna   AIIC, Italy
Stefan Brem   Federal Office for Civil Protection, Switzerland

Emiliano Casalicchio	Università di Tor Vergata, Italy
Michael Choras	University of Technology and Life Sciences, Poland
Jacques Colliard	Union Internationale des Chemins de Fer, France
Jorge Cuellar	Siemens, Germany
Gregorio d'Agostino	ENEA and AIIC, Italy
Geert Deconinck	K.U. Leuven, Belgium
Claudia Eckert	TU Munich and Fraunhofer SIT, Germany
Mohamed Eid	CEA, France
Katrin Franke	Gjøvik University College, Norway
Georgios Giannopoulos	European Commission Joint Research Centre, Italy
Stefanos Gritzalis	University of the Aegean, Greece
Bernhard Hämmerli	ACRIS and HSLU, Switzerland
Chris Hankin	Imperial College, UK
Pieter Hartel	University of Twente, The Netherlands
Leon Hempel	TU Berlin, Germany
Panayiotis Kotzanikolaou	University of Piraeus, Greece
Rafal Kozik	University of Technology and Life Sciences, Poland
Elias Kyriakides	University of Cyprus
Javier Lopez	University of Málaga, Spain
Eric Luiijf	TNO, The Netherlands
José Marti	University of British Columbia, Canada
Fabio Martinelli	IIT-CNR, Italy
Antonello Monti	RWTH Aachen, Germany
Igor Nai Fovino	European Commission Joint Research Centre, Italy
Eiji Okamoto	University of Tsukuba, Japan
Evangelos Ouzonis	ENISA, Greece
Stefano Panzieri	Università di Roma Tre, Italy
Erich Rome	Fraunhofer IAIS, Germany
Vittorio Rosato	ENEA, Italy
Andre Samberg	Sec-Control, Finland
Antonio Scala	CNR, Italy
Dominique Sérafin	CEA, France
Roberto Setola	Università CAMPUS Bio-Medico, Italy
Marianthi Theocharidou	European Commission Joint Research Centre, Italy
Paul Theron	Thales, France
Alberto Tofani	ENEA, Italy
Simona Louise Voronca	Transelectrica, Romania
Stephen Wolthusen	Royal Holloway, University of London, UK and Gjøvik University College, Norway
Christos Xenakis	University of Piraeus, Greece
Annette Zijderveld	Deltares, The Netherlands

Additional Reviewers

Abbasi, Ali
Caselli, Marco
Cazorla, Lorena
Di Pietro, Antonio
Flourentzou, Nikolas
Klaoudatou, Eleni

Kokolakis, Spyros
Levy-Bencheton, Cedric
Liveri, Dimitra
Mattioli, Rossella
McEvoy, Richard
Paterson, Kenny

Salako, Kizito
Samberg, Andre
Tonelli, Federico
Tsohou, Aggeliki

Supporting Institutions

Fraunhofer IAIS   Fraunhofer Institute for Intelligent Analysis
                     and Information Systems
CIPRNet   EU FP7 project
AIIC   Italian Association of Critical Infrastructures' Experts
JRC   European Commission Joint Research Centre

Sponsoring Institutions

Compass Security Deutschland GmbH

Contents

Selected Short Papers

Critical Information Infrastructure Protection

Security Architecture and Specification Framework for Safe and Secure Industrial Automation

Sergey Tverdyshev[1], Holger Blasum[1], Ekaterina Rudina[2(✉)], Dmitry Kulagin[2], Pavel Dyakin[2], and Stanislav Moiseev[2]

[1] Sysgo AG, Am Pfaffenstein 14, 55270 Klein-winternheim, Germany
{sergey.tverdyshev,holger.blasum}@sysgo.com
[2] Kaspersky Lab, Leningradskoe Shosse 39A/3, Moscow 125212, Russia
{ekaterina.rudina,dmitry.kulagin,pavel.dyakin,
stanislav.moiseev}@kaspersky.com

Abstract. Today policy specification and enforcement mechanisms are often interwoven with the industrial control processes on which the security policy is enforced. This leads to interferences and non-secure behaviour as well as increases system attack surface. This paper presents a security system architecture and a framework where the processes, policies, and enforcement are strictly separated. The security architecture follows separation and least-privilege principles. The policy framework is based on a formal language and tools to specify and generate components for the security architecture. We illustrate our approach on an technological process and present how this solution is implemented in practice where security is mixed with safety requirements such as real-time, worst case execution time and certification.

Keywords: Security policy · Linear Temporal Logic · Industrial control system · Separation kernel

1 Introduction

Weaknesses of modern industrial control systems are caused by multiple reasons. Networked systems with historically grown architectures, made up from heterogeneous devices are very difficult to maintain, support and update. Usage rules and policies sometimes do not provide the necessary level of security, because the system has to operate (i.e. functional safety) and provide technological management interface. Weakly controlled access to the control interface of the critical-purpose system may have dire consequences.

In all use-cases security of the technological process shall be provided. This security should be gained not only by restricting access to the system. The human factor can thwart all measures of controlling the remote or physical access to the system (e.g. angry net-admin), particularly if the system should have emergency personnel access.

© Springer International Publishing Switzerland 2016
E. Rome et al. (Eds.): CRITIS 2015, LNCS 9578, pp. 3–14, 2016.
DOI: 10.1007/978-3-319-33331-1_1

Even for all seemingly authorized accesses, operational control must comply with the policy that will keep the technological process within its safe execution boundaries, e.g. building up or reducing pressure or temperature, or a process with big inertial or sensitive thresholds.

There are plenty examples where technological process got out of safe boundaries. On August of 2010 at Millard Refrigerated Services, in Alabama, U.S. the hydraulic shock caused a roof-mounted 12-inch suction pipe to catastrophically fail. This led to the release of more than 32,000 pounds of anhydrous ammonia [1]. There were more than 150 exposed victims, 32 of which required hospitalization, and 4 were placed in intensive care. Except of the failure of roof-mounted piping it also caused an evaporator coil inside the facility to rupture.

The hydraulic shock occurred during the restart of the plant's ammonia refrigeration system following a 7-hour power outage. While this incident was not a cyberattack, it is disturbing that the control program didn't prevent the dangerous attempt to restart and diagnose the system that caused the momentary pressure rise in the pipes. In case of the unauthorized access to the system the catastrophe may repeat.

As described in recent report of German government's Bundesamt für Sicherheit in der Informationstechnik [2] there was an incident where a malicious actor infiltrated a steel facility. To gain access to the corporate network the attacker used the spear phishing email. Then he moved into the plant network (it isn't reported how, but he probably traversed through trusted zones and connections between the corporate and plant network). The adversary showed knowledge of industrial control systems (ICS) and was able to cause multiple components of the system to fail. This specifically impacted critical process components to become unregulated, which has resulted in massive physical damage. This is one more case where the security control of the process operations would help to mitigate the harmful consequences of unauthorized access to the industrial system network.

The incidents with gathering unauthorized access to Internet-exposed SCADA systems are quite common now. But the process can be impacted also by insiders such as in Maroochy in 2000 [3] or due to complicated malware attack as was demonstrated by Stuxnet in 2010 [4].

2   Related Work

Common ICS security approaches are often inherited from the real-world constraints. They are pretty close to the principles of the role-based access control except that the access control on its own is unable to guarantee the proper execution of the process. Role-based security principles are unable to take into account the constraints on operations sequence and time-based issues. Such constraints may be very important in industrial control systems.

Mossakowski et al. [5] concluded that classical role-based access control (RBAC) provides the separation of duties principle but it doesn't factor the sequence of states in making a security decision. They proposed a security model extended by temporal logic to specify the execution sequences. However, they don't describe any implementation of the extended security models.

A similar approach is proposed by Mondal et al. [6]. They described a formal technique to perform security analysis on the Generalized Temporal RBAC (GTRBAC) model [7–9]. This model can be used to express a range of temporal constraints on different RBAC components like role, user and permission. In GTRBAC time is represented by a periodic expression [10]. To validate the GTRBAC model authors map it to the state transition system built using timed automata. Each of the constraints of GTRBAC model is also mapped to the timed automaton. As shown in the paper all the features of GTRBAC model can be represented using timed automata.

An interesting approach to expressing information flow policies for imperative programs is demonstrated by Balliu et al. [11]. Authors connect temporal epistemic logic and several security conditions studied in the area of language-based security. They claim that temporal epistemic logic appears to be a well suited logical framework to express and study information flow policies.

The state-based security conditions related to noninterference for confidentiality (absence of "bad" information flows) and declassification (intended release of information) are addressed in the paper. The considered attack in this approach is basically reduced to observing the system activities and deducing the information about process execution. This approach may be quite useful for monitoring the safety-critical processes but the security objectives addressed in this work are not really applicable to industrial automation because in ICS security the confidentiality of process execution is not an issue and often can be found in public sources (e.g. in form of Process Hazard Analysis [12]). The only considered impact of an attack is the direct influence on technological process, whether it was intentional or not.

Today policy specification and enforcement mechanisms are often interwoven with the process on which the policy is to be enforced [13,14]. That makes it hard to separate policy from enforcement objectives and lead to non-secure behaviour.

Flux Advanced Security Kernel (FLASK) [15] implements the idea of separation of access computation and decision enforcement. This implementation is based on two key concepts: a security server, that contains policy implementations, and object managers which are responsible for querying the security server and enforcing access decisions. Such a separation is an important step towards more flexible and reusable policies. We employ and enhance this idea by offering a number of architectural and language concepts, which, applied together, form a flexible security specification and enforcement system.

The principle of separation between the resource and application layers with minimal trusted base for the enforcement of security policies has been studied since 80s [21]. This principles are well known as Multiple Independent Levels of Security (MILS) architecture. The recently published technical report in the EURO-MILS project [20] defines a template to specify and design a MILS system with a precise operation of concerns and use-cases. The proposed security architecture follows the ideas summarised in the template.

3   Main Contribution

The objective of this research is to provide a solution to keep the execution of technological process in industrial control system safe and secure even in case of malicious activity. In this paper we

- propose a generic comprehensive security architecture with separated application execution, policy computation, and policy enforcement
- define an adaptive security framework to specify security policies
- present an implementation of the security architecture and the framework which preserves safety, real-time execution, reliability, components and resources availability etc.

The cornerstone of the solution is a security system architecture and a framework which are designed to provide support for diverse security policies. Flexibility is an essential requirement because there cannot be a single definition of security, e.g. different deployments even with one site. capability-based systems), but in practice, it is insufficient to rely on a single security policy or a fixed list of policies. We achieve this flexibility by separating a security-related logic from applications implementing the business logic/technological process. This approach has a number of advantages. From application point of view

- there is no need for applications to implement security policies
- there is no need to change applications if the security policy changes
- security policy is not limited to the means supported by applications.

We also strengthen the security part (i.e. the security of the security mechanics themselves) because

- policies are abstracted away from applications
- policies operate over abstract domains
- policies are not aware of differences between applications, resources, etc.
- policy may remain stable even if applications change significantly
- system-wide security policy is a composition of smaller policies.

The paper is structured as follows. In Sect. 4 we propose the architecture that allows different objects and subjects interact and coexist in a secure way. In Sect. 5 we define a framework which enables the system designer specify his system for both safety and security and instantiate the security architecture with his configuration. We illustrate usage of our framework on a simple technological process in Sect. 6. Finally, in Sect. 7 we show how the security architecture and the framework are implemented, i.e. how a secure industrial control system is created.

4   Security System Architecture

The architecture consists of three separated layers (cf. Fig. 1).

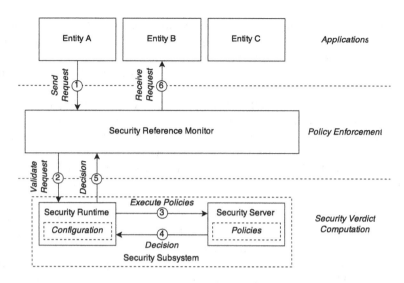

Fig. 1. Security system architecture

- Application layer: execution environments
- Security Reference Monitor (SRM): enforcement of the security verdict
- Security Subsystem: computation of a security verdict.

Application layer consists of separated execution environments, where technology specific applications are executed, e.g. interaction between processes, external communications, local computations, process control, human-machine interfaces etc. We employ the term *entity* to describe any part of application such as separated technological processes, domain, or subject whose behaviour can be described in terms of a security policy. Entities interact with each other by sending and receiving messages.

The layer for the security subsystem computes a verdict based on system state, input data, and configured security policy.

Each entity on its execution is associated with *a security context*. A security context is a data structure, which is used by stateful polices to keep security related attributes required to compute a decision. In fact, a policy knows nothing about the entity, except for its security context.

The security subsystem layer consists of two separated components a *security server* and a *security runtime*. The security runtime for each message, intercepted by SRM:

- builds the set of policies which have to be applied to this particular interaction according to security configuration
- requests the security server to compute those policies
- combines the results of the computation into the final access decision
- communicates the decision to the enforcement layer.

Security server is a component which contains implementations of all policies, manages security contexts and serves requests on policy calculation from security runtime. Security server provides interfaces to plug in external verdict engines for specific security requirements (e.g. file system with specific policy for files accesses).

The layer for the Security Reference Monitor (SRM) enforces the computed verdict on technological processes and the system as whole. The SRM controls the execution of entities, mediates interactions between entities, and communicates with the security runtime to receive and enforce the verdicts.

The verdict can be from simple "don't transfer this data", "don't allow open the file" to more complex such as "restart/pause/activate entities".

In short, the SRM can be viewed as the infrastructural level which enables entities to work, and sets up communication channels to let the information flow. SRM also guarantees that the channels do not leak, are correctly interconnected, and the channels endpoints are opened when it's allowed. The security subsystem is responsible to control content of the pipe with respect to the configured security policy. Thus, our architecture allows an easy separation of functionality, security policies, and security enforcement.

5   Framework for Security Policy Definition

The framework consists of a set of policies templates for the security server, interface definition language (IDL), security specification language (which is called CFG), and toolchain to translate specification into executable programs. Figure 2 illustrates how the framework works with the security architecture.

Security Server Templates. The framework provides a number of policies implementing specific access control approaches, e.g. type enforcement, time logic-based safety properties specifications, multilevel security. The security server can be easily extended with new policies.

Each policy may have its own, policy specific configuration, and thus, many policies operate domain specific notions (for example, multilevel security models operate by labels, sensitivities and categories, type enforcement operates by domains, types etc.). These notations require support for

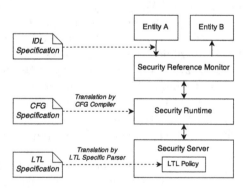

Fig. 2. Framework role in the security architecture

policy-specific configurations. The framework allows a policy developer to define such policy-specific configurations as well as to integrate a parser implementation for these configurations. In Sect. 6.2 we show how this approach to custom policy configuration works with a policy, which verifies a safety property specified as a temporal logic statement.

Interface Definition Language (IDL) is used to statically declare messages structure of every interaction between applications/entities in the system. Declared interfaces serves as anchor points in security specification to associate interactions and policies to validate them.

To configure system-wide security policy, the framework provides **specification language CFG**. It allows to specify for every interaction in the system, which policies should be applied. It also allows to specify custom policy configuration if a policy requires such a configuration. CFG is a declarative, suitable for static analysis language.

CFG compiler translates specification into C-code of security runtime component. Thus, the security runtime is a component, directly obtained from CFG specification.

6 Framework Application on a Typical Industrial Control System

6.1 Industrial Process Specification

In this section we introduce a simple processing unit which we use as the running example in this paper. This unit consists of the conveyor transferring the detail and the drill which makes a hole in this detail in the given location when the detail is under the drill.

The interesting part of the technological process consists of moving the belt to position the workpiece under the drill, running the drill, descending the drill (i.e. drilling itself), elevating the drill, and stopping the drill.

In this example, the system can be viewed as consisted of two communicating parties: entity, sending control commands (SCADA), and entity, responsible for command implementation and sending sensor information (Factory).

Control interface (IFactory) and sensor notification interface are defined using IDL:

```
package Factory
interface IFactory {      /* Factory control interface */
    BeltOn();             /* turn conveyor belt on  */
    BeltOff();            /* turn conveyor belt off */
    DrillOn();            /* turn drill on  */
    DrillOff();           /* turn drill off */
    DrillPlateDown();     /* let drill plate down */
    DrillPlateRaise();    /* raise drill plate */
    DrillPlateOn();       /* turn drill plate on */
    DrillPlateOff();      /* turn drill plate off */

}
interface IStatus {       /* Factory status interface */
```

```
BeltOn();              /* conveyor belt was turned on  */
BeltOff();             /* conveyor belt was turned off */
DrillPlateRaised();    /* drill plate is at the highest position */
DrillPlateDown();      /* drill plate is at the lowest position  */
}
```

Our purpose is to identify and specify safety properties for this small part of the process, thus, we are looking for conditions which are necessary to avoid breaking the drill or the detail. The identified constraints for this process are defined as follows:

- drilling is not allowed if the belt is currently moving on
- the conveyor can't be started while drilling
- the drill can't be descended if it is not run
- drilling can't be stopped if drill is not elevated.

Some conditions may depend on input provided by installed sensors. For example, drilling can't be run if the detail is not positioned properly, or the drill must be run at specific RPM.

6.2 Formalizing Safety Properties with Linear Temporal Logic

Linear Temporal Logic (LTL) is a useful tool in formal specification and runtime verification of temporal safety properties. LTL formulae define a set of event traces where each even has an index and an identifier of its type (such as observed command or action). In the running example, informal drilling safety properties for drilling (see Sect. 6.1) are expressed in LTL as a custom policy for security server and placed in a file "drill.tl":

```
C:DrillOn       ==> !S:BeltOn SINCE S:BeltOff
C:BeltOn        ==> !(!C:DrillOff SINCE C:DrillOn)
C:DrillPlateOn ==> !C:DrillOff SINCE C:DrillOn
C:DrillOff      ==> !C:DrillPlateOn SINCE S:DrillPlateRaised
```

where'|','!' and'==>' mean OR, NOT and IMPLY respectively.

6.3 Security Specification with CFG Language

So far we have two interacting entities SCADA and Factory, which use interfaces IFactory and IStatus to communicate. We have also formalized safety properties of the interesting part of the process encoded with LTL notation and stored in file "drill.tl". We have all pieces in place to provide CFG specification for the system.

```
01 use init policy drill_ltl_init = SecurityServer.LTL.init;
02 use call policy drill_ltl     = SecurityServer.LTL.call "drill.tl";
03 use call policy allow         = SecurityServer.Basic.allow;
```

```
04 entity Factory {
05    execute default = drill_ltl_init;
06    /* Status message */
07    send out IStatus.BeltOn          = drill_ltl "S:BeltOn";
08    send out IStatus.BeltOff         = drill_ltl "S:BeltOff";
09    send out IStatus.DrillPlateRaised = drill_ltl "S:DrillPlateRaised";
10    send out IStatus.DrillPlateDown  = drill_ltl "S:DrillPlateDown";
11    /* Control message */
12    receive in IFactory.BeltOn       = drill_ltl "C:BeltOn";
13    receive in IFactory.BeltOff      = drill_ltl "C:BeltOff";
14    receive in IFactory.DrillOn      = drill_ltl "C:DrillOn";
15    receive in IFactory.DrillOff     = drill_ltl "C:DrillOff";
16    receive in IFactory.DrillPlateDown  = drill_ltl "C:DrillPlateDown";
17    receive in IFactory.DrillPlateRaise = drill_ltl "C:DrillPlateRaise";
18    receive in IFactory.DrillPlateOff   = drill_ltl "C:DrillPlateOff";
19 }
20 entity SCADA {
21    execute default = allow;
22    send    in IFactory.* = allow;
23    receive in IStatus.*  = allow;
24 }
```

Let's each line in more detail. Line 1 declares that init policy SecurityServer.LTL.init is used in this specification under name drill_ltl_init. *Init policy* is a special kind of policy which is typically applied on entity execution and it's main purpose is to initialize the security context for newly created subject. Line 2 declares that call policy SecurityServer.LTL.call is used in this specification under name drill_ltl. The generic policy is parameterized with particular LTL statements from file "drill.tl". *Call policy* is used to control interactions. Line 3 declares usage of a very basic call policy, which just permits any interaction if applied. Lines 4–19 describe security specification for entity Factory. It has three parts: execute section, sent messages control and received messages control. Execute section at line 5 specifies that on Factory-entity creation newly created security context has to be initialized with policy drill_ltl_init. Lines 7–10 specify what type of event should be fed into LTL policy when Factory sends particular sensor notification. For example, when Factory sends notification BeltOn, the policy emits an event of type "S:BeltOn". Similarly, lines 11–18 specify what type of event should be fed into LTL policy when Factory accepts a command. But here, if a command violates safety properties stated in "drill.tl", policy prohibits its execution. Lines 20–23 specify very permissive configuration for SCADA (all communications are allowed), since all interesting events are handled on Factory side.

As one can see, CFG allows us easily to bind formal symbols from LTL statements to particular commands and sensor notifications in a very concise way.

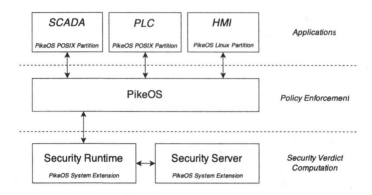

Fig. 3. Security system implementation (instantiation of Fig. 1)

7   Security System Implementation

The described solution is implemented as a security system collaboratively developed by SYSGO AG [16] and Kaspersky Lab [17]. Figure 3 depicts the implementation of the concept presented in Sect. 4.

The security system architecture is based on the virtualisation platform PikeOS [18] and covers safety and security aspects on resource and application execution layers. The PikeOS role is to

- implement the Security Reference Monitor (SRM)
- provide separated environment for entity execution
- provide separated and protected environment for execution of the security subsystem
- provide controlled communication channels between entities
- provide corset and interfaces for the security architecture defined in Sect. 4
- enforce safety policy for resource usage (e.g. memory, CPU) and guarantee real-time requirements
- provide high-assurance certification guarantees according to IEC61508 up to SIL4, IEC62443, and Common Criteria.

The implementation of the framework and security subsystem is based on a set of Kaspersky Lab technologies. The security runtime code is generated from CFG security specification for the SCADA and PLC domains as well as the domain for the operator's panel (HMI). The security runtime is a glue between SCADA, PLC, HMI and the security server and issues calls into the security server to calculate access decision with policies it contains. The verdict logic for the HMI is generated from a simple access control list.

The framework toolchain extensively uses model based specification and code generation (for both security runtime and parts of security server) to exclude human factor from the implementation of specification for the critical system.

8   Conclusions and Future Work

In this work we have presented a security system architecture for industrial control system which follows separation principles. We explicitly split between evaluation of security policies, enforcement of security verdicts, and safety critical computations. This approach allows system integrators to greatly reduce attack surface and increase security maintainability.

We have also proposed a framework accompanying the security system architecture to specify technological processes. We demonstrate the approach by employing LTL-based languages to express complex time- and event-based polices for the controlled processes.

Finally, we have implemented the security system architecture and the framework. The implementation of the security system architecture is based on the certified hypervisor PikeOS. The toolchain implementing framework is heavily utilising code generation and automatic deployment to decrease the human factor in critical parts to the minimum.

In the future we will explore and validate the developed solution on wider technological processes and adjacent domains such as railway automation, transportation and communications. We are already working on formal verification of the code generators of the security subsystem to provide ultimate correctness guarantees between the generated code and the specification. We will asses to bring formal semantics of the PikeOS as the Security Reference Monitor [19]. We will investigate how the framework's toolchain can be extended with deployment generation and interfaces to typical model-based integrated development environments.

Acknowledgement. A part of the research leading to these results has received funding from the European Union's Seventh Framework Programme (FP7/2007-2013) grant agreement no. 318353 (EURO-MILS, http://www.euromils.eu).

References

1. Hydraulic Shock Safety Bulletin. U.S. Chemical Safety Board, January 2015. http://www.csb.gov/assets/1/19/final_CSB_CaseStudy_Millard_0114_0543PM.pdf
2. Federal Office for Information Security. The IT security in Germany 2014 (Bundesamt für Sicherheit in der Informationstechnik. Die Lage der IT-Sicherheit in Deutschland 2014). https://www.bsi.bund.de/SharedDocs/Downloads/DE/BSI/Publikationen/Lageberichte/Lagebericht2014.pdf?_blob=publicationFile
3. Abrams, M., Weiss, J.: Applied Control Solutions. Malicious Control System Cyber Security Attack Case StudyMaroochy Water Services, Australia. http://csrc.nist.gov/groups/SMA/fisma/ics/documents/Maroochy-Water-Services-Case-Study_report.pdf
4. Langner, R.: To Kill a Centrifuge. A Technical Analysis of What Stuxnet's Creators Tried to Achieve. Langner Blog (2013). http://www.langner.com/en/wp-content/uploads/2013/11/To-kill-a-centrifuge.pdf

5. Mossakowski, T., Drouineaud, M., Sohr, K.: A temporal-logic extension of role-based access control covering dynamic separation of duties. In: TIME, pp. 83–90. IEEE Computer Society (2003)
6. Mondal, S., Sural, S., Atluri, V.: Towards formal security analysis of GTRBAC using timed automata. In: Proceedings of the 14th ACM Symposium on Access Control Models and Technologies, SACMAT 2009, pp. 33–42. ACM (2009)
7. Bertino, E., Bonatti, P.A., Ferrari, E.: TRBAC: a temporal role-based access control model. In: Proceedings of the Fifth ACM Workshop on Role-Based Access Control, Berlin, pp. 21–30. ACM, July 2000
8. Uzun, E., Atluri, V., Sural, S., Vaidya, J., Parlato, G., Ferrara, A.L., Madhusudan, P.: Analyzing temporal role based access control models. In: Proceeding of the 17th ACM Symposium on Access Control Models and Technologies (SACMAT), pp. 177–186. ACM, New York (2012)
9. Joshi, J.B.D., Bertino, E., Ghafoor, A.: Temporal hierarchies and inheritance semantics for GTRBAC. In: Proceedings of the 7th ACM Symposium on Access Control Models and Technologies, Monterey, pp. 74–83. ACM, July 2002
10. Joshi, J.B.D., Bertino, E., Latif, U., Ghafoor, A.: A generalized temporal role based access control model. IEEE Trans. Knowl. Data Eng. **17**(1), 4–23 (2005)
11. Balliu, M., Dam, M., Guernic, G.L.: Epistemic temporal logic for information flow security. CoRR abs/1208.6106 (2012)
12. Chemical Facility Security News. Control System Scenarios, April 2015. http://chemical-facility-security-news.blogspot.de/2015/04/control-system-scenarios.html
13. Banerjee, A., Naumann, D.A., Rosenberg, S.: Expressive declassification policies and modular static enforcement. In: IEEE Symposium on Security and Privacy, pp. 339–353. IEEE Computer Society (2008)
14. Rocha, B.P.S., Bandhakavi, S., den Hartog, J., Winsborough, W.H., Etalle, S.: Towards static flow-based declassification for legacy and untrusted programs. In: IEEE Symposium on Security and Privacy, pp. 93–108. IEEE Computer Society (2010)
15. Spencer, R., Smalley, S., Hibler, M., Andersen, D.: The flask security architecture: system support for diverse security policies. In: Proceedings of the Eighth USENIX Security Symposium, pp. 123–139, August 1999
16. SYSGO AG. www.sysgo.com
17. Kaspersky Lab. www.kaspersky.com
18. Brygier, J., Fuchsen, R., Blasum, H.: Safe and secure virtualization in a separation microkernel. In: Proceedings, Embedded World Conference. Nuremberg (2009)
19. Verbeek, F., Schmaltz, J., Tverdyshev, S., Blasum, H., Havle, O., Langenstein, B., Stephan, W., Wolff, B.: Formal functional specification of the pikeos separation kernel. In: Proceedings of 7th NASA Formal Methods Symposium. Pasadena (2015)
20. EURO-MILS Consortium: MILS Architecture, Technical report (2014). http://euromils.eu/downloads/2014-EURO-MILS-MILS-Architecture-white-paper.pdf
21. Rushby, J.: Design and verification of secure systems. In: Eighth ACM Symposium on Operating System Principles, pp. 12–21 (1981). http://www.sdl.sri.com/papers/sosp81/sosp81.pdf

Access Control Issues in Utilizing Fog Computing for Transport Infrastructure

Stavros Salonikias[1], Ioannis Mavridis[1], and Dimitris Gritzalis[2(✉)]

[1] Department of Applied Informatics, University of Macedonia,
156 Egnatia Street, 546 36 Thessaloniki, Greece
{salonikias,mavridis}@uom.gr
[2] Information Security and Critical Infrastructure Protection (INFOSEC) Laboratory,
Department of Informatics, Athens University of Economics and Business,
76 Patission Avenue, 104 34 Athens, Greece
dgrit@aueb.gr

Abstract. The integration of the information and communication technologies of cloud computing, Software Defined Networking (SDN) and Internet of Things (IoT) into traditional transportation infrastructures enables the evolution of Intelligent Transportation Systems (ITS). Moreover, the specific requirements for real-time applications and service provision near to consumers introduce the utilization of fog computing as an extension of cloud. However, such a movement affects security aspects and poses new access control challenges. In this paper, we study the operational characteristics of a proposed ITS paradigm utilizing fog computing and identify corresponding access control issues. To address these issues in such a versatile and highly distributed environment, we present the key pointers of an attribute-based access control scheme suitable for fog computing. This paper aims to set a basis for further work in refining, verifying and validating the proposed solution.

Keywords: Critical infrastructures · Transport infrastructure · Intelligent Transportation System · Internet of Things · Fog computing · Software Defined Networks · Access control · ABAC · Context-awareness

1 Introduction

The integration of information and communication technologies (ICT) into traditional transportation infrastructures enables the evolution of Intelligent Transportation Systems (ITS) [5] to support safe, efficient, sustainable and environmentally friendly transportation facilities. In ITS, the concept of device ubiquity [21] that refers to the ability to be present but not intrusive and yet interact with physical environment in a calm way, is extensively realized.

Actually, fabricating ICT in transport infrastructures using different kinds of devices (from sensors and actuators to computing systems embedded into vehicles) as well as various types of services to create a large transport ecosystem, depicts the concept of Internet of Things (IoT) [16]. A "thing" is a stakeholder (e.g. a sign mark or a milestone)

© Springer International Publishing Switzerland 2016
E. Rome et al. (Eds.): CRITIS 2015, LNCS 9578, pp. 15–26, 2016.
DOI: 10.1007/978-3-319-33331-1_2

which has been assigned an identity (e.g. RFID metal id, IPv6 address) and can pervasively be present and interact with other things within the scope of a network [3].

The ICT infrastructure that supports and utilizes the IoT contains various types of network connections in order to supply services that are provided from datacentres residing in the cloud. However, cloud-based infrastructure realizes a centralized model for service consolidation and offering through wired backbone connections. The fact that in IoT environments there may be an enormous number of stakeholders requesting services, producing and consuming data, likely leads to congestion and arbitrary delays in servicing all requests. Additionally, there are cases where time available for data transfer and decision making process is so critical that must be counted near to zero (i.e. vehicle collision avoidance).

An architecture that extends cloud to facilitate service deployment near the edge of the network, meet latency requirements, achieve context-awareness and accommodate large numbers of nodes was introduced in 2012 by Cisco Systems under the term "fog computing". Fog realizes a highly distributed virtualized platform that provides processing, storing and networking services between the cloud and the edge of the network [4]. Thus, fog can be considered as an extension of cloud, stretching it to utilize resources from devices near the edge.

Network devices are usually autonomous, configured via a web or command line interface, whereas all high level organizational policies should be transformed into low-level multiple configurations [8]. The fact that many vendors provide management controllers does not drastically improve the situation since in real world infrastructures there exist multi-vendor and even end-of-support devices. Software Defined Networking (SDN) decouples the control plane from the forwarding plane [6]. Thus, network traffic paths are no longer configured in every device but are centrally managed by the SDN controller.

Due to importance in economy, transport infrastructures face multiple threats [18]. Moreover, a single incident can cause cascading effects [9] on other critical infrastructures due to dependencies among them [10]. More specifically, ITS mainly suffer from ICT threats. To mitigate relevant risks, effective countermeasures should be taken in order for confidentiality, integrity and availability to be ensured. Thus access to system resources must be controlled in an authenticated and authorized manner.

The main contributions of this paper is to study the particular functional and non-functional requirements posed on an ITS paradigm utilizing fog computing, spot the corresponding access control issues and propose an approach to address them via an effective access control system based on proper mechanisms.

The structure of this paper is as follows. In Sect. 2 we present the ITS deployment that is utilising fog computing. Based on this paradigm, Sect. 3 presents identified access control issues. In Sect. 4, the stepping stones in defining a suitable attribute-based access control approach in fog computing are discussed. The paper concludes in Sect. 5.

2   ITS Paradigm

In this paradigm, we assume a transport environment supported by a proper ICT infrastructure to implement the ITS under consideration. In such an ITS, consumers (vehicles and humans as passengers or pedestrians) are provided with safety services (collision avoidance, emergency response), infotainment services (informatory services, advertising, multimedia entertainment content) and routing services (collision or congestion avoidance). We distinguish four main areas (Fig. 1): Core ICT (CI), Road Side (RS), Vehicles and Humans (VH), and Sensors and Actuators (SA).

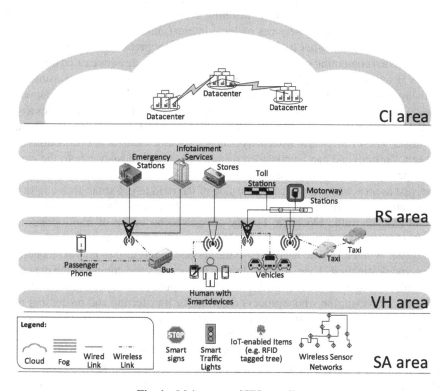

Fig. 1.   Main areas of ITS paradigm

CI provides a solid platform for applications that are used to provide services to consumers, according to the Software as a Service (SaaS) model of cloud computing. Content and infrastructure management along with resources for data processing and data warehousing are provided. CI services are mainly implemented in the cloud, which is built using a distributed architecture over high-bandwidth wired links between datacenters to provide high availability of operations.

Service consumers are inhibiting the VH area. More specifically, consumers are considered to be vehicles appropriate equipped or humans (pedestrians or passengers) carrying smart devices (e.g. smartphones) connected to the ITS network. From the network point of view, consumers are mobile nodes, connected wirelessly to access stations and are arbitrarily entering and leaving the system. For the consumers to obtain authenticated access to services provided by the CI, connections from VH area to CI area are established. In a heavily inhibited road though, vehicle or human requests to CI for services can readily escalate in a large number.

Between CI and VH areas, in close vicinity to the latter, RS area is deployed to mainly facilitate network connectivity between service providers and consumers. Servers and network nodes are usually connected in a wired manner, sometimes using redundant paths. Applications deployed to this area provide services to near consumers. By doing so, services can easily be localized and directly access context parameters. Moreover, by shortening network distance and lessening connected users, network latency is lowered. In order to provide services of local interest, instead of distant datacenters, servers can be installed either in various service provider premises (in the RS area) or in the embedded computing systems of vehicles and the smart devices carried by humans (in the VH area). An example scenario of providing such services to consumers is advertising offers in gas from stations in a particular city. This information is important to vehicle drivers in the same city but rather useless to a driver located many miles away.

In the SA area IoT enabled devices with temporal or permanent presence on the road are assumed. These devices are wirelessly connected using short-range connections (e.g. Bluetooth, ZigBee) and can be considered stationary nodes in relevance to the carrier (i.e. the speed meter of a bus). A sensor network attached to a car is stationary regarding the car, just as an actuator attached on the side of the road (e.g. a smart traffic light).

In a routine scenario, a cloud service deployed in CI area is used to provide alternative routes in case of traffic blockage. For the service to be aware of traffic conditions (contextual information), traffic data should be provided from sensors near the problematic area. When a vehicle needs to use the service, it has also to provide its current location and destination. Then, the cloud service processes and compares the data with similar datasets from other vehicles. Finally, the computed routes are transmitted back to vehicles. However, the whole process required for transferring and processing may take a significant amount of time making the returned information possibly obsolete. Regarding a first case when the vehicle is a tourist bus, if alternative routes are no longer possible (vehicle has already been blocked in traffic before receiving alternative routes), tourists may have to bear a delay in their vacation. In a second case, where the vehicle is an ambulance (or any other emergency vehicle) urging to a destination in an urban environment, alternative routes must be received as soon as possible, before the vehicle become stacked and rerouting is no longer possible. If additional contextual information like weather or road condition should also be sent to the service, computation time and data transfer time may become longer.

The above scenario indicates that direct accessing of services from CI suffers from the following limitations:

- CI area is physically located away from consumers,
- network congestions and arbitrary delays are likely to happen when a service is simultaneously offered to a vast number of consumers,
- quality of service can be negatively affected due to increased latency from network delays while a real-time service is being requested,

- increased volume of transmitted data after context-aware applications request for contextual information to be transmitted to the cloud,
- limited scope when a service is provided in a restricted area with local interest only.

To overcome the above limitations, fog computing can be utilized to extend cloud functionality in RS and VH areas, using resources from both. By extending cloud with fog computing, services can take advantage of both RS and VH area characteristics to achieve (1) low latency, (2) application localization and decentralization, (3) direct interference between applications and consumers (vehicles or humans). It is worth to make clear that by contributing their ICT resources to fog, vehicles and humans can act either as service consumers or providers.

More specifically, using fog computing to deploy services providing alternative routes, data would be uploaded to a nearby fog server, less congested than a cloud server. At the same time, a fog server located close to the scene could already be aware of contextual information like traffic conditions. Accordingly, total time for uploading, processing and downloading rerouting instructions to vehicle would be less.

Another fog advantage is that it can be used to create federations [4] between different administrative domains. Luan et al. [12] present a situation where a store using its fog server distributes a digital flyer. Vehicles near roadside access points get the flyer and push it further to other vehicles. Using federations, the same store can simultaneously provide additional services from another federated domain.

Fog computing is usually implemented over heterogeneous networks. This happens because in the RS area networks usually preexist. To substitute all devices to a single-vendor infrastructure is usually not an option mainly due to cost. Device heterogeneity though leads to high administrative costs and may pose a negative trend on fog adoption. To create a vendor-independent environment that permits unified management, SDN technology is an interesting option to be implemented [8]. Using SDNs in RS area allows for a centralized orchestration [19] of the fog underlying network via SDN controllers.

Table 1. Main characteristics for each ITS area

	CI	RS	VH	SA
Network area	Core	Field	Edge	Field - Edge
Architecture/Topology	Centralized	Distributed	Mobile	Wireless Sensor Networks (WSN) [2]
Bandwidth	Very High	High	Low	Very low
Latency	Low	Low	High	Low
Network Availability	High	Medium	Low	Low
Number of connections	Few	Many	Limited	Limited
Context awareness	No	Yes	Yes	No
Device heterogeneity	No	Yes	Yes	No
Geographic distribution	Moderate	High	Very High	Low
Access Medium	Wired	Wired	Wireless	Wireless
Mobility	No	No	Yes	No
Proximity to consumers	Far	Near	Near	Near
Implementation location	Datacenters	Roadside (Buildings or/and outdoors)	Outdoors	Outdoors
Connections	Controlled	Controlled and arbitrary	Arbitrary	Managed within WSN

The SDN Controller (control plane) implements two interfaces. The Southbound Interface (SBI) which logically connects controller with SDN-enabled hardware devices (data plane) and the Northbound Interface (NBI) which exposes controller API (application plane) to make network flows programmable by external applications.

In Table 1 we summarize the main characteristics that describe each area behavior in the ITS environment.

3   Access Control Issues

The utilization of fog computing in developing ITS, as presented in the paradigm of the previous section, results in arising a number of security and privacy considerations mainly regarding controlling permissions on the use of resources and services. Access control seeks to prevent activity that could lead to breach of security by ensuring in general that accesses to system's resources and services occur according to the rules defined in corresponding security policies [17]. Towards implementing a suitable access control solution various functional and non-functional system features must be taken under consideration.

In the dispersed fog environment presented in the previous section, vehicles and humans are entering and leaving domains arbitrarily. Service consumers and providers can act as access control subjects and objects interchangeably. In a gas station scenario, stores (located in RS area) are able to push information to vehicles (in VH area). Then, vehicles can pass this information to other vehicles etc. This indicates that in the ITS fog entities can dynamically operate either as subjects or as objects. The crossing of administrative domains is of special interest, as a vehicle or human moves, and appropriate administrative functions are needed. An administrative domain is a set of network entities on which a single security policy is employed by a single administrative authority [20].

Services are deployed by local providers from RS area, wherein a number of different administrative domains are interoperating and usually forming federations. These administrative domains provide, besides their own, services from other domains of the same federation. An important factor is that services can be deployed by local providers in RS area without the intervention of a particular administrative authority. Service owners should be able to set appropriate access control policies to limit services consumption. The propagation of access control policies can be delegated to administrative authorities, in order to enable interoperability between the rest of service providers and the whole ITS environment.

Ambient environment plays a key role in an ITS. For example, in a circumstance with a heavy rain, it is not desirable to distract the vehicle driver with non-critical information, such as the nearest museum (unless he specifically requests for such information). Hence, context awareness becomes a critical feature of access control. Abowd et al. [1] define context as any information that can be used to characterize the situation of an entity or environment. An entity is a person, place, or object that is considered relevant to the interaction between a user and an application, including the user and application themselves. Accordingly, a system is context-aware if it uses context to provide relevant information and/or services to the user, where relevancy depends on the current task of the user [1].

In order for an ITS to support context-aware services, information related to personal data (i.e. current location of vehicle or human) is transferred, processed and stored in the fog and the cloud. Thus, the transport infrastructure should ensure protection of privacy. Marx [13] perceives privacy violation when one of the four following borders is crossed:

- Natural Borders that protect a person from direct observation.
- Social Borders that protect a person's social life.
- Spatial Borders that protect periods of a person's life.
- Transitory/Ephemeral Borders that protect fleeting moment actions.

These borders indicate that privacy can be extended in many directions. Ephemeral borders can be crossed as access control logs expose a person's activity at a specific moment. Moreover, natural borders can be crossed when access control request sequence can indicate a set or actions. To protect privacy, access control should be implemented following a method where person's identity is not used or the contextual information cannot reveal it. Another important consideration is that privacy concerns should not prevent accountability.

The high mobility of sensors and actuators in the SA area, in conjunction with their limited power and computation resources, should also be taken under consideration during access control system development.

Table 2 summarizes access control issues in fog computing.

Table 2. Access control issues in fog computing

Privacy violation	Fog decentralization may require data interchange between adminis-trative domains. Private data should be protected
Coherency	A unique and coherent access control system should be end-to-end applied through multiple administrative domains
Context-awareness	Capturing, transferring, processing and storing of rich and quickly changing contextual information (e.g. weather conditions, tempera-ture, time, etc.) should be effectively managed to support access control decisions
Resource restriction	Access control system should not drain power or resources from devices with limited capacity
Network availability	Access control should be able to provide a level of functionality even in case of network unavailability
Decision latency	The system should minimize time required to grant or deny a request. Delays in the process may lead to undesirable effects for human safety and infrastructure integrity
Management	Policy management, which includes the ability to create, update and delete policies and to notify stakeholders for changes, should be supported
Accountability	Tracks concerning malicious activity should not be lost across admin-istrative domains

4   Proposed Approach for Access Control in Fog Computing

Based on the operational and security characteristics of utilizing fog computing in transport infrastructure, as presented and discussed in the previous sections, we propose the main features of a proper access control system.

4.1   Attribute-Based Authentication and Authorization

In traditional ICT systems, subjects are assigned with an identity. During user identification this identity is presented to the system and then is verified during authentication, usually by using a password. After a successful authentication process, access control involves the authorization process which is to decide whether an access request should be permitted or denied.

For the arbitrarily changing number of subjects and objects in VH area, assigning and verifying identities for every entity is not possible. On the one hand not all services might be publicly available. On the other hand some services might require consumer identification. Even for publicly available services, there are circumstances when access should be denied based on the contextual information. This urges the need for an access control system that can consider information describing subjects, objects and the context of operation.

NIST has released the Special Publication (SP) 800-162 [7] to provide a definition of Attribute-Based Access Control (ABAC), as an access control approach based on attributes, and a guidance in implementing it within an organization. Attributes are characteristics, defined as name-value pairs, which can contain information about subjects, objects and context. Context attributes, or environmental conditions, allow ABAC implementations to be context-aware, thus making it an ideal candidate for ITS applications, where context is a factor that affects the entire system behavior.

Identity-based authentication is not a prerequisite for ABAC. Nevertheless, when required, identities can be used provided they have been assigned to subjects as attributes. To ensure certified exchanging of attributes, the utilization of proper attribute certificates has already been proposed in previous work [14].

In an attribute-based access control system, authorization is performed according to a security policy that is mainly defined on the basis of subject and object attributes instead of any identities. Security policy refers to the set of rules, laws and practices that regulate how an organization manages, protects, and distributes sensitive information [15]. ABAC utilizes two sets of policies. Digital Policies (DP) and Meta Policies (MP). DPs dictate access control rules that access control system enforces. MPs are used for managing DPs. An example of MP is the definition of priorities that should be assigned for the case of conflicting DPs.

4.2   Reference Monitor Implementation

Reference monitor (RM) is consisted by the Policy Decision Point (PDP) and the Policy Enforcement Point (PEP). Access decisions are made in PDP and are then fed into the

PEP that enforces them, thus granting or denying subject access requests against objects. These decisions are based on DPs and corresponding MPs.

In traditional computing environments, the reference monitor is usually integrated with the objects to be protected or implemented in a central location to process all requests for distributed objects [11]. In a dynamic and highly distributed ITS environment, where access control decisions should be taken instantly, these approaches are both not viable. The former requires processing power that is not available in all entities and the latter would impose a significant latency for all access requests and access decisions to be sent over the network. Moreover, the number of requests can escalate to as high as to impose further delays in processing time. To overcome this issues, we propose a distributed reference monitor, based on ABAC, as presented in Fig. 2.

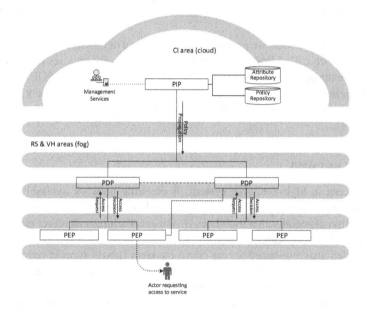

Fig. 2. Proposed ABAC implementation

In the proposed ABAC implementation, security administrators set policies that are stored in a logical Policy Information Point (PIP). Policies can be set using User Interface (UI) or another suitable method (e.g. via a web service). We characterize PIP as logical since it is presented as a single entity although it is more likely to be implemented in a distributed manner within the CI area. PIP contains all policy and attribute information for one or multiple domains and propagates policies to PDPs deployed mainly in RS area. A PEP enforces access decisions and can be implemented on every single device. For example, PEP can reside on a network switch, where it disables a port if attributes of a requestor subject lead to a deny decision by a PDP located in a fog server. PEP does not require significant computing resources to consume, since most of the required computation takes place in the PDP.

4.3 Policy Propagation

For system continuance and redundancy, PEPs can be bound to one or more PDPs. This can only be functional when all PDPs are simultaneously informed of any policy change. PDP policy synchronization requires a proper policy propagation control method. As mentioned above, MPs contain information for managing DPs. All policies are created, modified or deleted by policy managers in the scope of an administrative domain.

In case of a single PDP, all changes in policies stored in a PIP can directly be propagated to the PDP and then immediately be effective for the whole system. However, in case of distributed PDPs, where communication networks may impose delays due to outages or breakdowns, a change in the policy set (PIP) should be propagated based on specific rules that take under consideration, among others, the current network conditions. For example, it may be preferable not to send policy updates to any PDP unless all required PDPs are reachable.

To cope with such issues, we propose the introduction of propagation rules described by a new policy set, called Propagation Policies (PP). PPs are policies that define how PIP policies are updated, propagated to PDPs and exchanged between PDPs. Setting the propagation policies alone is not enough. DPs and MPs should be securely transmitted and verified. For this purpose, we aim at extending the definition and use of access rule certificates [14].

4.4 Offline Operation

A major concern in high-available systems is ensuring network availability. This is usually done by providing redundant links. Nevertheless, a case of network failure is still a possibility, especially in a mobile environment. Failures can affect either PIP-to-PDP or PDP-to-PEP communication.

The intended attribute-based access control system should support redundant links between PIP and PDPs, as well as between PDP and PEPs. When a connection between PDP and PIP fails, the PDP that cannot reach PIP should be able to use a neighbor PDP to fetch policy information required to answer requests. For the case of a complete communication failure, a small set of default policies could be locally stored. On the other hand when PEP cannot reach any PDP, a default action should be enforced.

5   Conclusion

Transport infrastructure, apart from the significant economic impact that justifies the characterization critical, accommodates a vast number of consumers as vehicles and humans. Integrating ICT to transport infrastructure can improve the overall experience and advance safety.

In this paper, we described an ITS paradigm that results in dividing the ICT environment into four areas (CI, RS, VH and SA). These areas facilitated our study for the adoption and utilization of fog computing in ITS scenarios that introduce specific requirements. Summarizing our study, fog enables ITS to extend services from the cloud near to consumers, overcoming problems that a centralized approach induces. Based on the ITS paradigm, a number of specific access control issues were located and discussed. Our proposed approach towards addressing these issues is to develop a distributed access control system that instead of identities only, will utilize attributes for authentication and authorization purposes.

Our future research effort aims at refining the access control deployment for single or multiple ITS domains, along with providing a solid theoretical basis, using appropriate formal methods, on which the proposed solution can be validated and verified. This will include effective solutions for reference monitor implementation, secure policy propagation and support for offline operation, with an utmost goal of a real-world implementation.

References

1. Abowd, G.D., Dey, A.K., Brown, P.J., Davies, N., Smith, M., Steggles, P.: Towards a better understanding of context and context-awareness. In: Gellersen, H.-W. (ed.) HUC 1999. LNCS, vol. 1707, pp. 304–307. Springer, Heidelberg (1999)
2. Akyildiz, I.F., Su, W., Sankarasubramaniam, Y., Cayirci, E.: Wireless sensor networks: a survey. Comput. Netw. **38**, 393–422 (2002)
3. Atzori, L., Iera, A., Morabito, G.: The Internet of Things: a survey. Comput. Netw. **54**, 2787–2805 (2010)
4. Bonomi, F., Milito, R., Zhu, J., Addepalli, S.: Fog computing and its role in the Internet of Things. In: Proceedings of the MCC Workshop on Mobile Cloud Computing, pp. 13–16. ACM, USA (2012)
5. ETSI - Intelligent Transport. http://www.etsi.org/technologies-clusters/technologies/intelligent-transport. Accessed 20 May 2015
6. Hakiri, A., Gokhale, A., Berthou, P., Schmidt, D.C., Gayraud, T.: Software-defined networking: challenges and research opportunities for Future Internet. Comput. Netw. **75**(Part A), 453–471 (2014)
7. Hu, V.C., Ferraiolo, D., Kuhn, R., Schnitzer, A., Sandlin, K., Miller, R., Scarfone, K.: Guide to Attribute Based Access Control (ABAC) Definition and Considerations. National Institute of Standards and Technology (2014)
8. Kim, H., Feamster, N.: Improving network management with software defined networking. IEEE Commun. Mag. **51**, 114–119 (2013)
9. Kotzanikolaou, P., Theoharidou, M., Gritzalis, D.: Assessing n-order dependencies between critical infrastructures. Int. J. Crit. Infrastruct. **9**, 93–110 (2013)
10. Kotzanikolaou, P., Theoharidou, M., Gritzalis, D.: Interdependencies between critical infrastructures: analyzing the risk of cascading effects. In: Bologna, S., Hämmerli, B., Gritzalis, D., Wolthusen, S. (eds.) CRITIS 2011. LNCS, vol. 6983, pp. 104–115. Springer, Heidelberg (2013)
11. Lampson, B., Abadi, M., Burrows, M., Wobber, E.: Authentication in distributed systems: theory and practice. In: Proceedings of the 13th ACM Symposium on Operating Systems Principles, pp. 165–182. ACM, USA (1991)
12. Luan, T.H., Gao, L., Li, Z., Xiang, Y., Sun, L.: Fog Computing: Focusing on Mobile Users at the Edge. arXiv:1502.01815 [cs] (2015)
13. Marx, G.T.: Murky conceptual waters: the public and the private. Ethics Inf. Technol. **3**, 157–169 (2001)
14. Mavridis, I., Georgiadis, C., Pangalos, G.: Access-rule certificates for secure distributed healthcare applications over the Internet. Health Inf. J. **8**, 127–137 (2002)

15. Mavridis, I., Pangalos, G.: Security issues in a mobile computing paradigm. Commun. Multimedia Secur. **3**, 60–76 (1997)
16. Miorandi, D., Sicari, S., De Pellegrini, F., Chlamtac, I.: Internet of things: vision, applications and research challenges. Ad Hoc Netw. **10**, 1497–1516 (2012)
17. Sandhu, R.S., Samarati, P.: Access control: principle and practice. IEEE Commun. Mag. **32**, 40–48 (1994)
18. Theoharidou, M., Kandias, M., Gritzalis, D.: Securing transportation-critical infrastructures: trends and perspectives. In: Georgiadis, C.K., Jahankhani, H., Pimenidis, E., Bashroush, R., Al-Nemrat, A., (eds.) Global Security, Safety and Sustainability & e-Democracy. pp. 171–178. Springer (2012)
19. Truong, N.B., Lee, G.M., Ghamri-Doudane, Y.: Software defined networking-based vehicular Adhoc Network with Fog Computing. In: 2015 IFIP/IEEE International Symposium on Integrated Network Management (IM), pp. 1202–1207 (2015)
20. Vázquez-Gómez, J.: Multidomain security. Comput. Secur. **13**, 161–184 (1994)
21. Weiser, M.: The computer for the 21st century. Sci. Am. **265**, 94–104 (1991)

A Cyber Forensic Taxonomy for SCADA Systems in Critical Infrastructure

Peter Eden[1(✉)], Andrew Blyth[1], Pete Burnap[2], Yulia Cherdantseva[2],
Kevin Jones[3], Hugh Soulsby[3], and Kristan Stoddart[4]

[1] Faculty of Computing, Engineering and Science,
University of South Wales, Pontypridd, UK
{peter.eden,andrew.blyth}@southwales.ac.uk
[2] School of Computer Science and Informatics, Cardiff University, Cardiff, UK
{p.burnap,y.v.cherdantseva}@cs.cardiff.ac.uk
[3] Cyber Operations, Airbus Group Innovations, Newport, UK
{kevin.jones,hugh.soulsby}@eads.com
[4] Aberystwyth University, Department of International Politics, Aberystwyth, UK
kds@aber.ac.uk

Abstract. SCADA systems are essential for the safe running of critical infrastructure but in recent years have increasingly become the target of advanced cyber-attacks through their convergence with public and corporate networks for easier monitoring and control. Cyber-events within critical infrastructure can have devastating consequences affecting human life, the environment and the economy. Therefore, it is vital that a forensic investigation takes place to provide remediation, understanding and to help in the design of more secure systems. This paper provides an overview of the SCADA forensic process, within critical infrastructure, and discusses the existing challenges of carrying out a SCADA forensic investigation. It also discusses ways in which the process may be improved together with a suggested SCADA incident response model. This paper is part of an ongoing research project that is working towards the creation of best practice guidelines for the forensic handling and incident response of SCADA systems.

Keywords: SCADA · Critical infrastructure · Digital forensics · Incident response · Cyber security lifecycle · SCADA forensics

1 Introduction

Much of the world's critical national infrastructure, including oil refineries, power grids, nuclear plants and water distribution, rely upon SCADA (Supervisory Control and Data Acquisition) for its safe operation through monitoring, automation and control. The requirement for these systems to remain continuously operational and with minimal interference is inflexible and means that many of today's SCADA systems were actually designed and implemented

© Springer International Publishing Switzerland 2016
E. Rome et al. (Eds.): CRITIS 2015, LNCS 9578, pp. 27–39, 2016.
DOI: 10.1007/978-3-319-33331-1_3

decades ago. They were originally designed to operate on closed networks, prioritising data availability over security and confidentiality. As technology has progressed, more and more SCADA systems have been interconnected with corporate and public networks for a more efficient process, communicating over TCP/IP, wireless IP and Bluetooth, leaving them vulnerable to outside attacks.

Recent years has seen a dramatic increase in the number of attacks on SCADA Systems, which have come along way since the Trans-Siberian gas pipeline explosion of 1982. [1] Stuxnet proved a new level of sophistication to dedicated attacks on critical infrastructure and many more have followed in its footsteps such as Duqu, Flame, Guass and Wiper. When a cyber-attack is carried out on critical infrastructure it is essential for a forensic incident response to follow immediately after. However, conventional computer forensic methodologies cannot simply be applied to SCADA systems because of the difference in their nature. As a result, the development of a SCADA forensic triage process is required to successfully remediate against such attacks.

The paper is split into four main sections. The first section initially discusses the generic SCADA system architecture commonly found in critical infrastructure. Section two outlines a taxonomy of SCADA system forensics, including current challenges and forensic readiness as well as the applicability of non-standard acquisition techniques. The third section describes a more developed SCADA incident response model for critical infrastructure. The final section identifies further areas of research to be carried out following this paper.

2 SCADA System Architecture

Critical infrastructure, based around the SCADA architecture, can consist of varying physical components, from a variety of manufactures, communicating across multiple zones and using a range of different SCADA protocols in the process.

2.1 Physical Assets

In a forensic investigation of a critical infrastructure incident hardware devices become the data sources for forensic artefacts. The main hardware devices exist within two main sections of a typical SCADA environment; Field Sites (of which there can be many covering huge geographical areas); and the Control Centre. [2] Field sites consist mainly of PLCs (Programmable Logic Controllers) and RTUs (Remote Terminal Units) and are normally attached to physical processes such as thermostats, motors, switches etc. The Control Centre is responsible for collecting data relating to the state of field instruments and interacting with the field sites. Components found at the control centre typically consist of an HMI (Human Machine Interface), Historian and MTU (Master Terminal Unit).

Field Sites:

PLC (Programmable Logic Controller): Computerised automated devices connected to physical sensors to control processes.

RTU (Remote Terminal Unit): Performs virtually the same function, and is very similar, to a PLC but is generally more robust and reliable in difficult terrain and also tend to have faster CPUs with more support for communication [3].

Control Centre:

HMI (Human Machine Interface): Provides a way of visually interpreting the data received by field devices and allows for human interaction with the SCADA system by providing a control panel interface. The size and design of an HMI can vary dramatically from something as small as a mobile phone to a much larger control-panel, which is more common amongst critical infrastructure.

Historian: A database management system that provides audit logging for SCADA system activity as well as storing and archiving of information that is sent to the control centre [4].

MTU (Master Terminal Unit): Often referred to as the SCADA server and whose responsibilities include receiving and processing communication information between field devices and control centre. The MTU also provides a graphical representation of the data which can then be transferred and displayed on the HMI. Data may be pre-processed before being sent to the Historian [5].

2.2 Networking

Due to the demand for a more efficient monitoring and control process, within critical infrastructure, SCADA systems have become massively complex through their interconnectivity with other networks (corporate, Internet etc.) and are now far different from their original monolithic architecture. Although this is not true for all SCADA networks, many of the more complex architectures found in critical infrastructure can be split into four main zones; External; Corporate; Data; and Control, as described by [6]. These are based around the type of data being communicated, access and locations. It is the multiple layers and communication across the multiple zones that makes forensic acquisition of specific forensic artefacts extremely challenging [7].

2.3 Protocols and Their Vulnerabilities

Critical infrastructure can typically see a wide range of protocols, both proprietary and non-proprietary, being utilised across its SCADA network. However, there are a specific group of protocols that are becoming standard or more common than others; MODBUS; DNP3; and PROFIBUS. Other widely used protocols include RP-570, Conitel, IEC 60870, PROFINET IO and many more.

A major problem within critical infrastructure security is the distinct lack of security-integrated mechanisms within the SCADA protocols being used. This lack of protection in communication was not a great issue for the earlier isolated SCADA networks but due to the integration with corporate networks and communication across TCP/IP, critical infrastructure vulnerability has increased significantly. The main problems with implementing security features into the SCADA protocols is that is risks introducing latency into communication with processes. In critical infrastructure this could have catastrophic consequences. The problem with leaving security mechanisms out of SCADA protocols is that it can be vulnerable to packet manipulation which could lead to packet modification, packet replay, packet deletion, latency, eavesdropping and spoofing [9,10].

3   SCADA Forensics Within Critical Infrastructure

A forensic analysis of any system will involve certain mandatory phases. These include the collection, preservation, analysis and reporting of digital evidence that is suitable and admissible in a court of law. Forensic artefacts across a network may be collected and analysed from both volatile and non-volatile data sources and although the same can be said for SCADA, conventional methods and forensic tools are somewhat inadequate for a SCADA systems [15].

3.1   Conventional Forensic Methodologies and Critical Infrastructure

One of the main reasons that deny the application of traditional forensic methods being applied to critical infrastructure systems is due to the sheer scale of proprietary and legacy equipment that can be found within a typical SCADA environment. If we compare the rate of replacing technology within a standard business to that of a SCADA system found in critical infrastructure we would see that they are very different. The rate of change for a typical SMB might be three to five years, which would see hardware, software and networks being updated to reflect business needs. Techaisle's white paper, entitled 'The Ageing PC effect - Exposing Financial Impact for Small Businesses', describes a survey of 736 businesses spanning six countries, and shows that the average cost of maintaing systems that were four years or older is actually more costly than to upgrade them. [17] Comparing the typical SMB to that of a nuclear plant, the rate of change is considerably slower. The main reason for this is due to the characteristics of SCADA systems and the need for these systems to run continuously without interference. Updating the system would involve interrupting critical processes causing them to fail. As a result some SCADA systems within critical infrastructure have been left to run continuously, untouched and unpatched for decades, running legacy hardware and software that is no longer supported and using proprietary protocols instead of more widely used open standard protocols.

[8] Attempting to use conventional forensic tools on such a fragile infrastructure would not only have compatibility issues but could have the potential to introduce latency or cause interference with critical running processes.

Challenges: Because of the complex structure and characteristics of a typical SCADA system found within critical infrastructure there are many challenges that make the forensic triage process very difficult. These challenges include:

Live Acquisition - SCADA systems controlling critical processes demand the need for live data acquisition due to their requirement to run continuously. This creates many problems for the forensic investigator as carrying out the process of data acquisition live could cause latency resulting in the delayed operation of critical processes . Establishing an order of volatility, much like that stated in RFC3227 [21], would be essential to perform live acquisition that makes minimal changes to data in memory [15].

Response Time - We can compare a SCADA forensic investigation to a jig-saw. At the time an incident occurs the jigsaw is complete as all the pieces are present. As time goes by, pieces of the jigsaw are removed as forensic evidence is overwritten by newer processes and it becomes more difficult to see the whole picture, therefore, it is vital to respond as quickly after an incident has occurred as possible. [16] The challenge here lies within SCADA systems that contain many field sites spanning thousands of square kilometres.

Verification - It is essential that any digital evidence acquired in an investigation is extracted using forensically sound methods and in traditional forensics any acquired data is normally verified by comparing a hash value of the original evidence against its acquired copy. As many SCADA systems need to remain live, data is continuously being updated. This poses a problem for verifying data that is being copied out of memory during a live extraction as the state of the data can change from the start of the copying process to completing a calculated hash, resulting in the hash being unusable.

Logging and Storage - According to Fabro et al. [15], SCADA System software that have audit and logging functionality built-in are often deployed without these functions enabled. Logs can be crucial in a forensic investigation and help to provide a timeline of events post incident. Another problem is that even when these functions are enabled, the storage capacities are sometimes so small that logs of forensic value do not remain in storage long enough before being overwritten [15].

Absence of Dedicated SCADA Forensic Tools - Research has identified a distinct lack of dedicated SCADA forensic tools and methodologies for data extraction on specific SCADA components. [2] This could result in forensic investigators being forced to use unconventional data extraction methods on SCADA Systems such as JTAG or Chip off.

3.2   SCADA Forensic Readiness

Understanding, developing and incorporating the following discussed ares into SCADA systems will ultimately improve the forensic process for the forensic investigator.

SCADA Forensic Artefacts and Their Half-Lives: Forensic artefacts within a SCADA system may exist on a variety of different components and in an array of different formats. The goal of SCADA system forensic analysis within critical infrastructure is to identify and collect forensic artefacts from the system under investigation to ultimately recognise the current state of the environment at the time the event occurred. An artefact will have a logical structure and exist on one or more data sources. If the logical structure is known then the artefact could potentially be extracted via data-carving, otherwise acquiring a complete image of that data source and thorough analysis would be necessary.

If the forensic investigator has already identified the data sources needed for investigation, based on the type of incident that has occurred, it is essential for the investigator to understand how long an artefact will exist on that particular device before it is overwritten by newer information. The half-life of an artefact within a PLC, that is continuously running and with minimal built-in storage, will inevitably be overwritten faster than that an artefact stored in a historian. Identifying the half-life of data for each data source within that particular SCADA system will allow for data sources, that can be investigated, to be prioritised.

Asset Classification: SCADA system classification can be identified at a component level. This will help the investigator to identify exactly which areas and devices can be accessed and interrogated and those that can't. The classification of SCADA assets has been adopted from [18] and is described in Table 1.

Table 1. SCADA Asset Classification

Classification	Failure of component may result in:
Process-Critical	loss of life, injury or damage to the environment
Time-Critical	loss of life, injury or damage to the environment after a specific length of time
Location-Critical	loss of life or injury in attempt to access/repair component
Mission-Critical	failure of some global-directed activity
Business-Critical	high economic losses

Asset Prioritisation: By combining SCADA asset classification with asset half-lives the forensic investigator is able to compile a prioritisation list of data sources to investigate, increasing the amount of forensic evidence available for recovery. Methods for calculating a priority list have been proposed by Knijff [14] where a specific formula is applied to calculate an asset's priority based on certain factors such as evidential value, the volatility of that evidence, and asset accessibility. Incorporating asset half-life and asset classification into Knijff's formula will ultimately maximising the amount of forensic artefacts recovered.

3.3   Data Acquisition via Non-standard Invasive and Non-invasive Methods

Although there are no specifically designed data acquisition forensic tools aimed solely at SCADA systems there are various methodologies that could be used to extract data from SCADA system components in certain circumstances and, in some cases, as a last resort.

Non-invasive Physical Data Acquisition of PLCs Using JTAG (Joint Test Access Group): Embedded devices like PLCs consist of on-board flash memory chips that could potentially hold vital information such as memory status and issued commands. Due to the lack of dedicated SCADA forensic tools available to the investigator a technique known as JTAG allows for a lower level of data extraction by interacting directly with the on-board micro-controllers via their test access points (TAPs). These points are normally used at the production level for debugging purposes but can be manipulated into handing over complete raw copies of the controller data and any connected flash memory chips. [19] This extraction of raw data will allow for a hex dump of the current state of that device which could then be interrogated offline by an investigator. This could be useful to determine if a PLC has been infected and to acquire current data in memory but would be dependent upon its half-life and classification status.

Invasive Physical Data Acquisition of PLCs Using Chip-Off: In the event that an incident results in a field device being shut down or the need to be powered off there is the opportunity to perform a physical extraction of the memory chips within the embedded device, known as chip-off. This requires the memory chip to be de-soldered from the PCB, or removed using specific tools that apply heat to the chip. Once removed, depending on the type of chip i.e. BGA chips, reballing may need to be carried out in order to repair the connectors on the underside of the chip. The repaired chip can then be placed into a hardware device designed to support the given chip and read [20].

4   Developed SCADA Forensic Incident Response Model

SCADA forensic process models have been suggested in the past, such as that proposed by Wu et al. [7], which adapts the traditional IT system forensics investigation process and applies it to SCADA systems. However, the incident response model proposed in this paper is an alternative, original model, first submitted to ICS-CSR [18], and now further developed, that treats SCADA forensics as an ongoing life-cycle, using the entire process to influence the next event.

Figure 1 shows the SCADA forensic incident response model consisting of six main stages; Prepare; Detect; Isolate; Triage; Respond; and Report. The final stage helps to improve the preparation for the next time an investigation is needed, therefore continuing the cycle.

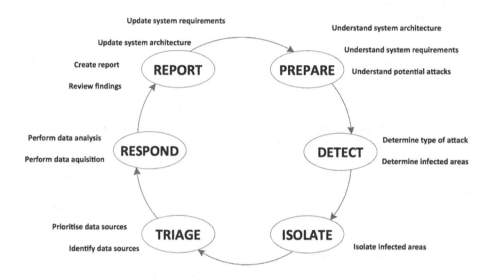

Fig. 1. SCADA Forensic Incident Response Model

Stage 1: PREPARE It is vital that the preparation stage starts before an event takes place. This will involve ensuring all documentation relating to the particular SCADA system is accurate and should comprise of understanding the following areas:

Understand system architecture: As each SCADA system will be unique in its configuration it is essential that detailed documentation regarding its architecture is recorded. Networking information should involve network configurations and all entry points into the system. Hardware documentation should include all SCADA components, including manufacturers, makes and models. Software documentation should include all software running on each device across all zones.

Understand System Requirements: Given the classification of certain SCADA devices it is also essential for the forensic investigator to have access to specific system requirements for the SCADA system being investigated. Documented here should be the types of systems and devices that need to remain continually running without fail, those that can be switched to a back-up, and finally those devices that can be powered down.

Understand Potential Attacks: It is also important to gather threat intelligence and to understand the types of attacks that can occur on the system. It has already been discussed by Zhu et al. [12] and further acknowledged by Stirland et al. [11], that the types of possible SCADA related attacks can be divided into 3 sections. These are hardware, software and the communication stack. Detailed information relating to these types of attacks can be found at [12].

Stage 2: DETECT

Determine type of attack: When an event has taken place, or is in the process of taking place, an investigator should try to determine the type of attack based on assessments of real-time data and any unusual behaviour that may have occurred.

Determine potential infected areas: Attempt to determine potential infected areas based on assessments made from the previous step. This will help in the next stage when identifying possible data sources.

Stage 3: ISOLATE One of the improvements from the previous model, described in [18], was to separate and develop the isolation phase. This is due to it's significance within the incident response model in containing an incident from creating further destruction to the SCADA network. It should naturally follows the detection stage.

Isolate infected areas: After detecting potential infected areas an attempt can be made to isolate those networks and devices, dependant upon their system requirements within the SCADA environment and business operations. It should be carried out with an effort to minimise disruption to other operations within the critical infrastructure.

Stage 4: TRIAGE

Identify data sources: The triage stage should start by identifying possible data sources of interest. This will be influenced by the documentation from stage 1 and stage 2. The list should include the device location within the network; device make, model and serial number; and classification status i.e. process critical [13].

Prioritise data sources: Prioritising data sources needs to be ordered in a way that reflects their value, volatility and accessibility in order to maximise the potential evidence available for recovery. [14] The time taken to assemble a priority list could also have an effect on the amount of evidence recovered as certain SCADA systems in critical infrastructure can span huge geographical areas and contain hundreds of data sources.

Stage 5: RESPOND

Perform data acquisition: With a priority list established the next stage involves forensically acquiring the data from the relevant data sources, which can either come from data stored in components or from data across the network. [14] Data needs to be admissible in court and therefore, should be acquired using forensically sound methods. The types of data acquired at this stage should include memory dumps, disk imaging and chip imaging from across the system. Traditional IT forensic tools can be used against engineering workstations, servers and historians but for embedded devices such as PLCs and RTUs, flashing software may be required from the manufacturer to extract a raw memory dump using JTAG ports and ensuring that no affect is made to the operation of the device if required to remain operational. [11] Invasive methods such as chip-off forensics may be used to extract data as a last resort but would be dependant on a component's classification. Clear guidelines would have to be established for each type of asset. The data acquisition stage should also include acquiring network data through retrieving logs data captures.

Perform data analysis: Data analysis will involve separating the forensic artefacts from other SCADA system data. This may be carried out with the use of traditional forensic analysis tools.

Stage 6: REPORT
Another development from the original model described in [18] was to introduce a separate 'Report' stage. This was to not only recognise its importance but to introduce further needed steps.

Review findings: Based on the analysis stage relationships can be correlated between the recovered forensic artefacts to ultimately create a timeline of events and to establish the root of an incident.

Create report: Based on the analysis of recovered artefacts a report should be compiled regarding results and findings. Inferences should be made between relationships of the gathered data, which should also include validation and integrity of data records such as chain of custody reports. It should also include any recommendations towards the development or patching of the SCADA system.

Update system architecture: The final steps of the reporting stage should be to update the documentation relating to the SCADA system architecture, post incident. This is due to the fact that after an event has taken place the overall configuration of the SCADA environment may have changed and will need to be accurate for the next investigation.

Update system requirements: Similar to the previous step, in the light of an incident occurring and system configurations changing, SCADA system requirements may also need to be revisited and, therefore, would need to be recorded.

5   Further Research

Further development of the SCADA forensic process is essential and this paper provides a good base from which to work from. Future research areas will include:

Developing the forensic triage process with practical implementation: This will include looking at the incident response model at a lower level and exploring each of the six stages in more depth. It will also include testing the IR model against real-world scenarios with half-lives of data on commonly used PLCs being calculated to influence the prioritisation of data sources.

Developing Forensic Hardware for SCADA Systems: Other research will include exploring the notion of developing dedicated forensic hardware, from an SBC (single-board computer), to incorporate into SCADA systems in order to improve upon the recovery of forensic artefacts from PLCs.

Such a device could act as a 'black box' for field devices that are perhaps restricted due to their classification, or located in an area that response time is far greater than the half-life of information within that device. This could, therefore, lengthen the time that forensic artefacts, such as memory status, modifications and issued commands, can be stored. Although datasets are generally quite large for forensic data capture, such a device would hope to extend the half-life of data by storing it long enough for an active response to take place.

6   Conclusion

As more and more SCADA systems are becoming susceptible to cyber-attacks it is clear that there is a distinct lack of focus on SCADA forensic incident response. A forensic investigation is an essential part of the cyber-security lifecycle that provides remediation post-incident and helps in the design of more secure systems of the future. Developing a forensic readiness plan for critical infrastructures is a timely, complex process, but is a necessity in the modern age for improving on security and remediation.

This paper has described the typical architecture of SCADA systems found in critical infrastructure and presented a forensic taxonomy of SCADA system investigations.Further to this it also suggests a more developed SCADA forensic incident response model.

Acknowledgments. This work is funded by the Airbus Group Endeavr Wales scheme under the SCADA Cyber Security Lifecycle (SCADA-CSL) programme with the ultimate goal of improving the forensic handling and incident response process for SCADA systems.

References

1. Miller, B., Rowe, D.C.: A survey of SCADA and Critical Infrastructure Incidents. In: Proceedings of the 1st Annual conference on Research in information technology (2012)
2. Ahmed, I., Obermeier, S., Naedele, M., Richard, G.G.: SCADA systems: challenges for forensic investigators. IEEE Comput. **45**(12), 44–51 (2012)
3. Boyer, S.: SCADA: Supervisory Control and Data Acquisition, 4th edn. ISA, Texas (2009)
4. McNamee, D., Elliott, T.: Secure Historian Access in SCADA Systems. Galios, White Paper, June 2011
5. Stouffer, K., Falco, J., Kent, K.: Guide to Industrial Control Systems (ICS) security. NIST (National Institute of Standards and Technology), U.S, Department of Commerce (2011)
6. Stouffer, K., Falco, J., Kent, K.: Guide to supervisory control and data acquisition (SCADA) and industrial control systems security. NIST (National Institute of Standards and Technology), U.S, Department of Commerce (2006)
7. Wu, T., Disso, J.F.P., Jones, K., Campos, A.: Towards a SCADA Forensics Architecture. In: 1st International symposium for ICS and SCADA cyber security research (ICS-CSR 2013) (2013)
8. McCarthy, J., Mahoney, W.: SCADA threats in the modern airport. Int. J. Cyber Warfare Terrorism **3**(4), 32–39 (2013)
9. Kang, D., Robles, R.J.: Compartmentalization of protocols in SCADA communication. Int. J. Adv. Sci. Tech. **8**, 27–36 (2009)
10. Ingure, V.M., Williams, R.D.: A Taxonomy of Security Vulnerabilities in SCADA Protocols. University of Virginia Charlottesville, USA (2007)
11. Stirland, J., Jones, K., Janicke, H., Wu, T.: Developing cyber forensics for SCADA industrial control systems. In: Proceedings of the International Conference of Information Security and Cyber Forensics (2014)
12. Zhu, B., Joseph, A., Sastry, S.: A taxonomy of cyber attacks on SCADA systems. In: Proceedings of the International Conference on Internet of Things and 4th International Conference on Cyber, Physical and Social Computing, pp. 380–388. IEEE Computer Society, Washington, DC (2011)
13. Wilhoit, K.: ICS, SCADA, and Non-Traditional Incident Response, Trend Micro, Digital forensics and incident response summit, July 2013
14. van der Knijff, R.M.: Control systems/SCADA forensics, what's the difference?, digital investigation. Int. J. Digit. Forensics Incident Response **11**(3), 160–174 (2014)
15. Fabro, M.E.C.: Recommended practice: creating cyber forensics plans for control systems, Homeland Security, Technical report, August 2008
16. Taveras, P.: Scada live forensics: Real time data acquisition process to detect, prevent or evaluate critical situations. Eur. Sci. J. (3), 253–262 (2013)
17. Techaisle White Paper: The Ageing PC Effect - Exposing Financial Impact for Small Businesses, May 2013. www.techaisle.com

18. Eden, P., Blyth, A., Burnap, Cherdantseva, Y., P., Jones, K., Soulsby, H., Stoddart, K.: A forensic taxonomy of SCADA systems and approach to incident response. In: Proceedings of the 3rd International Symposium for ICS and SCADA Cyber Security Research (ICS-CSR 2015) (2015)
19. Breeuwsma, I.: Forensic imaging of embedded systems using JTAG (boundary-scan). Digit. Invest. **3**(1), 32–42 (2006)
20. Hoog, A., Forensics, A.: Investigation, Analysis and Mobile Security for Google Android, 1st edn. Syngress, New York (2011)
21. Network Working Group, Internet Engineering Task Force. Guidelines for Evidence Collection and Archiving, RFC 3227 (2002)

Critical Infrastructure Resilience Assessment

Resilience Assessment of Interdependent Critical Infrastructure

Abdullah Alsubaie[1,2]([⊠]), Khaled Alutaibi[1,3], and José Martí[1]

[1] Department of Electrical and Computer Engineering, UBC, Vancouver, Canada
{alsubaie,alkhaled,jrms}@ece.ubc.ca
[2] King AbdulAziz City for Science and Technology, Riyadh, Saudi Arabia
[3] Civil Defence, Ministry of Interior, Riyadh, Saudi Arabia

Abstract. Recent extreme events have shown that total protection can not be accomplished. Therefore, Critical Infrastructure Protection (CIP) strategies should focus not only on the prevention of these events but also on the response and recovery following them. This shift in CIP strategies has put more interest on the concept of infrastructure resilience. In this paper, we address the problem of assessing critical infrastructure resilience. We first define the infrastructure attributes that make it resilient. Then, we propose a modeling framework to capture these attributes. After that, a resilience index is introduced to quantify the resilience of infrastructure systems. Finally, the usefulness of the proposed framework is demonstrated through an illustrative example.

Keywords: Critical infrastructure protection · Resilience assessment · Infrastructure interdependencies

1 Introduction

Our modern societies are dependent on the functioning of infrastructure systems that support economic prosperity and quality of life. These infrastructure systems face an increasingly set of threats, natural or man-made disasters, that can cause significant physical, economic, and social disruptions. The impact of these disasters could be limited to local communities, such as earthquakes, or global such as the Iceland volcano ash cloud which affected global air travel. Infrastructure systems operators have been continuously working on improving systems safety and security through traditional risk and reliability frameworks and guidelines. Infrastructure systems are large and complex which makes it impractical to consider all possible failure scenarios. It is then acknowledged that if total security cannot be achieved more effort should be devoted to planning effective response and recovery. As a result, there has been a paradigm shift in recent years from risk and reliability concepts toward resilience concepts [31]. This shift was realized by several governmental initiatives such as The Critical Infrastructure Resilience Study by the US National Infrastructure Advisory Council (NIAC) [3] and The Critical Infrastructure Preparedness and Resilience Research Network (CIPRNeT) program established by the European Union (EU) [1].

© Springer International Publishing Switzerland 2016
E. Rome et al. (Eds.): CRITIS 2015, LNCS 9578, pp. 43–55, 2016.
DOI: 10.1007/978-3-319-33331-1_4

Resilient infrastructure systems such as electric power, water, and health care are essential for minimizing impact of extreme events. Building a resilient infrastructure is an important goal for every nations' Critical Infrastructure Protection (CIP) program. One of the first steps toward this goal is developing an evaluation methodology that enables decision makers to quantify the infrastructure's resilience. The methodology is then used to evaluate the possible measures for improving infrastructure resilience.

As infrastructure systems are interdependent, failures can propagate from one infrastructure system to another. The systems are typically integrated and controlled in distributed and loosely manner. Haimes et al. [19] describe them as 'emergent systems' and show that while the cost of protecting emergent systems is high, more attention should be paid to improving their resilience. An effective resilience assessment approach must incorporate the interdependencies among infrastructure systems into the analysis. However, this incorporation is not an easy task. Although modeling and simulation tools are available for studying different aspects of infrastructure systems [32], conducting a comprehensive cross infrastructure resilience analysis poses several challenges. One of these challenges is the absence of universal measures that articulate the resilience of an infrastructure. Another challenge is finding the appropriate data for the study. Infrastructure systems operators are reluctant to sharing information due to regulation, competition, and security.

In this paper, we propose a simple yet an effective cross-infrastructure resilience assessment framework. It incorporates three main steps: definition of resilience attributes, modeling critical infrastructure, and measuring resilience. The assessment framework can be then used to evaluate preparedness, response and mitigation plans against natural and man-made disasters.The paper consists of six sections. Section 2 presents a literature review on existing resilience definitions and assessment methods. The proposed resilience assessment framework is presented in Sect. 3. Section 4 discusses cyber-physical interactions within resilience assessment. An illustrative example is discussed in Sect. 5 while a conclusion remarks are presented in Sect. 6.

2   Literature Review

2.1   Resilience Definition

The word Resilience? has been used in different disciplines such as ecology and health sciences for a long time. It was first defined at the system level by Holling in 1973 [22]. He defined resilience as measure of the persistence of systems and their ability to absorb change and disturbance and still maintain the same relationships between populations or state variables? [7]. Since this definition was proposed, researchers in social, ecological, and economic systems have proposed different definitions. Some are general while others are domain specific. Francis et al. [17] presented a survey of resilience definitions from different disciplines.

Within the CIP community, much effort has been devoted to explore and study the concepts of risk, reliability and security. However, the concept of resilience is still relatively new. In a survey conducted by the NIAC, many power companies executives indicated that "while reliability is relatively easy to define and measure, resilience is more difficult" [3].

The definitions of resilience in the context of critical infrastructure systems have evolved from existing definitions in other fields. Infrastructure system resilience is generally regarded as the ability of the system to withstand a disturbance and recover back to its initial state [7]. Dalziell et al. [13] describes resilience as the overarching goal of a system to continue to function to the fullest possible extent in the face of stress to achieve its purpose. Based on this definition, resilience is a function of the systems vulnerability and its adaptive capacity, where adaptive capacity is the ability of the system to respond to external changes and recover from internal damages [13]. Haimes et al. [19] proposes a definition that is more related to disaster response: Resilience is the ability of the system to withstand a major disruption within acceptable degradation parameters and to recover within acceptable cost and time. Recently, several governmental reports defined resilience as a key component in their CIP programs. For instance, the US National Infrastructure Advisory Council (NIAC) defines infrastructure resilience as [3]:

> the ability to reduce the magnitude and/or duration of disruptive events. The effectiveness of a resilient infrastructure or enterprise depends on its ability to anticipate, absorb, adapt to, and/or rapidly recover from a potentially disruptive event.

Looking at the different definitions, one can notice commonalities and differences. Figure 1 shows the key resilience characteristics as identified by the CIP community and other disciplines. Attributes such as ability to recover and adapt were incorporated in several proposals. Some consider the long term resilience by including a planning component [2,3], others think about resilience as an emerging behavior? after a disturbance [7]. Most of the proposed definitions include 'the ability to withstand' or 'absorb' a disturbance as a key attribute. However, Madni et al. [25] argues that this attribute is the definition of survivability while resilience is the ability to bounce back. In general, it is difficult to select any of the discussed definitions as 'the best' or 'the global' definition for resilience as they were developed to serve different objectives and perspectives.

2.2 Resilience Assessment

Since the introduction of system resilience definition by Holling in 1973 [22], researchers have proposed different approaches and methodologies for assessing and evaluating system resilience. In the context of critical infrastructure systems, Biringer et al. [7] classify resilience assessment approaches into three general categories: structural, performance based, and hybrid. Structural approaches use the structure or topology of the system to evaluate its resilience. Performance based approaches evaluate the system resilience by measuring its performance before and after a disruption. Hybrid approaches combine both: structural and performance based. It has been acknowledged that resilience assessment or evaluation

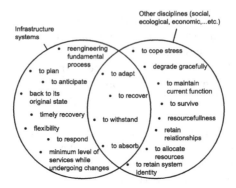

Fig. 1. Key characteristics of resilience definitions from different disciplines.

Table 1. Literature survey of resilience assessment in infrastructure.

Reference	Year	Approach	Context/System
[8]	2003	Hybrid (Quantitative)	Seismic/Infrastructure
[11]	2004	Performance (Quantitative)	Seismic/Infrastructure
[27]	2006	Performance (Quantitative)	Transportation
[9]	2007	Structural (Quantitative)	Seismic resilience
[6]	2009	Structural (Quantitative)	Risk/Transportation
[5]	2009	Performance (Quantitative)	Infrastructure
[28]	2009	Performance (Quantitative)	Telecommunication
[33]	2009	Hybrid (Quantitative)	Hurricane/Infrastructure
[12]	2010	Performance (Quantitative)	Seismic/Health Care Facilities
[24]	2010	Structural (Quantitative)	Risk/Transportation
[20]	2010	Performance (Quantitative)	Transportation
[14]	2011	Structural (Quantitative)	Risk/Transportation
[34]	2011	Performance (Quantitative)	Transportation
[35]	2011	Performance (Quant. &Quali.)	Petrochemical
[21]	2012	Performance (Quantitative)	Generic
[30]	2012	Performance (Quantitative)	Infrastructure
[18]	2012 7	Performance (Quantitative)	Transportation
[29]	2012	Performance (Quantitative)	Power Transmission Grid
[15]	2014	Hybrid (Quantitative)	Infrastructure

is not an easy task. It requires not only the static and dynamic properties of the systems but also other factors such as economic and human factors [25]. A survey of resilience assessment methods and frameworks for infrastructure systems is presented in Table 1. Several conclusions can be drawn from this survey. First, civil (structural) engineering community is one of the earliest areas in engineering discipline to adapt the resilience concept and use it in seismic related research. Therefore, there is more contribution in the literature from the civil (structural) engineering community than other areas. Second, the resilience assessment approach is highly dependent on the study definition and scope. Moreover, more work is being done on quantifying the resilience level using some performance indices. Finally, most of the work in assessing infrastructure systems resilience is recent (last few years) which reflects the increased attention to this topic within the research community.

3   Resilience Assessment Framework

Resilience assessment is needed for decision support to quantify the effectiveness of preparedness investments and activities. An effective preparedness plan improves the reaction of critical infrastructure following a disruption. Prior to conducting resilience assessment, one needs to define what aspects of the system under study constitute a resilient system. A proper modeling is also required to study the behavior of the system after disruptions. Then, a metric (or metrics) needs to be formulated to measure resilience. In this paper, we propose a resilient assessment framework consisting of three stages: defining resilience attributes, building infrastructure model, and measuring resilience, as shown in Fig. 2. More details are given in the following subsections.

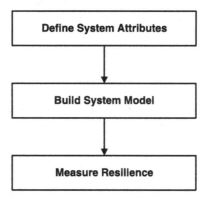

Fig. 2. Proposed resilience assessment framework.

3.1   Critical Infrastructure Systems Attributes

Since resilience is a multifaceted concept, it is imperative to assess resilience within the context of interest. The context of this paper is critical infrastructure systems, such power networks, water networks, and health facilities, with a particular interest in disaster response operations. Therefore, it is essential to define the systems attributes that constitute their resilience. The proposed framework focuses on the physical systems but it can be used to complement the financial aspects such as business continuity assessment. From the perspective of this paper, a resilience assessment framework should encompass the following attributes:

Static. This attribute measures the physical static parameters of the infrastructure. These parameters provide information about the components and topology of each system. Examples of these parameters include electrical network topology, capacity parameters of water pumps, and number of routs leading to a specific site. The interdependencies between the different systems are also described by this attribute. We should point out here that the interdependence relationships related to systems structure are measured here. Other interdependencies are captured by the other two attributes defined in the proposed framework.

Dynamic. This attribute describes the dynamic behavior of the infrastructure systems. Aspects such as emergency preparedness, response management, and recovery activities can all be measured in this attribute. For example, how the available resources are allocated, how failures propagate through the infrastructure, and how long it takes the infrastructure to return to its normal performance level.

Decision. This attribute measures the decision factors whose contributions are essential to the overall infrastructure resilience. Example of these factors include: decisions to allocate scarce resources, policies dictating command and control during disastrous events, and scheduling of available maintenance (or rescue) teams.

The above attributes are defined as linearly independent Eigen-attributes that influence the overall Critical Infrastructure (CI) resilience. The information given by these attributes provides insights on the systems capabilities to withstand, absorb, and recover from a disruption. The next section describes how these attributes can be modeled within the proposed resilience assessment framework.

3.2   System Modeling

Prior to measuring resilience, an infrastructure model needs to be constructed. There are a number of requirements that a model should satisfy. Some of these requirements are highlighted below:

- It should include the required parameters for measuring the specified attributes for system resilience. i.e. static, dynamic, and decision.
- As time is an integral part of resilience assessment, the model should capture the temporal behavior of the infrastructure.
- The model should be able to include both external and internal parameters.

To meet the above requirements, this paper uses the modeling framework proposed by Marti [26], namely the Infrastructure Interdependencies Simulator (i2Sim) framework. The i2Sim framework has been used in modeling critical infrastructure systems in disaster response applications [4,16,23]. The i2Sim defines a common ontology to capture the interactions between dissimilar systems using multiple simulation layers. It is based on a cell-channel approach. Infrastructure systems, such as power substations, water stations, and hospitals, are modeled using the i2Sim components: cells, channels, tokens, distributors, aggregators, sources, sinks, and modifiers. The input-output relationships is represented by a function (or a table) describing the operation of the cell. The output level is determined by the availability of input resources, level of physical damage to the cell, and the effect of possible modifiers. The availability of the input resources is determined by solution of the i2Sim solver every time step. The level of physical damage is modeled in i2Sim using the Physical Mode (PM) parameter which can be an external or internal. The i2Sim simulation layers shown in Fig. 3 are used to model the system attributes described in Sect. 3.1. The structure attribute can be modeled within the physical layer. For example, the topology of the infrastructure is represented by the arrangement of cells, channels, distributors, and aggregators. The physical parameters such as power substation capacities, and required manpower resources to operate a hospital are used to build the input-output functions. The dynamic attribute can be modeled by simulating the impact of resources allocation decisions on the performance of the infrastructure. Decision attribute can be modeled as modifiers inputs to the cells. It is worth noting that, in many cases, an attribute is not necessarily captured within a single layer but can be modeled across different layers. For example, in the decision attribute, one can model an emergency response policy within the decision layer while a maintenance team schedule is modeled in the physical layer.

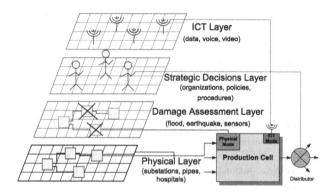

Fig. 3. i2Sim simulation layers [26].

3.3   Resilience Measure

An index (or metric) reflecting the defined resilience attributes is needed for decision support in planning for or designing resilient infrastructure. One approach is to use a performance indicator (or indicators) that captures the required attributes. In the context of CIP, the performance indicator is usually related to the functionality (output) level of the system.Thus, infrastructure resilience can be defined in terms of the deviation from the normal (healthy) performance level. We define the normal performance level as the pre-event level. This is represented graphically in Fig. 4. PL_N is the normal performance level (without any disruption) while PL_0 is the performance level immediately after the event. t_0 is the initial time of the event. t_R is the recovery time when the infrastructure returns to its normal performance level.

In this paper, we propose the use of i2Sim cell's output as a basis for defining an infrastructure resilience index. The output of an i2Sim cell is a measure of the operability of the modeled system. Moreover, it incorporates all the resilience attributes, static, dynamic, and decision, through the modeling approach described in Sect. 3.2. We define R as a resilience measure which can be defined mathematically as follows:

$$R = \int_{t_0}^{t_R} y(t)/t \, dt \tag{1}$$

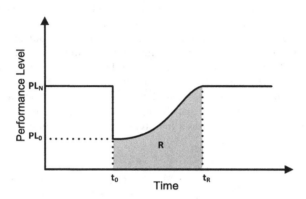

Fig. 4. Graphical representation of resilience

where $y(t)$ represents the i2Sim cell's output in per unit and $t = t_R - t_0$ is the duration of the event. R is measured in pu i.e. $R \in [0, 1]$. A higher R value indicates more resilient infrastructure. The integral represents the area under the curve between t_0 and t_f in Fig. 4. As t increases (longer time to recover), the value of R decreases (less resilient infrastructure). This is in accordance with the general concept of resilience. The performance level evaluation using i2Sim ensures that the defined attributes of resilience are measured by the proposed index.

4   Cyber-Physical Interactions Within Resilience Assessment

Many of Critical Infrastructure Protection tools and strategies focus on the physical infrastructures such as power networks, water networks, and transportation. On the other hand, Information Infrastructure is typically treated separately. Due to its complex and diverse nature, specific tools and strategies are developed for Critical Information Infrastructure Protection (CIIP) activities. The International CIIP Handbook 2008/2009 [10] summarizes the initiatives undertaken by different countries and organizations for CIIP related issues.

Concepts such as risk, reliability, security, and resilience are studied within CIP in terms of the physical infrastructure attributes such as flows, pressure, and voltages. Although these attributes could give good insights on the protection level, the cyber-physical interactions need to be considered. A large body of the existing research on cyber-physical systems highlights the difficulty of cyber-physical modeling.

In this paper, we outline a general approach for studying impact of cyber-physical interactions on critical infrastructure. First, we utilize the i2Sim simulation layers to

Table 2. Types of cyber-physical failures.

Failure type	Definition	Example
Control	Fail to maintain control functionality	Loss of a control signal (e.g. opening a circuit breaker)
Monitor	Fail to maintain monitor functionality	Loss of a monitoring signal (e.g. water level in a tank)
Time	Fail to send/receive information within acceptable time frame	Delay of a monitoring signal
Value	Fail to send/receive the correct value	Error in a monitoring signal (e.g. voltage value)

construct an Information and Communication Technologies (ICT) layer. The ICT layer can be designed using the i2Sim cell-channel approach or can be implemented using a domain specific modeling approach. After that, the interactions between the ICT layer and the physical layer can be modeled using the i2Sim parameters in the physical layer such as modifiers and distributors. For example, SCADA control signals can be interfaced to an i2Sim distributor to map the corresponding topology changes into the i2Sim distributor parameters. Since the focus of this paper is resilience assessment, we consider the impact of ICT failures on the physical systems. For this purpose, we define four failure types of cyber-physical interactions as shown in Table 2. Each failure is mapped into i2Sim model using the appropriate parameter. For example, a delay in one of the ICT signals can be implemented using an i2Sim channel with a delay.

5   Illustrative Example

In this section, we demonstrate the use of the proposed resilience assessment framework by applying it to a large university campus. The critical infrastructure of the campus were modeled using the i2Sim modelling approach described in Sect. 3.2. In this model, there are two power substations cells, one water station cell, one steam plant cell, and one hospital cell. The disaster events are taken from a heavy snow fall that occurred during the winter in 2006. Figure 5 depicts the sequence of events for the simulated scenario. The infrastructure and events data was collected during previous projects.

The objective of this example is to show that the proposed framework can model the defined resilience attributes and measure their impact on the resilience index. In this example, we assume the hospital's output as the performance level. Four cases are

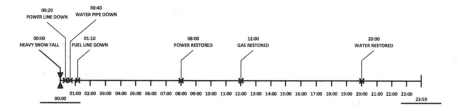

Fig. 5. Time line of the simulated events.

considered to study different resilience attributes. The results are shown in Fig. 6. Case (a) represents the original sequence of events as depicted in Fig. 5. In this case, the i2Sim model represents the structure and topology of the infrastructure. The resilience index for this case is R = 0.38. In case (b), we assume a dynamic behavior where the available resources are redistributed to increase the functionality of the hospital. The resilience for this case is R = 0.62 which is higher than case (a) as expected. In case (c), we assume that some of the resources allocation are done automatically (power distribution network is reconfigured through SCADA). The resilience index for this case increased slightly R = 0.70. Finally, we assumed a human factor in case (d) where a maintenance crew is required to perform switching operation instead of automatic reconfiguration as in case (c). The resilience index for this case is R = 0.66 which is lower than case (c). This example only shows that different actions (related to different attributes) bring different resilience. Whether they are better actions or how to find the best action is outside the scope of this paper and it is a future research direction.

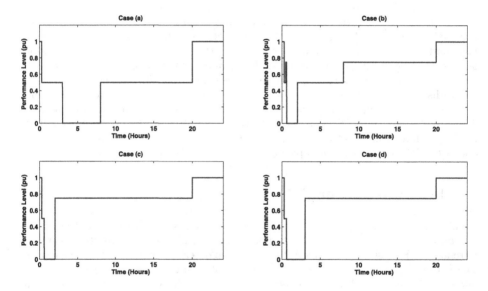

Fig. 6. Simulated results for the four cases in the illustrative example.

6   Conclusion

The primary focus of this paper is infrastructure resilience assessment. In this paper, we propose a resilience assessment framework consisting of three main components. First is the definition of the attributes that make an infrastructure resilient. Second is the modeling approach which is built upon the Infrastructure Interdependencies Simulator (i2Sim) framework. The third component is the resilience index that is measured using the system performance level. As highlighted in the relevant literature, the definition and quantification of resilience is highly dependent on the context and dimensions of the study. For the proposed framework, the context is emergency management in physical infrastructure. Its applicability is dependent on the modeling approach, which is shown to be able to capture the required resilience attributes. Also, we study the impact of cyber-physical interactions on the physical infrastructure resilience. The current framework can be extended in several ways. For example, the comparison between different resilient index values can include the cost associated with each resilience level. A multi-criteria decision technique such as Multi-Attribute Utility Theory (MAUT) can be applied to rank the resilience levels with their costs. Another extension is to use this framework within a comprehensive risk analysis in which the resilience toward events with high probability is studied.

References

1. Critical infrastructure preparedness and resilience research network (ciprnet)
2. Definitions of community resilience: an analysis. Technical report, Community and Regional Resilience Institute
3. A framework for estabilishing critical infrastructure resilience goals: final report and recommendations. Technical report, National Infrastructure Advisory Council, October 2010
4. Alsubaie, A., Di Pietro, A., Marti, J., Kini, P., Lin, T., Palmieri, S., Tofani, A.: A platform for disaster response planning with interdependency simulation functionality. In: Butts, J., Shenoi, S. (eds.) IFIP Advances in Information and Communication Technology. IFIP Advances in Information and Communication Technology, vol. 417, pp. 183–197. Springer, Heidelberg (2013)
5. Attoh-Okine, N.O., Cooper, A.T., Mensah, S.A.: Formulation of resilience index of urban infrastructure using belief functions. IEEE Sys. J $3(2)$, 147–153 (2009)
6. Berche, B., Von Ferber, C., Holovatch, T., Holovatch, Y.: Resilience of public transport networks against attacks. Eur. Phys. J. B $71(1)$, 125–137 (2009)
7. Biringer, B., Vugrin, E., Warren, D.: Critical Infrastructure System Security and Resiliency. CRC Press, Boca Raton (2013)
8. Bruneau, M., Chang, S.E., Eguchi, R.T., Lee, G.C., O'Rourke, T.D., Reinhorn, A.M., Shinozuka, M., Tierney, K., Wallace, W.A., von Winterfeldt, D.: A framework to quantitatively assess and enhance the seismic resilience of communities. Earthq. Spectra $19(4)$, 733–752 (2003)
9. Bruneau, M., Reinhorn, A.: Exploring the concept of seismic resilience for acute care facilities. Earthq. Spectra $23(1)$, 41–62 (2007)
10. Brunner, E.M., Suter, M.: International ciip handbook 2008/2009. Center for Security Studies, ETH Zurich (2008)
11. Chang, S.E., Shinozuka, M.: Measuring improvements in the disaster resilience of communities. Earthq. Spectra $20(3)$, 739–755 (2004)
12. Cimellaro, G.P., Reinhorn, A.M., Bruneau, M.: Framework for analytical quantification of disaster resilience. Eng. Struct. $32(11)$, 3639–3649 (2010)
13. Dalziell, E., McManus, S.: Resilience, vulnerability, and adaptive capacity: implications for system performance (2004)
14. Dorbritz, R.: Assessing the resilience of transportation systems in case of large-scale disastrous events. In: Proceedings of the 8th International Conference on Environmental Engineering, Vilnius, Lithuania, pp. 1070–1076 (2011)
15. Filippini, R., Silva, A.: A modeling framework for the resilience analysis of networked systems-of-systems based on functional dependencies. Reliab. Eng. Syst. Saf. 125, 82–91 (2014)

16. Formicola, V., Di Pietro, A., Alsubaie, A., DAntonio, S., Marti, J.: Assessing the impact of cyber attacks on wireless sensor nodes that monitor interdependent physical systems. In: Butts, J., Shenoi, S. (eds.) Critical Infrastructure Protection VIII. IFIP Advances in Information and Communication Technology, pp. 213–229. Springer, Heidelberg (2014)

17. Francis, R., Bekera, B.: A metric and frameworks for resilience analysis of engineered and infrastructure systems. Reliab. Eng. Syst. Saf. **121**, 90–103 (2014)

18. Freckleton, D., Heaslip, K., Louisell, W., Collura, J.: Evaluation of transportation network resiliency with consideration for disaster magnitude. In: 91st Annual Meeting of the Transportation Research Board, Washington (2012)

19. Haimes, Y.Y., Crowther, K., Horowitz, B.M.: Homeland security preparedness: balancing protection with resilience in emergent systems. Syst. Eng. **11**(4), 287–308 (2004)

20. Heaslip, K., Louisell, W., Collura, J., Urena Serulle, N.: A sketch level method for assessing transportation network resiliency to natural disasters and man-made events. In: Transportation Research Board 89th Annual Meeting. Report No. 10-3185 (2010)

21. Henry, D., Ramirez-Marquez, J.E.: Generic metrics and quantitative approaches for system resilience as a function of time. Reliab. Eng. Syst. Saf. **99**, 114–122 (2012)

22. Holling, C.S.: Resilience and stability of ecological systems. Annu. Rev. Ecol. Syst. **4**, 1–23 (1973)

23. Khouj, M.T., Sarkaria, S., Marti, J.R.: Decision assistance agent in real-time simulation. Int. J. Crit. Infrastruct. **10**(2), 151–173 (2014)

24. Leu, G., Abbass, H., Curtis, N.: Resilience of ground transportation networks: a case study on melbourne (2010)

25. Madni, A.M., Jackson, S.: Towards a conceptual framework for resilience engineering. IEEE Syst. J. **3**(2), 181–191 (2009)

26. Marti, J.R.: Multisystem simulation: analysis of critical infrastructures for disaster response. In: D'Agostino, G., Scala, A. (eds.) Networks of Networks: The Last Frontier of Complexity. Understanding Complex Systems, pp. 255–277. Springer International Publishing, Switzerland (2014)

27. Murray-Tuite, P.M.: A comparison of transportation network resilience under simulated system optimum and user equilibrium conditions. In: Simulation Conference, 2006, WSC 2006. Proceedings of the Winter, pp. 1398–1405. IEEE (2006)

28. Omer, M., Nilchiani, R., Mostashari, A.: Measuring the resilience of the transoceanic telecommunication cable system. IEEE Syst. J. **3**(3), 295–303 (2009)

29. Ouyang, M., Dueñas-Osorio, L.: Time-dependent resilience assessment and improvement of urban infrastructure systems. Chaos: Interdisc. J. Nonlin. Sci. **22**(3), 033122 (2012)

30. Ouyang, M., Dueñas-Osorio, L., Min, X.: A three-stage resilience analysis framework for urban infrastructure systems. Struct. Saf. **36–37**, 23–31 (2012)

31. Pant, R., Barker, K., Zobel, C.W.: Static and dynamic metrics of economic resilience for interdependent infrastructure and industry sectors. Reliab. Eng. Syst. Saf. **125**, 92–102 (2014)

32. Pederson, P., Dudenhoeffer, D., Hartley, S., Permann, M.: Critical infrastructure interdependency modeling: a survey of us and international research. Idaho National Laboratory, pp. 1–20 (2006)

33. Reed, D.A., Kapur, K.C., Christie, R.D.: Methodology for assessing the resilience of networked infrastructure. IEEE Syst. J. **3**(2), 174–180 (2009)

34. Serulle, N.U., Heaslip, K., Brady, B., Louisell, W.C., Collura, J.: Resiliency of transportation network of santo domingo, dominican republic. Transp. Res. Rec.: J. Transp. Res. Board **2234**(1), 22–30 (2011)
35. Vugrin, E.D., Warren, D.E., Ehlen, M.A.: A resilience assessment framework for infrastructure and economic systems: quantitative and qualitative resilience analysis of petrochemical supply chains to a hurricane. Process Saf. Prog. **30**(3), 280–290 (2011)

A Methodology for Resilience Optimisation of Interdependent Critical Infrastructures

Luca Galbusera[1]([✉]), Ivano Azzini[2], and Georgios Giannopoulos[1]

[1] Institute for the Protection and Security of the Citizen, European Commission,
Joint Research Centre, Via E. Fermi 2749, 21027 Ispra, VA, Italy
{luca.galbusera,georgios.giannopoulos}@jrc.ec.europa.eu
[2] GFT Italia s.r.l., Via A. Campanini 6, 20124 Milano, Italy
ivano.azzini@ext.jrc.ec.europa.eu

Abstract. Many methodologies proposed in the literature for modelling and simulating the behaviour of critical infrastructures (CIs) in
response to disruptive events are based on exhaustive analytic models,
require extensive amounts of data and suffer from high computational
burden. These factors restrain their applicability in practical policy making processes, which often require higher flexibility and efficiency in the
delivery of analysis and prediction results. Taking these constraints into
consideration, in this paper we propose a resilience-oriented framework
for the high-level analysis of networked CIs, based on the concept of
functional representation of interdependencies. We also show the usefulness of the proposed methodology to improve the operability of the
network by appropriately tuning relevant parameters of selected assets
according to an optimisation algorithm aiming at the improvement of
the overall resilience of the CI network. This feature ultimately provides
a guidance for selecting proper strategies to bound the propagation of
damages across interdependent assets/infrastructures.

Keywords: Critical infrastructures · Resilience · Interdependencies ·
Optimisation · Simulated annealing

1 Introduction

Critical infrastructures (CIs) are those infrastructures whose operability is
reputed of paramount importance in order to maintain security, economics, and
social welfare. Communication, banking, water supply, health, energy, and emergency services are examples of sectors wherein inoperability can lead to great
impact on the quality of life of the general public [1,2]. Related safety and security concerns resulted in a series of programs, both at national and international
levels, addressing the protection and resilience of CIs against different classes of
hazards (see for instance the FACIES[1] and CIPRNet[2] projects).

---

[1] http://facies.dia.uniroma3.it.
[2] https://www.ciprnet.eu/summary.html.

© European Union, 2016
E. Rome et al. (Eds.): CRITIS 2015, LNCS 9578, pp. 56–66, 2016.
DOI: 10.1007/978-3-319-33331-1_5

A necessary step towards protection, preparedness and resilience is represented by detecting interdependencies and modelling the complex behaviours that CIs, as systems of systems, can exhibit [3]. Through the years, such a purpose has to cope with the gradual shift from vertically-integrated systems towards different types of network structures, wherein interaction among the components can embrace numerous and variable kinds of physical, cyber, logical, and geographic dependencies [4]. More and more with time, alongside with other forms of interdependence, information flow also contributes to enrich the inter-linkage between different infrastructures and to determine the emerging resilience properties, as for instance in the electrical domain [5,6]. Assuming that each part of a networked infrastructure can be assessed by means of specialised models, nevertheless the emerging behaviour of the overall network can't generally be inferred by a simple combination of sectoral modelling frameworks [7]. Integrative approaches are thus looked for in order to assess large scale, complex CIs. See [8] for a recent review of different approaches to CI modelling.

This article comprises an effort towards a generic modelling method for resilience optimisation, wherein the focus in not on the differences between types of assets and infrastructures, but on their interdependencies expressed in terms of service and disservice propagation. Based on the representation method proposed in [9], we characterise a given set of CIs as a dynamical network, wherein binary output variables are associated to the nodes and depend on their internal dynamics. Interaction and inoperability propagation across different infrastructures are mediated by these binary variables and their combinations. This kind of description realises a number of contexts wherein the concept of asset in/out of service is considered. Furthermore, in this paper we also discuss how our modelling approach can serve towards resilience optimisation with respect to critical events affecting some components of a given CI network. This contribution is supported by the construction of an ad-hoc optimisation algorithm based on meta-heuristic methods. The proposed approach seems to present some advantages, as: it can be implemented at different scales to networks of CIs; it refers to a functional modelling of interdependencies; it exploits a representation based on a limited amount of variables, which can be advantageous in a high-level optimisation perspective. Referring to the latter point, it has to be observed that the proposed framework can also be combined with a great gamut of different underlying models available in the literature or developed ad-hoc.

The rest of this article is organized as follows: Sect. 2 introduces our approach to modelling CI networks from a resilience point of view; in Sect. 3 we address the network resilience enhancement through optimisation, also introducing our numerical algorithm; in Sect. 4 we apply the proposed modelling and optimisation methods to a numerical example.

2 Modelling CIs and Interdependencies from a Resilience Perspective

According to [10], "given the occurrence of a particular disruptive event (or set of events), the resilience of a system to that event (or set of events) is the ability to reduce effectively both the magnitude and duration of the deviation from targeted system performance levels". In order to address resilience analysis and optimisation, in this paper we represent CIs (either individually, in parts or as conglomerates) as the set $\mathcal{N}$ of nodes of a directed graph, and the functional dependencies through the associated edge set $\mathcal{E} \subseteq \mathcal{N} \times \mathcal{N}$, where edge $e_{ij} \in \mathcal{E}$ connects source node i to destination node j.

Typically CIs produce, store, transform and/or deliver specific types of resources/services. Correspondingly, we will attach to each node $i \in \mathcal{N}$ of the network an inner dynamics associated to a generic operability state variable $x_i(t) \in [0,1]$, where 1 denotes full operability. Defining $\bar{x}_i \in (0,1)$ as the minimum acceptable value of x_i ensuring service, we also introduce the output variable

$$y_i(t) = \begin{cases} 1 \text{ if } x_i(t) \geq \bar{x}_i \\ 0 \text{ otherwise} \end{cases} \tag{1}$$

where $y_i(t) = 1$ indicates that node i is providing service at time t, while $y_i(t) = 0$ the opposite. This output variable is transmitted to all nodes in $\mathcal{N}$ connected to i through its outgoing edges. For simplicity, in this representation we assume that the same output signal is transmitted through all these edges. Correspondingly, as detailed below in this section, the inner dynamics of the nodes in the network will depend on the output variables of the respective source nodes and their combinations. An example of such an architecture is provided in Fig. 1, where interdependency relationships can take the form of logical combinations of the outputs of source nodes. The latter, binary representation of interdependences is a peculiar feature which we exploit to represent the operability of the different nodes in a serviceability perspective. This allows the introduction of new semantics substituting traditional modelling paradigms based on the exchange of physical quantities (e.g. electricity, water, traffic flow, etc.) between assets and infrastructures.

We assume that the operability state $x_i(t)$ of each node $i \in \mathcal{N}$, when exposed to the effects of a critical event affecting the network, depends on the following factors:

– its *static resilience*, which refers to the ability of node i to continue its operation despite the event, ensuring $x_i \geq \bar{x}_i$ as long as possible;
– its *dynamic resilience*, describing the ability of node i to promptly recover to a serviceable status after the impacting event.

The dynamics of each node $i \in \mathcal{N}$ is assumed to be described by one of two possible operational modes, which are associated to the concepts of static and dynamic resilience introduced above:

$$\dot{x}(t) = \begin{cases} F_i(x_i(t), f_i), & \text{if } u_i(t) = 0 \\ R_i(x_i(t), r_i), & \text{if } u_i(t) = 1 \end{cases} \tag{2}$$

Herein, $f_i > 0$ is the static resilience parameter of node i and $r_i > 0$ its dynamic resilience parameter. For all $x_i \in [0,1]$, we have $F_i(x_i, f_i) \leq 0$, $F_i(0, f_i) = 0$

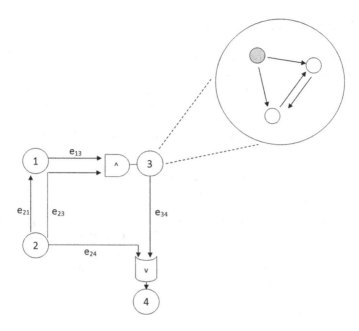

Fig. 1. Representation of a CI network including AND and OR interdependency relationships. The figure emphasizes that a network structure may represent the considered CI network at different levels of abstraction, depending on the scope and objectives of the modelling process as well as on the amount of the available data. Thus, we may associate a node to a specific asset of a particular CI, a component of a CI network, a region inside a country, an entire country or even to a set of cross-country CIs.

and $R_i(x_i, r_i) \geq 0$, $R_i(1, r_i) = 0$. These functions can be suitably specified to describe the failure mode and recovery mode, respectively. The choice of the active mode is determined by $u_i(t)$, which we define as follows:

$$u_i(t) = B_i \left(\{ y_j(t) : \ j \in \mathcal{N}, \ e_{ji} \in \mathcal{E} \} \right) \wedge (\neg d_i(t)) \tag{3}$$

Herein, B_i is a boolean function having as arguments the outputs of the source nodes associated to the incoming edges of node i. Finally, boolean signal $d_i(t)$ is associated to external perturbations inducing triggering events and causing the activation of the failure mode of node i, when active (i.e. while $d_i(t) = 1$).

To conclude, observe that the proposed representation is in accordance with the modelling framework proposed in [9]. In this paper, anyway, we use the terms of static and dynamic resilience in order to provide a pragmatic dimension to these concepts: static resilience reflects the prevention measures that a CI operator puts in place in order to absorb the impact of a disruption affecting this node, while dynamic resilience reflects the response measures exploited in order to recover as quickly as possible from a disruptive event.

3   Resilience Optimisation

In this section, we describe an optimisation problem whose objective is to improve the configuration of the static and dynamic resilience parameters of a CI network. The idea is to take into account both the features of the functional interdependency description we refer to in this paper and the generally large dimensionality of the problem. Furthermore, we will introduce an associated optimisation algorithm based on simulated annealing [11,12].

3.1   Optimisation Problem Formulation

Consider a single-disruption scenario wherein k is the node affected by critical event and assume that the resilience parameters of nodes $i \in \mathcal{N} \setminus \{k\}$ are involved in the optimisation process. Associate to each of these nodes nominal values $\bar{f}_i$ and $\bar{r}_i$ for the static and dynamic resilience parameters, representing a system configuration we are interested in improving. Then, we introduce the following minimisation problem over the finite time horizon $[T_0, T_f]$:

$$\min_{f_i, r_i, i \in \mathcal{N} \setminus \{k\}} J$$

$$J = \int_{T_0}^{T_f} \sum_{i \in \mathcal{N} \setminus \{k\}} [J_{i1}(x_i(t)) + J_{i2}(f_i) + J_{i3}(r_i)] \, dt \tag{4}$$

s.t.

$$f_i \in [f_i^-, f_i^+], \ r_i \in [r_i^-, r_i^+], \forall i \in \mathcal{N} \setminus \{k\}$$

and subject to the dynamical model described in Sect. 2. Herein, we define

$$J_{i1}(x_i) = \alpha_i \left(\frac{x_i - \bar{x}_i}{\bar{x}_i} \right)^2 \Theta(\bar{x}_i - x_i)$$

$$J_{i2}(f_i) = \beta_i \left(\frac{f_i - \bar{f}_i}{\bar{f}_i} \right)^2$$

$$J_{i3}(r_i) = \gamma_i \left(\frac{r_i - \bar{r}_i}{\bar{r}_i} \right)^2$$

where $\Theta(\cdot)$ is the Heaviside function and α_i, β_i, $\gamma_i > 0$ are weights. Observe that, in the definition of J_{1i} provided above, any value $x_i \geq \bar{x}_i$ does not contribute to J. Furthermore, terms J_{2i} and J_{3i} represent reconfiguration costs related to the modification of the static and dynamic resilience parameters associated to node i. This definition of the cost function complies with some of the most recent definitions of the concept of resilience, which account for the control costs as well as for the serviceability of the system [13,14]. Finally, in (4) we included bounds f_i^-, f_i^+, r_i^- and r_i^+ on the optimisation variables, to be adequately specified.

Main:
1. Input: $x(0), \bar{x}, \bar{f}, \bar{r}, \text{JPar}, \text{SPar}, \Delta_{min}, \Delta_{step}, \Delta_{max}$
2. Init $f = \bar{f}, r = \bar{r}$
   $NetModel(n, x(0), f, r, \bar{x}, \bar{f}, \bar{r}, k)$
   $NetModelR1 = \textbf{Prune}(NetModel)$
3. for $\Delta = \Delta_{min} : \Delta_{step} : \Delta_{max}$
   $out_1 = \textbf{OptProc}(\textbf{Jfun}(NetModelR1, \text{JPar}, \Delta), \text{SPar})$
   if $\#NetModelR1(out_1.unreach) \neq 0$
   $NetModelR2 = \textbf{Prune}(NetModelR2)$
   $out_2 = \textbf{OptProc}(\textbf{Jfun}(NetModelR2, \text{JPar}, \Delta), \text{SPar})$
   end if
   $\text{BestSol}(\Delta) = \textbf{Best}(out_1, out_2)$
   $f = \text{BestSol.f}(\Delta); r = \text{BestSol.r}(\Delta)$
   end for
4. save **BestSol**
end

Fig. 2. Optimisation algorithm.

3.2 Numerical Algorithm

In Fig. 2 we report the pseudo-code of the algorithm we apply to the solution of the optimal control problem (4) in the case of the considered single-disruption scenario affecting node $k \in \mathcal{N}$, assuming that the external perturbation induces $y_k(t) = 1, \forall t \in [T_0 + \Delta_{min}, T_0 + \Delta_{max}]$ with $0 \leq \Delta_{min} \leq \Delta_{max} \leq T_f - T_0$, and $y_k(t) = 0$ out of this interval.

At Step 1 we initialize the following parameters: the initial states $x(0)$, the threshold vector $\bar{x}$ and the vectors $\bar{f}$ and $\bar{r}$ collecting the nominal static and dynamic resilience parameters; the optimisation and simulation parameters $JPar = \{\alpha_i, \beta_i, \gamma_i, \forall i \in \mathcal{N} \setminus \{k\}\}$ and $SPar$; parameters $\Delta_{min}, \Delta_{step}, \Delta_{max}$, specifying the iterative search process at Step 3; the triggering node k.

At Step 2, we initialize the variables involved in the computation as well as the model *NetModel* of the dynamical network constructing according to the model presented in Sect. 2. Thanks to the **Prune** function, when relevant we derive a reduced model *NetModelR1* wherein the nodes structurally unreachable by the disruption are eliminated from the optimisation problem.

Step 3 is built taking into account the intuition that a higher value of Δ, describing the operability perturbation horizon affecting the output of node k, is likely produce larger displacements of the optimisation variables from the nominal values in many cases. Thus, the optimum search is performed iteratively, by progressively increasing the value of Δ starting from Δ_{min}. Inside this cycle, we make use of the optimal control search procedure **OptProc**, based on a simulated annealing method. By this technique we are able to explore extensively the search space, which in general represents a non-trivial task due to the network size and the possible presence of many local minima. Simulated annealing is intended to avoid the solution search process to be trapped too sensitively by such minima. Once the simulated annealing procedure is completed, we are able to evaluate the disturbance propagation associated to the best solution found. As one possible outcome of the process consists in a network wherein some nodes are unaffected by the perturbation, we can further refine the optimisation process by resetting the associated control variables to the nominal values and repeating **OptProc** over an even smaller search space, related to the affected nodes alone as specified in model *NetModelR2*. Finally, we select the best solution found in the cycle. Note that solution out_2, when computed, outperforms solution out_1 form an optimisation viewpoint. The best solutions found for the relevant resilience parameters are then used to initialize the next iteration.

4 Numerical Experiments

In this section, we propose an application of the methodology to a dynamic network of homogeneous CIs, whose topology is represented in Fig. 3. The network comprises 32 nodes and we focus here on a single-damage scenario wherein node $k = 28$ is inoperative for $t \in [0, \Delta]$ and introduces a propagating effect. The inoperability propagation is assumed to be regulated by AND type functions involving the incoming edges of each node, while the considered time horizon is $[T_0, T_f] = [0, 1]$. The dynamical model associated to nodes $i \in \mathcal{N} \setminus \{k\}$ is described by

$$F_i(x_i(t), f_i) = -f_i x_i(t)$$
$$R_i(x_i(t), r_i) = r_i (1 - x_i(t)) \tag{5}$$

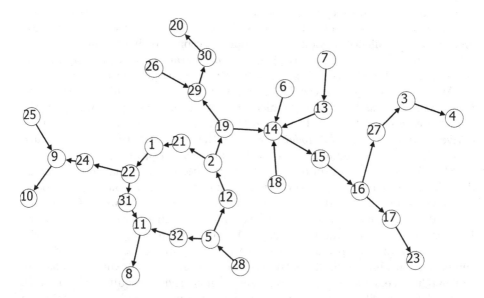

Fig. 3. The topology of the system of critical infrastructures that is used in the present analysis

The usage of exponential failure and recovery models is in accordance with fault classification reported in [15] and it reveals high adaptable to many practical contexts. In our example, $\forall i \in \mathcal{N} \setminus \{k\}$, the operability threshold is $\bar{x}_i = 0.5$ while the nominal static and dynamic resilience parameters are $\bar{f}_i = 5$ $\bar{r}_i = 1$. We apply the optimisation algorithm described in Sect. 3 assuming $\alpha_i, \beta_i, \gamma_i = 1, \forall i \in \mathcal{N} \setminus \{k\}$.

Define the initial optimum search space $\mathcal{S}_C^0(28) = \{f_i, r_i \geq 0 : i \in \mathcal{N} \setminus \{28\}\}$ associated to the algorithm variable *NetModel*. The **Prune** function applied at Step 2 serves to reduce the search space by suitably eliminating from this set the control variables which are unaffected by the disruption due to the unreachability of the associated nodes, which depends on the network topology in Fig. 3. The set of unreachable nodes is $\mathcal{N}_u(28) = \{6, 7, 13, 18, 25, 26\}$. Thus, the optimum search space for *NetModelR1* will be reduced to $\mathcal{S}_C(28) = \{f_i, r_i \geq 0 : i \in \mathcal{N}_r\}$, where $\mathcal{N}_r = \mathcal{N} \setminus \{\{28\}, \{\mathcal{N}_u(28)\}\}$, while we set $f_i = \bar{f}_i$ and $r_i = \bar{r}_i, \forall i \in \mathcal{N}_u(28)$.

The search procedure at Step 3 of the algorithm is based on *NetModelR1*. Iterations start at $\Delta = \Delta_{min} = 0$ from the initialization $f_i = \bar{f}_i$ and $r_i = \bar{r}_I$, $\forall i \in \mathcal{N}_r$. Once the simulated annealing procedure in **OptProc** (first call) has produced its best estimate of the optimisation parameters in the space $\mathcal{S}_C(28)$, we can identify the corresponding set of nodes $\mathcal{N}_a(\Delta)$ unaffected by the disruption of node 28. Consequently, we can refine the optimum estimate by setting $f_i = \bar{f}_i$ and $r_i = \bar{r}_i, \forall i \in \mathcal{N}_a(\Delta)$ and repeating the simulated annealing procedure in **OptProc** on a further reduced search space. Iteration by iteration, as

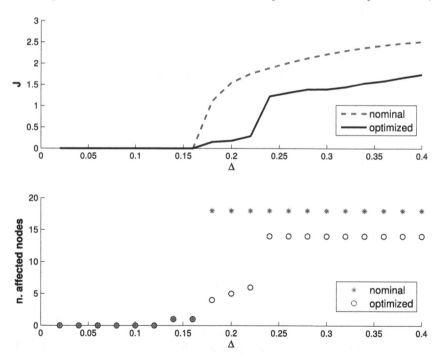

Fig. 4. Value of the cost function J and number of nodes affected by disruption over the simulation horizon as functions of Δ.

the disruption duration Δ increases, the search is initialized at the best values of f_i and r_i previously found, while the search space is re-initialized to $\mathcal{S}_C(28)$.

Figure 4 reports the value of J and the number of nodes affected by disruption over the simulation horizon, expressed as functions of Δ. We report both the cases of the nominal system (i.e., $f_i = \bar{f}_i$ and $r_i = \bar{r}_i$, $\forall i \in \mathcal{N} \setminus \{k\}$) and the system reconfigured according to the optimisation procedure described above. It appears clearly that our parameter choice consistently outperforms the nominal configuration in terms of damage propagation mitigation and recovery. Finally, we focus on the case with $\Delta = 0.2$ and detail the disruption propagation for the nominal and optimised plant along the node sequence $\{28, 5, 12, 2, 19, 14, 15, 16, 17, 23\}$, which represents a key CI ridge in the network under consideration. In Fig. 5 we can observe that, while the nominal network displays increasing inoperability intervals along this sequence, the optimally re-tuned network is able to confine the spread of the damage.

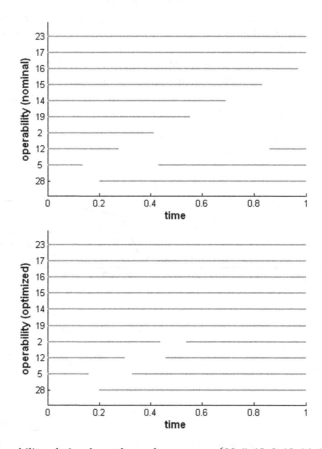

Fig. 5. Inoperability chain along the node sequence $\{28, 5, 12, 2, 19, 14, 15, 16, 17, 23\}$. The operability of node i at time t is represented by a line segment when $y_i(t) = 1$.

5   Concluding Remarks

In the present paper, we introduced a framework for the analysis and resilience optimisation in networked CIs. We expressed the dynamics of the nodes in terms of synthetic resilience indicators, namely their static and dynamic resilience parameters, which describe the ability of the associated infrastructures to withstand and recover from a disruptive event. Furthermore, infrastructure serviceability and inoperability propagation across the network were represented at a functional level, by exploiting boolean interdependence relationships. Based on this representation, we also formulated an optimisation problem supporting the improvement of the network resilience by means of a reconfiguration of the static and dynamic resilience parameters. The algorithm we proposed for its solution exploits a meta-heuristic search procedure, which can be helpful to cope with the high dimensionality of the parameter search space often found in applications.

Acknowledgment. This work is supported by the Annual Work Programme 2010 and 2012 for the specific programme on the "Prevention, Preparedness and Consequence Management of Terrorism and other Security-related Risks (CIPS)", which is financed by Directorate General Home Affairs of the European Commission. The authors would like to express their gratitude for this support.

References

1. Bashan, A., Berezin, Y., Buldyrev, S.V., Havlin, S.: The extreme vulnerability of interdependent spatially embedded networks. Nat. Phys. **9**(10), 667–672 (2013)
2. Edwards, M.: Critical Infrastructure Protection, vol. 116. IOS Press, Amsterdam (2014)
3. Eusgeld, I., Kröger, W., Sansavini, G., Schläpfer, M., Zio, E.: The role of network theory and object-oriented modeling within a framework for the vulnerability analysis of critical infrastructures. Reliab. Eng. Syst. Saf. **94**(5), 954–963 (2009)
4. Rinaldi, S.M., Peerenboom, J.P., Kelly, T.K.: Identifying, understanding, and analyzing critical infrastructure interdependencies. IEEE Control Syst. **21**(6), 11–25 (2001)
5. Locke, G., Gallagher, P.D.: NIST framework and roadmap for smart grid interoperability standards, release 1.0. National Institute of Standards and Technology, p. 33 (2010)
6. Galbusera, L., Theodoridis, G., Giannopoulos, G.: Intelligent energy systems: introducing power-ICT interdependency in modeling and control design. IEEE Trans. Ind. Electron. **62**(4), 2468–2477 (2015)
7. Woods, D.D., Leveson, N., Hollnagel, E.: Resilience Engineering: Concepts and Precepts. Ashgate Publishing Ltd, Farnham (2012)
8. Ouyang, M.: Review on modeling and simulation of interdependent critical infrastructure systems. Reliab. Eng. Syst. Saf. **121**, 43–60 (2014)
9. Filippini, R., Silva, A.: A modeling framework for the resilience analysis of networked systems-of-systems based on functional dependencies. Reliab. Eng. Syst. Saf. **125**, 82–91 (2014)

10. Vugrin, E.D., Turnquist, M.A., Brown, N.J.: Optimal recovery sequencing for critical infrastructure resilience assessment. Sandia National Laboratories (SNL-NM), Albuquerque. Technical Report SAND2010-6237 (2010)
11. Kirkpatrick, S., Gelatt Jr., C.D., Vecchi, M.P.: Optimization by simulated annealing. Science **220**(4598), 671–680 (1983)
12. Press, W.H.: Numerical Recipes: The Art of Scientific Computing. Cambridge University Press, New York (2007)
13. Vugrin, E.D., Camphouse, R.C., Sunderland, D.: Quantitative resilience analysis through control design. Sandia National Laboratories (SNL-NM), Albuquerque, NM, USA. Technical Report SAND2009-5957 (2009)
14. Vugrin, E.D., Camphouse, R.C.: Infrastructure resilience assessment through control design. Int. J. Crit. Infrastruct. **7**(3), 243–260 (2011)
15. Deckers, J., Jepsen, O.N., Latzel, S., Metz, H., Stuecher, R.: Condition monitoring and failure diagnosis in plants of the metals industry. In: Fault Detection, Supervision and Safety of Technical Processes 2003 (SAFEPROCESS 2003): A Proceedings Volume from the 5th IFAC Symposium, Washington, DC, 9–11 June 2003, vol. 1, p. 453. Elsevier (2004)

PPP (Public-Private Partnership)-Based Business Continuity of Regional Banking Services for Communities in Wide-Area Disasters

Limitation of Individual BCP/BCM Ensuring Interoperability Among Banks Cooperation with Local Governments for Socioeconomic Resilience in Japan

Kenji Watanabe[(⊠)] and Takuya Hayashi

Graduate School of Engineering, Nagoya Institute of Technology,
Gokiso-Cho, Shouwa-Ku, Nagoya, Aichi 466-855, Japan
kewatanabe@nifty.com, 22117049@stn.nitech.ac.jp

Abstract. Traditionally, banks have developed Disaster Recovery Plan (DRP), Business Continuity Plan (BCP), and implemented structure of Business Continuity Management (BCM) for their business continuity as regulators required. However, once a wide-area disaster occurs, it is difficult for each bank only with individual BCP/BCM to continue local banking services at a limited but necessary level for vital activities and socioeconomic recoveries. Based on the actual experiences and discussions in the Kyoto Prefecture, the importance of Public-Private Partnership (PPP)-based Area BCM is recognized and actual procedures and systems concept are overviewed.

Keywords: Business Continuity Plan · Business Continuity Management · Public-Private partnership · Retail banking · Interoperability · Socioeconomic resilience

1 An Overview of Resilience Building in the Banking Industry

Before actual industry-wide damages occurred to the banking business due to the World Trade Center bombing in New York in 1993, main part of the resilience enhancing efforts of banking industry had been Disaster Recovery Plan (DRP) which mainly focused on Information and Communication Technology (ICT) readiness with data back-up, redundant networks, or back-up computer systems. However, the industry experienced the limitation of DRP in feasibility of recovery operations with not only operational element but also other elements such as human resources, operational sites, and external dependencies such as ICT vendors, and critical infrastructure and utility service providers.

© Springer International Publishing Switzerland 2016
E. Rome et al. (Eds.): CRITIS 2015, LNCS 9578, pp. 67–76, 2016.
DOI: 10.1007/978-3-319-33331-1_6

Based on the recognition of the limitations of DRP after the bombing disaster, Business Continuity Plan (BCP), which identifies an organization's exposure to internal and external threats and synthesizes hard and soft assets to provide effective prevention and recovery for the organization, while maintaining competitive advantage and value system integrity, had started to penetrate into bank's management [1].

After the banking industry acquired "lessons learnt" from experiences in preparations for the Year 2000 problem (Y2K) and in another industry-wide severe disruptions caused by the 9.11 attacks in 2001, BCP had been shifted into Business Continuity Management (BCM) as a management system with strategic continuous improvement [2].

Addition to the adoption to the above development of resilience enhancement in global banking industry, the Japanese banks had extra experiences with wide-area natural disaster oriented disruptions in retail banking services with the Great Hanshin earthquake in 1995, the Niigata-Chuetsu earthquake in 2004, the Great East Japan earthquake in 2011, and other disasters along with major floods or severe snow storms.

From among a wide range of banking services, this paper focuses on retail banking services, especially on accessibility of the deposit account, which will be highly demanded in wide-area disasters to secure vital activities and recovery efforts in the affected areas.

2   Emerging Limitations of Individual BCP/BCM

2.1   BCP/BCM Limitations and Challenges for Japanese Banks

As banking industry is highly regulated, most of the banks from the largest banks to small regional banks have been required to prepare BCP and operate it as BCM. They have been directed by the regulators such as the Financial Services Agency (FSA) and the Bank of Japan through guidelines and periodical regulatory inspections. As a result, BCP/BCM has been equipped at each bank. However, many of them are just to meet the necessary formal requirements from the regulators and lack of feasibility. On the other hand, banking operations have been getting heavily dependent on ICT and their operations are highly connected with each other through networks especially in nationwide settlement operations, wire-transfer transactions, and interoperation of Automated Teller Machines (ATMs).

Because of the interdependencies among the networks and individual BCP/BCM, there have been several industry-wide incidents caused by a single bank but spread through the nation-wide banking network. Each BCP/BCM is limited to an individual bank, and elements of interdependencies among banks are not much considered.

2.2   Emerging Importance of Industry-Wide Efforts to Build Interoperability Among Local Banks

As discussed in the previous section, banking operations are well networked and highly dependent each other, the limitations of individual BCP/BCM at each bank have a possibility to cause critical service disruptions at an industry-wide level when they have been damaged by severe disasters and any single bank could not response to by themselves. After the Japanese banking industry and regulators experienced several industry-wide incidents, the industry has introduced street-wide exercises to make sure interoperability among banks. [3] The Bank of Japan is playing a proactive role to lead the efforts to ensure the availability of banking services as one of critical infrastructures for their local community even in wide-area disasters.

2.3 Recognized Needs for Changes After the Great East Japan Earthquake in 2011

In the Great East Japan Earthquake which occurred in March, 2011, the three banks, the Bank of Iwate, the Tohoku Bank, and the Kita-Nippon Bank, were severely damaged by the earthquake and tsunami. After the three banks recognized the limitations of business continuity by individual banks, the three CEOs immediately discussed and agreed to consider cooperation with sharing remaining resources as much as they could to recover their banking services to the minimum level that was required for the community to secure vital activities and recovery efforts.

The fields they considered for co-operation were [3]:

(1) Mutual back-up for cash availability management
(2) Private armored cars for cash and valuables transportation
(3) Telecommunication equipment
(4) Tools, stationaries, water, foods, and gas
(5) Employees transportation to the affected areas
(6) Coordination in office hours and exemption of inter-bank transaction fees
(7) Supporting shared corporate customers' recovery
(8) Media messages and public communications
(9) Governmental bill colleting operations
(10) Tentative shared branch operations

(2), (3), and (10) were actually implemented and effectively worked to recover and keep their banking operations at limited but required level for the community (Table 1).

Table 1. Implemented inter-bank cooperation

	Fields for cooperation among the three banks	Actions taken
(2)	Private armored cars for cash and valuables transportation	Because of the lack of gas for cars in the affected area, private armored car operator could not dispatch their cars to their bank clients. The three banks and the armored car operator agreed to share operations and also to transport essential commodities for their employees' lives in the disaster situation.
(3)	Telecommunication equipment	Each bank had telecommunication problems with the branches in the affected areas and the three

(Continued)

Table 1. (*Continued*)

	Fields for cooperation among the three banks	Actions taken
		banks agreed to share their telecommunication tools and equipment such as cell phones, satellite phones, or MCA (Multi-channel Access) radio systems.
(10)	Tentative shared branch operations	Some of their branches were heavily damaged by the earthquake and tsunami, and also some employees including management had become victimized or missing. The three banks agreed to set up tentative branches at templary sites.

After the earthquake, the three banks have worked with the Bank of Japan and established a council to continue discussions on an agreement for mutual backup in disasters, to execute street-wide exercises, and also to have collective negotiating with authorities to get necessary governmental support in disasters [4].

2.4   Implications from the Discussion Case

Through the discussions in the previous sections, the following points have been recognized and those should be taken into considerations in further development of local banking resilience;

- limitations of individual BCP/BCM at a single bank
- effectiveness of inter-bank operations at local level
- some difficulties to have accountability of co-operation
- need more understandings and supports from regulators
- need support from local government in priority transportation, public communication, and resource arrangements

3   Case: Kyoto BCP and Availability Enhancement of Regional Baking Services in Wide-Area Disasters

3.1   Kyoto BCP and Cooperative Efforts with Regional Banks

Based on the experiences of unexpected disruptions of social functionalities in the Great East Japan earthquake, the Kyoto Prefectural Government recognized the importance of an area-based BCP/BCM and developed the Kyoto BCP – Guideline for actions to establish socioeconomic resilience in Kyoto based on PPP (Fig. 1).

They illustrates the expected risks surrounding Kyoto as below [5]:

One of the key elements of the guideline is to maintain cash flows for residents and companies in the affected areas through activate individual BCP/BCM, cooperation among regional banks, special arrangement requests to governments, and public-private partnerships.

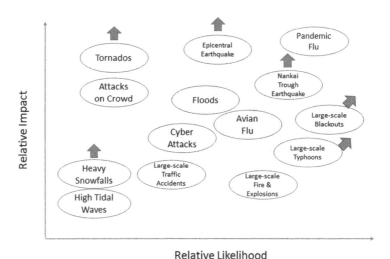

Fig. 1. Illustrated risk map defined in the Kyoto BCP

3.2   Conceptual Structure of the PPP-Based Efforts for Regional Banking Availability

The Kyoto BCP committee has several working groups and one of them is for regional banks and regulators (the Kinki Finance Bureau and the Bank of Japan – Kyoto Branch) to discuss possible cooperation in wide-area disasters. The working group started their discussions with the actual experiences of business disruptions with the flood caused by the concentrated heavy rain in August, 2012. In the disaster, some of the banks' branches with full services and only ATM machines were affected but the information was not shared among banks and local governments. This resulted in the lack of information to the residents and companies that wanted to know the accessibility to their deposit in the banks.

The banking industry is highly regulated and troubles in their businesses have to be reported to the local regulator, the Kinki Finance Bureau, that also have to report to the Financial Services Agency (FSA) However, the information is never shared with the local governments in the affected areas.

Based on the above experiences and situations, the regional banks and the Kyoto Prefectural government tried to expand their scope of BCP/BCM with the concept of Kyoto BCP [6].

Each local banks in Kyoto is expanding its BCP/BCM scope to its corporate group, supply chain, industry associations and regulators, and local community (Fig. 2).

The Kyoto Prefectural government is also expanding its BCP/BCM scope to local agencies, neighboring and remote prefectural governments, central government and agencies, and local business community (Fig. 3).

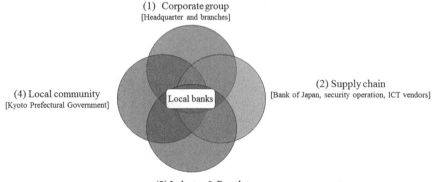

(1) Corporate group
[Headquarter and branches]

(2) Supply chain
[Bank of Japan, security operation, ICT vendors]

(4) Local community
[Kyoto Prefectural Government]

Local banks

(3) Industry & Regulators
[Other local banks, industry associations and Kinki Local Finance Bureau]

Fig. 2. Extended BCP/BCM scope for the local banks

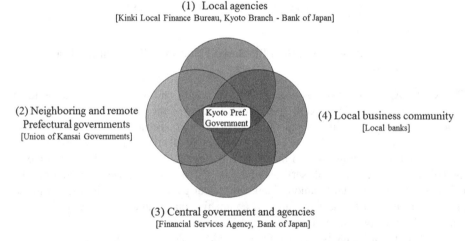

(1) Local agencies
[Kinki Local Finance Bureau, Kyoto Branch - Bank of Japan]

(2) Neighboring and remote
Prefectural governments
[Union of Kansai Governments]

Kyoto Pref. Government

(4) Local business community
[Local banks]

(3) Central government and agencies
[Financial Services Agency, Bank of Japan]

Fig. 3. Extended BCP/BCM scope for the Kyoto prefectural government

And the both sides, private sector and public sector agreed to work together to continue banking services at a limited but minimum required level in wide-area disasters based on PPP. Those activities are positioned as "Area BCM" (Fig. 4).

In the working group, detailed considerations, process designs, and actual agreements are ongoing. For example, several key points for discussions and coordination are defined at each phase for business continuity (Fig. 5).

(1) Preparedness phase (before a disruptive incident occurs)

- Criteria for activation of the shared headquarters for disaster management
- Organizational structure and contact lists
- Contact information maintenance and exercise schedule

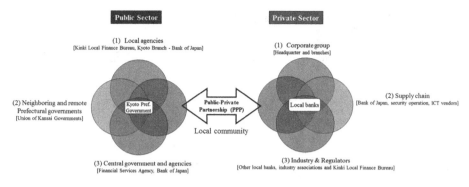

Fig. 4. Local community as a field for PPP-based Area BCM

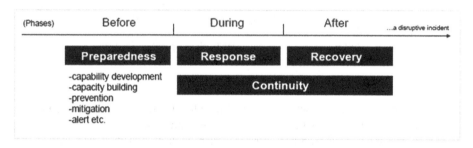

Fig. 5. Phases for BCP/BCM

(2) Response phase (during a disruptive incident is ongoing)

- – Data format for disaster information from the Kyoto Prefectural government
- – Format of information to be shared among banks and the Kyoto Prefectural government
- – Monitoring operational situations at the banks
- – Impact analysis with zoning and decision making on requests to other critical infrastructures

(3) Recovery phase (after a disruptive incident is convergent) Cooperation in:

- – Mutual back-up for cash availability management
- – Private armored cars for cash and valuables transportation
- – Tentative shared branch operations

4 GIS-Based Decision-Support System for Area-BCM with Local Banking Service Resilience

Based on the discussions and agreements in the working group, a trial development of Geographic Information System (GIS)-based decision-support system.

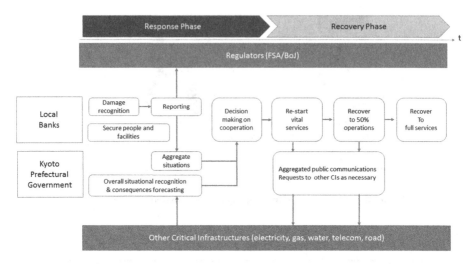

Fig. 6. PPP-based processes for inter-bank cooperation in disasters

(1) Once a disaster occurs, each local bank immediately starts damage assessment at the same time they starts securing their people and facilities.

(2) After activating the shared headquarters, each bank reports their damages to the headquarters and the aggregated situations are reported to the Kyoto Prefectural government at the same time each bank reports to their regulators.

(3) With information fed from the Kyoto Prefectural government on the overall situation (availability information from other critical infrastructure service providers) and consequences forecasting, the local banks make decisions on cooperation for shared business continuity [7–9]

(4) Based on the decisions and agreements, cooperation of banking services starts at the limited but required level for vital activities and socioeconomic recovery (Fig. 6).

(5) The Kyoto Prefectural Government inform their local residents, companies, and any other stakeholders about the banking service situations and negotiate other critical infrastructures that have interdependencies with banking services for support to the banking operations if necessary. [10] In this decision, a zoning analysis tool for leveling of banking service recoveries without any unnecessary geographical biases (Fig. 7).

The development project is still ongoing with some challenges:

- Feasibility of actual operations of the shared headquarters
- Currently four banks joined but branches of national brand banks have not joined yet
- Resources for this structure at the Kyoto Prefectural government is limited

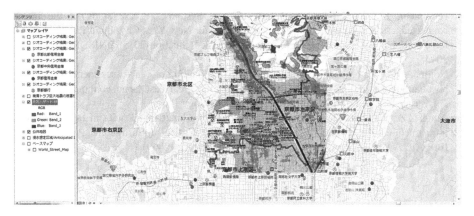

Fig. 7. Sample image of integrated map of flooded damages and bank locations

5 Conclusions and Next Steps

In order to continue local banking services at the limited but necessary level for vital activities and socioeconomic recoveries, taking individual BCP/BCM efforts at each bank is not enough. Based on the actual experiences and discussions in Kyoto Prefecture, the importance of PPP-based Area BCM is recognized. The Area BCM system concept and procedures are overviewed.

Next steps are moving the committee discussions and trial development of the decision support system forward and trying to use them in the incoming mid-small size disasters. It also can be used for a dynamic decision making exercise system for preparedness using hazard maps.

References

1. Elliott, D., Swartz, E., Herbane, B.: Just waiting for the next big bang: business continuity planning in the UK finance sector. J. Appl. Manag. Stud. **8**(1), 43–60 (1999)
2. International Standards Organization, ISO 22301:2012 Societal security – Business continuity management systems — Requirements, Geneva (2012)
3. The Bank of Japan, Case: Street-wide Exercise organized by the Bank of Iwate, the Kita-Nippon Bank, and the Tohoku Bank (in Japanese), October 2013
4. Sayanagi, Y., Watanabe, K.: A study on the practical ways of implementing a street-wide bcp exercise in the banking industry. J. Disaster Res. **10**(2), 252–262 (2015). Fuji Technology Press
5. Kyoto Prefectural Government, Kyoto BCP – Guideline for Action (in Japanese), June 2014
6. Watanabe, K.: Developing public-private partnership-base business continuity management for increase community resilience. J. Bus. Continuity Emerg. Plann. **3**(4), 335–344 (2009). Henry Stewart
7. Comes, T., Van de Walle, B.: Measuring disaster resilience: the impact of hurricane sandy on critical infrastructure systems. In: Proceedings of the 11th International ISCRAM Conference, pp. 195–204, May 2014

8. Haraguchi, M., Kim, S.: Critical Infrastructure Systems: A case study of the inter-connectedness of risks caused by Hurricane Sandy for New York City, Input Paper prepared for the Global Assessment Report on Disaster Risk Reduction 2015, UNISDR, March 14, 2014

9. Nojima, N., Kato, H.: Modification and validation of an assessment model of post-earthquake lifeline serviceability based on the great east japan earthquake disaster. J. Disaster Res. **9**(2), 108–120 (2014). Fuji Technology Press

10. Aung, Z.Z., Watanabe, K.: A framework for modeling interdependencies in Japan's critical infrastructures. In: Palmer, C., Shenoi, S. (eds.) Critical Infrastructure Protection III. IFIP AICT, vol. 311, pp. 243–257. Springer, Heidelberg (2009)

Emergency Management: Critical Infrastructure Preparedness

Critical Infrastructure Assessment
by Emergency Management

Marieke H.A. Klaver[1](✉), H.A.M. Luiijf[1], Albert N. Nieuwenhuijs[1],
Nico van Os[2], and Vincent Oskam[3]

[1] Netherlands Organisation for Applied Scientific Research TNO,
Den Haag, The Netherlands
{marieke.klaver,eric.luiijf,
albert.nieuwenhuijs}@tno.nl
[2] Veiligheidsregio Zuid-Holland Zuid, Dordrecht, The Netherlands
n.van.os@vrzhz.nl
[3] Veiligheidsregio Rotterdam-Rijnmond, Rotterdam, The Netherlands
vincent.oskam@veiligheidsregio-rr.nl

Abstract. Large scale emergencies such as a large scale flooding or a devastating storm can severely impact Critical Infrastructures (CI). Since a subsequent disruption or even destruction of CI may increase the severity of an emergency, it is important for emergency management organizations to include an impact assessment of CI in their risk management, emergency planning, and emergency preparation.

This paper describes a methodology for emergency management organizations to assess the impact of CI disruptions. The methodology takes into account common cause failures affecting multiple CI concurrently, cascading effects as well as the potential disruptive impact on emergency management operations. The methodology builds on earlier CI assessment approaches at the national level and has been tested in a case study.

Keywords: Critical infrastructure · Emergency management · Risk management · Preparation · Common cause failure · Cascading · Resilience

1 Introduction

In case of large scale emergencies such as a large scale flooding or a devastating storm, Critical Infrastructures (CI) can be severely impacted. Since the disruption or even destruction of CI may increase the severity of the emergency, it is important for emergency management (EM) organizations to include an impact assessment of CI in their risk management, emergency planning, and preparation. Emergency preparation comprises joint training and exercises by EM and CI organizations.

Critical Infrastructure Protection (CIP) has been a research topic in the Netherlands for some fifteen years. Until recently, most of the CIP research was aimed at the national level e.g. on identifying CI, performing risk assessment, and analyzing dependencies. This paper describes a CI impact assessment methodology for use by EM organizations at the local EM level. In the case of the Netherlands, the local EM

© Springer International Publishing Switzerland 2016
E. Rome et al. (Eds.): CRITIS 2015, LNCS 9578, pp. 79–90, 2016.
DOI: 10.1007/978-3-319-33331-1_7

level is that of the Safety Region ("Veiligheidsregio") responsible for EM in an area of 1500 to 2000 km^2. This methodology builds on earlier methods developed and validated in assessing CI at the national level.

The outline of this paper is as follows. Section 2 provides a set of definitions used in this paper. Section 3 describes earlier work. The methodology and its main steps are discussed in Sect. 4. Section 5 describes the application and testing of the approach in a case study. Based on the results of the case study, the next steps for further refinement of the methodology and making it applicable are described in the concluding Sect. 6.

2 Definitions

The following definitions come from CIPedia© [1]. The chosen definitions are the ones most relevant in the EM - CI context:

Cascading effect is a sequence of events in which each individual event is the cause of the following event; all the events can be traced back to one and the same initial event.

Critical Infrastructure is an asset, system or part thereof which is essential for the maintenance of vital societal functions, health, safety, security, economic or social well-being of people, and the disruption or destruction of which would have a significant impact as a result of the failure to maintain those functions.

Emergency management is the overall approach preventing and managing emergencies that might occur [2].

Vulnerability: intrinsic properties of something resulting in susceptibility to a risk source that can lead to an event with a consequence [2].

3 Earlier Work on CI and Emergency Management

Empirical evidence from reports about emergencies and disasters in various regions in the world [7, 8] shows that CI disruptions may cause unwanted extensions of the duration and size of emergencies with more casualties, more suffering of the population, and more damages as reported by [5, 6]. Therefore, it is of utmost importance for EM organizations to assess the possible impact of CI disruptions.

Moreover, one of the main lessons learned from CI disruptions all over the world [4] is that the set of CI dependencies may change with the mode of operations [3]. When an organization enters a non-normal mode of operations, its operational continuity may critically depend on a complete different set of CI as in normal operations. For example, the availability of diesel, roads and oil trucks are of no importance to the daily operation of a hospital until it has to rely on its backup generators due to a power grid failure. Empirical evidence shows that the business continuity planning by CI operators and EM organizations mostly understand and plan for possible CI disruptions critical to their normal mode of operations, e.g. they install a backup generator. However, it is much harder to understand and prepare for CI dependencies which occur in the non-normal modes of operations [5, 6]. This crucial kind of dependency analysis is beyond the scope of continuity planning of most public and private sectors.

In addition to the direct impact on CI, more damage may occur due to cascading effects, e.g., the loss of electricity may lead to loss of all information and communication technology (ICT) dependent services and in turn impact the functioning of hospitals and the transport system. Such so-called cascading effects may impact different CI within the local EM area, but may also refer to effects outside the directly affected area.

The observations mentioned above were used to develop the methodology described in the next section.

4 Description of the Methodology

This section describes the seven steps of the CI assessment methodology for local EM (as defined in Sect. 1) in the cold phase of EM operations. These seven steps have been synthesized from the analysis of earlier CI approaches by The Netherlands at the national level [10] as well as from the lessons about CI disruptions and EM identified by [5–8]. The methodology consists of the following steps:

1. Identify the threats to be taken into account for the area of responsibility of the local EM organization;
2. Identify the CI in this area;
3. Identify the key CI elements in this area;
4. Characterize the vulnerability of the key CI elements to each of the threats identified in step 1;
5. Assess the first order impact of each of the threats on the key CI elements identified in step 3;
6. Describe the dependencies between the identified CI elements:
   (i)   describe the required input and output of all identified key CI elements,
   (ii) distinguish between the different modes of operation,
   (iii) include the temporal and spatial factors;
7. Assess the CI cascading effects.

This remainder of this section describes the seven steps at a high level. More details can found in the next section which demonstrates these steps when applied to a specific case study.

4.1 Step 1: Identify the Threats to Be Considered

The assessment of the risk of cascading effects starts with the assessment of the set of threat(s) e.g., an earthquake or a large scale flooding, to the area of responsibility of the local EM organization. Hereafter, we use the term area to describe the area which will be assessed. The output of this step will include:

- an assessment of the area that is threatened;
- an understanding of the expected temporal and spatial development of the threat;
- an assessment of the (expected) severity of the threats.

4.2   Step 2: Identify the CI in the Area

Once the spatial area that is threatened is known, the second step of the methodology identifies the most important CI within that area. In identifying the relevant CI, the following perspectives can be used:

- the CI in the area that are essential to the life-support of the population within and outside the affected area, e.g. electricity, transport, drinking water, communication, food, health, financial services;
- the CI in the area that can pose a risk to the population or EM response within or outside the affected area when compromised, e.g. chemical plants or storage facilities;
- the CI that directly support the EM operations, e.g. energy, communication, and transport for EM services;
- the CI which have a footprint in the affected area which is not directly of use to the area but is essential to the population outside the directly affected area such as the nation, cross-border region or adjacent area(s).

As discussed in the previous section, the set of CI that are essential for the area may shift during the different phases of the threat exposure [3]. For example, before flooding reaches a specific place, transport will be an important CI to evacuate (parts of) the population and to distribute food and bottled water to emergency shelters. Thereafter, other transport modalities will become critically important. Therefore, this step takes track in identifying CI for each of the threat development phases that can be discerned (e.g., before the flooding, during the flood, and during the recovery phase).

4.3   Step 3: Identify the Key CI Elements

For each of the relevant CI identified in the previous step, this step identifies the most relevant key CI elements (objects, services) in the area. The perspectives for identification of these key CI elements are similar to the perspectives used in step 2:

- the key CI elements that are essential to the CI to function properly;
- the key CI elements that are in direct support to sustaining life of the population within the affected area;
- the key CI elements that can pose a risk to the population within or outside the affected area when compromised;
- the key CI elements that are in direct support to the EM operations in the area;
- the key CI elements that are essential to the population outside the area.

4.4   Step 4: Characterize the Vulnerability of the Key CI Elements for the Threat

For each of the key CI elements identified in the previous step and the threat(s) identified in step 1, the vulnerability of the key CI elements for these threats is assessed. This includes, for example, an assessment whether the CI element is vulnerable for a storm or for flooding. In general, the vulnerability depends on the type of element, the type of threat, and the severity and duration of the threat. If sufficient data is available, one may even use expected time-sequences and disruption and failure characteristics.

4.5   Step 5: Assess the First Order Impact of the Threats to the Key CI Elements

Based on the vulnerability of the element and the severity of the threat(s), an assessment can be made on the first order impact for each CI element. The assessment of first order effects will indicate which critical CI services will be disturbed by the threat(s) and what the impact will be. The impact includes all negative impacts that are deemed relevant and can include the number of casualties and wounded people as well as financial, physical, ecological, mental and intangible damages (e.g. disrupted societal cohesiveness) [10]. Only the direct impact is accounted for in this step. Impacts due to CI dependencies are accounted for in the next steps.

4.6   Step 6: Describe the Dependencies Between the CI Elements

The disruption to the CI elements as assessed in step 5 may lead to cascading effects due to CI dependencies. For assessing the CI dependencies, the following factors are of importance:

- different modes of operations: as explained above and in [3] the set of CI dependencies may shift depending on the mode of operations,
- the temporal effects (e.g. the time that a mobile mast will function is based on its disruption and recovery characteristics and the capacity of its battery power[1]).

4.7   Step 7: Assess the CI Cascading Effects

Based on the CI dependencies established in step 6 and the CI elements directly impacted by the threat(s) as established in step 5, the potential CI cascading effects can be determined. This seventh assessment step provides the basis for the estimated probability and potential extent of cascading effects.

5   Application of the Methodology in a Case Study

This section describes a case study in which the methodology is applied to assess the effect of a large scale flooding in a part of the Netherlands. In this paper we will only highlight the seven steps, the information needed to perform this analysis, and the most relevant findings.

---

[1] E.g., a power grid failure occurs in less than a second; the recovery process is a stepwise balancing process which may take hours or even days depending on the size of the impacted area and the potential to balance the bringing online of power generation units in balance with enough demand to maintain the voltage-frequency requirements.

5.1 Scenario Description

The town of Gorinchem in the Netherlands, with about 35.000 inhabitants, is situated adjacent to the river Boven Merwede bordering the Alblasserwaard polder with its bottom level at an average of about two meters below sea level (Fig. 1).

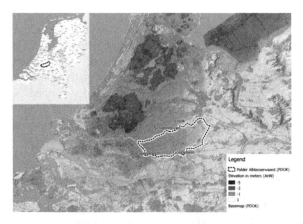

Fig. 1. Location of Gorinchem and the Alblasserwaard polder on the elevation map (meters below sea level) of the Netherlands

In the use case, a developing dike breach near Gorinchem is assessed, which directly leads to failure of the quays directly behind the dike. As a result, the influx of water will threaten the polder 'Alblasserwaard'. We will demonstrate the seven-step method below for this threat scenario using information from earlier flooding studies of the polder [11] and regional risk assessment [12].

5.2 Step 1: Identify the Threats to Be Considered

Step 1 ensures a good awareness of the threat(s). For the flooding threat the spread of the water front can be calculated as a function of time by using detailed flooding models. A breach of the dikes and quays will rapidly lead to water levels rising to heights of 2.5 m and more above street level in the city of Gorinchem. After an hour, the water flows into the Alblasserwaard polder and after seven hours water heights rise up to four meters above ground level in the polder.

The water front moves to the north along both sides of the A27 motorway and reaches Lopik within sixteen hours after the event, spreading gradually over the west side of the polder flooding the cities of Papendrecht, Alblasserwaard, Nieuw-Lekkerland, and Sliedrecht. A canal running from Lopik to Gorinchem abates the spreading of the waterfront to the east for seven days after which the eastern part of the polder also inundates. On day eight, the A27 and A2 motorways as well as the railways running in parallel to them are flooded, leading to the flooding of the eastern area of the polder [11]. This assessment shows:

- The western area of the polder will flood over a period of approximately sixteen hours.
- The affected area is initially limited to the polder west of the canal until day eight.
- The affected area contains several cities, scattered inhabitants, some commercial installations, and extensive agricultural activities which would be severely flooded.

5.3 Step 2: Identify the CI in the Area

Step 2 identifies the CI in the affected area. For the case area, this includes:

- infrastructures in support of the EM operations including the EM communication radio network (C2000) and power generators;
- transport infrastructure including road, water and rail transport;
- the energy infrastructures electricity, gas and oil;
- drinking water infrastructure;
- the ICT infrastructure including the fixed and mobile communication infrastructures carrying voice, video and data;
- water management infrastructure (e.g. dikes, pumping stations, sluices, bridges);
- food services including production, processing and distribution;
- financial infrastructure;
- healthcare infrastructure including hospitals, homes for the elderly, and the medicine supply chain;
- facilities with hazardous material such as chemical plants and storage facilities.

5.4 Step 3: Identify the Key CI Elements

In step 3, the key CI elements will be identified for each of the identified CI, including its geographical location. Note that these key CI elements should be identified in a dialogue with the CI operators and the EM organization in the local EM area. As an illustration, we include a table (Table 1) with a small selection of CI sectors and identified key CI elements leaving out sensitive location information.

5.5 Step 4: Characterize the Vulnerability of the Key CI Elements for the Threat(S)

For the case at hand, some typical vulnerabilities for flooding are listed in Table 2.

Table 1. A selection of identified CI sectors and their identified elements in the area.

CI sector	Key CI elements
Electricity	• Transmission lines (three 50 kV and one 150 kV lines) and two switch stations • A high to medium-voltage transformer station • High/medium voltage cables (in area: above ground) • Low voltage local substations (many) • Low voltage distribution cables (in area: underground)
Telecommunication	• Mobile antennas and control systems • C2000 antennas (EM communication system) • ICT
Drinking water	• Processing plants • Distribution system and transport pipelines • (one transport pipeline feeding a neighboring area)
Transport	• Main motorways (A15, A27, A2) • Main railways (Betuwelijn, Dordrecht-Geldermalsen) • Pipelines (gas to Rotterdam, Antwerp and Germany) • Ferries (Schoonhoven, Ameide, Beneden Merwede, Boven Merwede, Brakel) • Waterways (Beneden Merwede, Boven Merwede, Waal, Lek, Noord) • Inland shipping terminals (for fuel)

Table 2. Some examples of key CI elements in the affected area that are vulnerable to flooding

CI sector	Vulnerability of key element
Electricity	The power transmission network will be switched off at water levels above 2,5 m above ground level. The power distribution system will stop functioning at water heights of 0,5 m above ground level.
Mobile communication	The mobile telecommunication antennas will stop functioning at water levels of approximately 0,2 m above ground level. Some of the antennae that are not affected by flooding (e.g. masts on high buildings) will function as long as electrical (emergency) power is available.
Drinking water	The water inlet stations and water pressure pumps will stop functioning. The pressure drop might cause seeping of flood waters into the water distribution network resulting in chemical and biological contamination.
Main roads	Roads will be closed when the water level reaches the road surface or even earlier when the road bed becomes instable. Road use by emergency trucks depends on the water level above the road and the speed of the water flow.
Emergency communication (C2000)	The antenna controlling equipment will stop functioning when water levels reach approximately 0, 2 m above ground level.

5.6   Step 5: Assess the First Order Impact of the Threats to the Key CI Elements

As the vulnerability data shows, the direct impact of the flooding may lead to the loss of functioning of almost all CI in the affected area. The timeline for this to happen depends on the location of the key CI elements and the water levels at these locations. This can be determined by combining the threat assessment of step 1 with the geographical locations and vulnerability determined in step 4.

The analysis for this case shows that the western part of the Alblasserwaard will flood within eight hours after the dike breach which causes almost all CI in the area to cease functioning.

5.7   Step 6: Describe the Dependencies Between the CI Elements in the Area

The main dependencies between the CI elements can be modelled by a matrix that, describes the main dependencies. Due to the extent and speed of the flooding, a detailed analysis of the cascading effects of CI as part of this specific case analysis is less relevant, since most of the CI will stop functioning in a matter of hours due to the direct vulnerabilities to the flooding threat. The added value of this type of analysis, even in this extreme scenario, follows from the analysis result that one of the cascading effects is the loss of electricity in the eastern side of the area while it isn't yet flooded, due to the topology of the electricity network in the area. Some examples of CI dependencies to take into account are listed in Table 3.

Table 3. Examples of CI dependencies identified

CI sector/element	Function delivered	Dependent on
Emergency services/ C2000 communication masts	Emergency communications	Electricity, fixed telecommunications grid
ICT/GSM antennas	Communications for population, back-up communication for emergency responders	Electricity, fixed telecommunications grid
Drinking water/water inlet station	Supply of drinking water	Electricity
Gas/compressor station	Pressure for transport pipelines	Electricity, fixed telecommunications grid, mobile telecommunications grid (backup)
Transport/lifting bridge	Alternating passage for road or water transport	Electricity, fixed telecommunications grid

(*Continued*)

Table 3. (*Continued*)

CI sector/element	Function delivered	Dependent on
Healthcare/hospitals and homes for the elderly	Health care	Gas, drinking water, electricity (normal operation), diesel (emergency generator), fixed telecommunication, mobile communication (remote monitoring of patients)

5.8   Step 7: Assess the CI Cascading Effects

Based on the identified CI dependencies (step 6), and the key CI elements directly impacted by the threats (step 5), the CI cascading effects are determined.

Sector (elements)	Effects	Timeline
Electricity/ voltage transformer and switch station	Loss of electricity also in part of the neighboring region (area to the north and east of Gorinchem, up to the town of Vianen)	After 3 to 6 hours
Stop functioning of the Drinking water supply (inlet stations and processing)	One of the neighboring areas will not have drinking water	After 24 hours, will last for days to months
Transport by Road (motorways A2, A15, A27)	Large scale disruptions and delays of road traffic over the national motorway system due to the unavailability of the main North-South motorways. International transport will require rerouting – economic loss due to extra costs and delays.	A15 is blocked after 1 to 3 hours; the A2 and A27 after 8 days. Effect will last for weeks if not months
Transport by Rail (Betuwelijn)	Betuwelijn Rotterdam - Germany will be stopped. International transport will require rerouting – economic loss due to extra costs, capacity problems, and delays.	Immediately after or before breach. Effect will last for weeks/ months if not years when tunnels flood and rail infrastructure requires major repairs

It is important to identify the societal functions outside the affected area that are dependent on the functioning of key CI elements in the affected area. In this case, the supply of drinking water to population in an area far outside the affected area depends on a water inlet station in the affected area. Moreover, the uncontrolled shutdown of an industrial site outside the affected area due to its dependence on power supply from the affected area would result in irreparable damages and the loss of that entire industry to the region.

5.9   Impact on the EM Response Effort

The steps above provide an analysis of the non-normal-mode of operation in which the EM responders must operate. It should be noted that the location of a dike breach is unknown up to the moment of failure. Thereafter, the spatial and temporal development of the inundation can be estimated. It is unlikely for EM responders to be able to evacuate all those not yet evacuated in the area prior to any CI failures. Search and rescue efforts will have to operate in the absence of power and the C2000 EM communication system. The population that takes refuge on rooftops and high rise buildings will lack CI, e.g. drinking water, heating, medicine distribution and emergency healthcare. Efforts to recover affected CI are required to support the non-evacuated population and may be needed when such CI are essential to the surrounding areas [5].

These impacts illustrate the need for EM to include an impact assessment of CI in their risk management, emergency planning and preparation.

6   Conclusions and Further Work

6.1   Reflection on the Methodology

Each of the steps of the proposed methodology may be performed either in great detail, or by a more qualitative approach. In order for the methodology to be useful, the desired and attainable level of detail is determined in an iterative process in which the desired output of the assessment is described and the required information is gathered.

While performing the case study, discussions with the EM organizations and CI operators in the affected area showed that for the specific case the analysis does not require a high level of detail. The assessment should support EM and CI decision makers by providing the main CI impacts, and the affected temporal and spatial effects. For such an assessment to be usable neither exact locations nor exact water levels are needed; just a quick first order assessment is preferred.

Due to the extent of the flooding and the serious impact on all CI, the analysis steps 5 and 6 provide only limited added value in this case study.

6.2   Reflection on the Available Data

The use of the methodology in the case study showed that most of the data needed to perform the analysis steps is available. Although some of the data is available in open sources, it is recommended to determine the main data in a collaborative dialogue between the main stakeholders: CI operators and the EM organization.

6.3   Next Steps

In order to further test and refine the methodology another case study will be performed on a scenario describing a large scale power outage. Other researchers are also encouraged to apply this methodology and to provide feedback to the authors.

Moreover, the methodology provides a strong basis for supportive tooling using an agent based approach. Part of this tooling will be developed as part of the EU project PREDICT.

Acknowledgement. The EU project PREDICT has received funding from the European Union's Seventh Framework Programme for research, technological development and demonstration under grant agreement no. 607697. This article reflects only the authors' views. The EU is not liable for any use that may be made of the information contained therein.

References

1. CIPEdia©. www.cipedia.eu
2. ISO, ISO 22300:2012(en): Societal security — Terminology, ISO, Geneva, Switzerland
3. Nieuwenhuijs, A., Luiijf, E., Klaver, M.: Modeling dependencies in critical infrastructures. In: Papa, M., Shenoi, S. (eds.) Critical Infrastructure Protection II. The International Federation for Information Processing, vol. 290, pp. 205–213. Springer, Heidelberg (2008). ISBN 978-0-387-88523-0
4. Van Eeten, M., Nieuwenhuijs, A., Luiijf, E., Klaver, M., Cruz, E.: The state and the threat of cascading failure across critical infrastructures: the implications of empirical evidence from media incident reports. Public Admin. **89**(2), 381–400 (2011)
5. Luiijf, H.A.M., Klaver, M.H.A., Expand the Crisis? Neglect Critical Infrastructure! (insufficient situational awareness about critical infrastructure by emergency management – Insights and Recommendations). In: Tagungsband 61. Jahresfachtagung der Vereinigung des Deutsches Brandschutzes e.V., 27–29 May 2013 Weimar, Germany, pp. 293–304 (2013)
6. Luiijf, E., Klaver, M.: Insufficient situational awareness about critical infrastructures by emergency management. In: Proceedings Symposium on C3I for Crisis, Emergency and Consequence Management, Bucharest 11-12 May 2009, NATO RTA, Paris, France (2009)
7. Von Kirchbach, H-P. et al.: Bericht der Unabhängigen Kommission der Sächsischen Staatsregierung Flutkatastrophe 2002 (2003)
8. Pitt, M.: The Pitt Review: Learning Lessons from the 2007 Floods, Cabinet Office, United Kingdom, June 2008. http://www.environment-agency.gov.uk/research/library/publications/33889.aspx
9. Deltaprogramma 2015, Werken aan de Delta, de beslissingen om Nederland veilig en leefbaar te houden, September 2014
10. Ministry of Security and Justice, The Netherlands, Working with scenarios, risk assessment and capabilities in the National Safety and Security Strategy of the Netherlands. http://www.preventionweb.net/files/26422_guidancemethodologynationalsafetyan.pdf
11. Vergouwe, R., van den Berg, M.C.J., van der Scheer, P.: Veiligheid Nederland in kaart 2 (VNK2 study): Overstromingsrisico dijkring 16 Alblasserwaard en Vijfheerenlanden, HB2310976, Rijkswaterstaat (2014)
12. VRZHZ, Regionaal Risicoprofiel Veiligheidsregio Zuid-Holland Zuid, Dordrecht (2011)

Knowledge-Driven Scenario Development for Critical Infrastructure Protection

Jingquan Xie[1]($\boxtimes$), Marianthi Theocharidou[2], and Yohan Barbarin[3]

[1] Fraunhofer IAIS, Sankt Augustin, Germany
jingquan.xie@iais.fraunhofer.de
[2] EC Joint Research Centre, IPSC, Ispra, Italy
marianthi.theocharidou@jrc.ec.europa.eu
[3] CEA Gramat, Gramat, France
yohan.barbarin@cea.fr

Abstract. Scenarios play a central role in developing novel modelling and simulation based systems for Critical Infrastructure Protection. Well-developed scenarios can be used to accelerate system development in different phases including requirements engineering, functional testing and system validation. Developing scenarios, in particular cross-border scenarios, is however a time-consuming task requiring a significant amount of contributions from end-users, system developers and domain experts. Existing approaches for scenarios development are mainly ad-hoc and heavily dependent on texts and diagrams scattered in various documents and data sheets. This introduces more vagueness and ambiguities which are intrinsic in natural languages. Furthermore to fully benefit from modern simulation technology, an extra modelling step is often needed to translate the text-based scenario descriptions into a computer model for domain-specific simulators. Most of the translation work needs intensive interaction between system developers and domain experts and hence can only to be done manually in a tedious and error-prone way. In this paper a knowledge-driven scenario development method is proposed to tackle the problem mentioned above. The core component is a formal knowledge base CISO constructed with Description Logics ($\mathcal{DL}$), which covers the essential elements and their relations of a crisis scenario. Based on CISO a new scenario development workflow is proposed together with a software tool suite to facilitate scenario generation and visualisation. A concrete crisis scenario is presented based on the proposed method to demonstrate its potential for generating precise scenario definitions.

1 Introduction

Critical Infrastructures (CI), like power grids, telecommunication networks and public transportation systems, etc., play a central role in modern societies. One of the commonly used techniques to test and validate new methods developed for Critical Infrastructure Protection (CIP) is using computer-based Modelling, Simulation and Analysis (MS&A) [15] together with crisis scenarios [6]. A *scenario* for CIP can contain real crisis data from history or realistic fictitious events

© European Union, 2016
E. Rome et al. (Eds.): CRITIS 2015, LNCS 9578, pp. 91–102, 2016.
DOI: 10.1007/978-3-319-33331-1_8

that are not likely to happen in real life. During the last decade, several European research projects [12, 19] have investigated and successfully applied the scenario-driven approach to facilitate the development and validation of new methods, models and systems for CIP. Meanwhile this approach is also a recommendation of the European Commission in its 2010 guidelines for disaster management [5] focusing on national risk assessments and covering risk identification, analysis and evaluation.

Well-developed scenarios involve a substantial amount of work contributed by end-users, domain experts and system developers. They need to cooperate together to get a common understanding about a specific domain, with respect to the terminology used. The description of scenarios is mostly provided as text documents and data sheets using ad-hoc schema. To our best knowledge, there are no well-accepted standards available on how to construct and represent scenarios for CIP. This makes the scenarios extremely difficult to be reused. Moreover texts in natural languages are intrinsically ambiguous. The lack of formal representation of scenarios makes computer-based reasoning virtually impossible. To tackle the problems mentioned above, a formal knowledge-driven approach based on Description Logics ($\mathcal{DL}$) [1] for scenario development is proposed in this paper. This knowledge-driven approach is designed to be generic enough to facilitate developing a variety of CIP scenarios with fine-grained modelling capability. The whole framework is designed to be extensible, i.e. support of different CI can be added in the future. The rest of this paper is structured as follows: Sect. 2 gives a detailed description of essential elements of crisis scenarios. The core knowledge base is presented in Sect. 3 followed by the scenario development workflow in Sect. 4. In Sect. 5 an example scenario is given. The related work of scenario development is discussed in Sect. 6. Finally, Sect. 7 concludes this paper and provides insight on potential future directions.

2   Essential Elements of CIP Scenarios

The word *scenario* is extensively used in different contexts with different meanings. In Oxford dictionary, it is defined as *"a postulated sequence or development of events."* Some projects have tried to give different definitions [12, 19] based on their understanding. We will not argue which one is better or scientifically more precise. For the purposes of this work, we consider the following elements of a crisis scenario for CIP as essential: the *static models*, the *dynamic behaviours*, and the *context information* (see Fig. 1). In the rest of this section, some of the core elements of a CIP scenario are explained with more details.

CI Models. Building fine-grained CI models is a challenging task, especially in the context of cross-border scenarios. Because of the confidential level of real CI data, domain experts usually construct an artificial model that is realistic enough to validate new methods. CI models are simulator-specific. Mainstream simulators, in particular commercial simulators, use their own proprietary scheme to represent CI models. This makes the interchangeability and portability of CI models in practice extremely difficult.

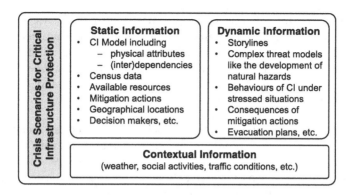

Fig. 1. Static, dynamic and contextual information in a CIP scenario

Decision Makers. Decision makers are roles responsible for performing mitigation actions. They can be crisis managers on local and national level, or on-site rescue forces. They are well trained to deal with crisis. Under crisis situation they take decisions based on their expertise, the situation assessment, the resources available and, if possible, the predictive consequences of decisions. In Europe, each country has its own organisational structure of crisis management and decision making responsibilities. In general crisis management has a hierarchical structure with different levels of decision making responsibilities and functionalities. They communicate with each other intensively to keep a consistent overview of the whole crisis situations.

Resources. Crisis scenarios for CIP may contain numerous categories of resources like rescue forces, polices, CI operators, hospitals, ambulances, etc. Decision makers need to know the availability of these resources at any time during crisis situations. Resources are dynamically changing during scenario running. In real cases, crisis management is normally conducted in a distributed way with different teams using different systems. Therefore resource changes need to be reflected in all systems to keep a consistent view of available resources to all participants of crisis management teams.

Threat Models. Threats, as triggers of crisis, are essential parts of crisis scenarios. Different kinds of natural and man-made threats exist like flooding, earthquake, hurricane, cyber-attacks, nuclear pollutions, etc. They can be organised in categories based on different criteria [8,14,20]. For crisis scenarios, one or more threats need to be identified. Developing threat models is labour-intensive task requiring specific expertise about the targeted threat simulators. The ability to reuse existing threat models in a federated simulation system is one of the key factors for a well-defined crisis scenario for CIP.

Mitigation Actions. At certain time point of crisis, depending on the resilience of CI systems, damages start to appear in CI components. Before serious consequences occur, some actions need to be performed to minimise or even eliminate the negative effects. In real crisis situations, decision makers - rescue forces and crisis managers - often have a handful of candidate mitigation actions against certain threats. During scenario running with simulators, several mitigation actions can be chosen by decision makers with adjustable parameters. The decision criteria are either based on their expertise, fixed regulations and checklists, or computer-based consequence analysis.

Storyline. Storylines describe the dynamic behaviours of a crisis scenario. A storyline contains a sequence of pre-defined events or happening with time stamps. Complex CIP scenarios can contain more than one storylines. In particularly, this is the case for scenarios involving decision making and execution of mitigation actions. Depending on the courses of actions, the whole scenario may evolve in different directions. For instance, some pre-defined critical events may not occur if certain actions are performed.

Consequence Analysis. Consequence Analysis (CA) is the entire process of assessing and evaluating impacts caused by threats and their cascading effects. Different criteria are available. For instance, the Cross Cutting Criteria of the 2008 Directive on European Critical Infrastructures [7] is one of early criteria:

- Casualties criterion (assessed in terms the potential number of fatalities or injuries);
- Economic effects criterion (assessed in terms of the significance of economic loss and/or degradation of products or services; including potential environmental effects);
- Public effects criterion (assessed in terms of the impact on public confidence, physical suffering and disruption of daily life; including the loss of essential services).

Due to page limitation, the detailed procedure of performing CA will be elaborated in another paper.

Context Information. Scenarios are not isolated - they exist in a sophisticated context. Contextual information like weather conditions, sport events, traffic situation, etc. can be of critical importance in crisis situations for decision making. Situation assessment during crisis should not neglect these kinds of information, in particular when evacuation plans need to be carried out. Nowadays most of these types of contextual information are available as web services, i.e. can be consumed directly by other software systems with minimum human interventions. This makes it possible to automatically assess contextual information under crisis situations in a more effective way.

3   CISO - the Core Knowledge Base

To improve the reusability, consistency and interchangeability, the essential elements of crisis scenarios described in Sect. 2 need to be consolidated into a scenario definition in a structured way. A knowledge-based approach is proposed to achieve this goal. The core knowledge base is developed as a formal ontology - the Crisis Scenario Ontology (CISO).

3.1   Design Focus

The primary goal of CISO is to provide a formal basis for developing richer crisis scenarios in CIP, focusing on improved semantic unambiguity, interchangeability, reusability and consistency. For large-scale scenarios these characteristics are of the utmost importance.

Semantic Unambiguity. One of the primary drawbacks of traditional ad-hoc scenario development method is semantic ambiguity. The unstructured information cannot be processed by computers *directly* on a semantic level - at least not with today's artificial intelligence technology. That means internal logics of scenarios can neither be discovered nor extracted by computers automatically to form a sound scenario model. With the help of CISO, scenarios for CIP are forced to conform a rigorous schema with little or even no ambiguities.

Interchangeability. Well-developed crisis scenarios are normally shared by different institutions and organisations for various research and development purposes. Traditional text-based scenario descriptions, which are more intuitive to create, are nightmares for sharing: people from different areas normally have different backgrounds and use different terminologies for the same thing or they use the same terminology for different things. CISO targets this issue by providing a formal way with sufficient syntax checking and expressive power. Sufficient tool support makes the collaboration of scenario development and sharing even more effective.

Reusability. Well-developed crisis scenarios for CIP are valuable assets. They should be reused in different projects dealing with similar topics or possessing similar objectives. Text documents based scenario descriptions with isolated scenario data, like CI models, do not provide sufficient support for scenario reusability. Huge amount of work still needs to be invested to modify old scenarios to adapt them to new projects. With CISO and sufficient software support, reusability can be improved significantly. Fine-grained models built with CISO provide adequate support for parameterising the whole scenario.

Consistency. Consistency checking is a classic task for knowledge-intensive systems. Crisis scenarios comprise by nature plenty of information that is derived by human expertise. Though it is possible to discover some internal conflicts for traditional scenario definitions via proof reading; it is however not effective and efficient enough. CISO is based on $\mathcal{DL}$, which per se provides automatic consistency checking to form a sound formal knowledge base. Various $\mathcal{DL}$ reasoners, both commercial [16] and open source [11], are available for that purpose.

3.2   CISO in $\mathcal{DL}$

To provide efficient reasoning capability without sacrificing too much expressivity, we have carefully designed the knowledge base without using *expensive* $\mathcal{DL}$ features like *role hierarchy* and *complex concept negation*. The knowledge base, which captures $\mathcal{DL}$ expressivity $\mathcal{ALEQ}$, contains 129 axioms of which 44 are class assertions, 10 are property assertions, 15 are individual assertions and other relations. A top-level concept named CI is created to denote all kinds of critical infrastructures. In the current version three sub-concepts are defined for specific CI types: Electric for electricity network, Teleco for telecommunication network and Railway for railway network:

$$\text{CI} \sqsubseteq \text{Electric} \sqcup \text{Teleco} \sqcup \text{Railway}$$

The semantics of the above is that if x is an instance of CI, then it is either a electricity network or a telecommunication network or a railway network. This can be easily extended in the future by adding other CI. Similar to the VITA taxonomy [14], threats are organised as hierarchies. Basically there are two types of threats: nature and man-made. For instance, the following is a detailed taxonomy of the man-made threats:

$$\text{Threat} \sqsubseteq \text{HumanMadeThreat} \sqcup \text{NaturalThreat}$$

$$\text{HumanMadeThreat} \sqsubseteq \text{CyberAttack} \sqcup \text{NuclearPollution} \sqcup \text{TransportAccident}$$

$$\text{TransportAccident} \sqsubseteq \text{TrainDerailment}$$

$$\text{TrainDerailment} \sqsubseteq \text{CargoTrainDerailment}$$

In a similar way, other elements of crisis scenarios like decision makers, contextual information, etc. are defined. The storyline however is defined in a different way. A property with value constraints is used to formally specify the concept Storyline:

$$\text{Storyline} \equiv \exists \text{containsEvent.Event}$$

$$\text{Event} \equiv \ = 1 \ \text{hasTimePoint TimePoint}$$

The semantics of the above statements is as follows: a storyline contains at least one event and each event contains exactly one time point. The concept CIPScenario is the major concept for defining a scenario. This concept needs to be enriched by end-users and domain experts. It is formally defined as follows:

$$\text{CIPScenario} \equiv \exists \text{containsMitigationAction.MitigationAction}$$
$$\sqcap \exists \text{hasContextInformation.ContextInformation}$$
$$\sqcap \exists \text{hasResource.Resource}$$
$$\sqcap \exists \text{hasStoryline.Storyline}$$
$$\sqcap \exists \text{involvesCI.CI}$$
$$\sqcap \exists \text{involvesDecisionMaker.DecisionMaker}$$
$$\sqcap \ = 1 \text{hasThreat Threat}$$
$$\sqcap \ = 1 \text{useConseqAnalysisCriterion Criterion}$$

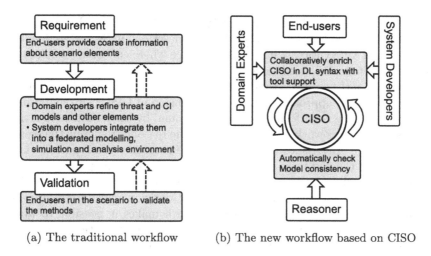

(a) The traditional workflow   (b) The new workflow based on CISO

Fig. 2. The side-by-side comparison of two workflows

This definition specifies the essential elements of a CIP scenario with cardinalities. With this formal definition, reasoners are able to check the consistency of a scenario definition with sufficient explanations if error occurs.

4 Scenario Development Workflow

The development of crisis scenarios is a time-consuming task requiring a significant amount of work of domain experts and system developers. To our best knowledge there exist several guidelines [2] and tools [13] of workflows focusing on crisis management training; however no standard available covering the entire development workflow. The traditional scenario development workflow illustrated in Fig. 2a focuses on the generation of text documents and data sheets with minimum software support. Based on agreed document structures, end-users provide the information as text documents, where some of the scenario elements described in Sect. 2 are identify. After several iterations, domain experts and system developers start to develop fine-grained models, identify the involved CI and decision makers, design the mitigation actions, and choose appropriate consequence analysis criteria. Finally, end-users are asked to use the scenario to test methods that need to be validated in a federated simulation environment. All work is done manually with E-Mail exchange or face-to-face meetings without dedicated tools.

4.1 Workflow Based on CISO

The knowledge-driven approach enables a new scenario development workflow depicted in Fig. 2b. It focuses on collaborative scenario development by enriching CISO.

The workflow starts with extending CISO by end-users. Based on the scenarios they have in mind, all the scenario elements described in Sect. 2 are identified and specified in $\mathcal{DL}$ syntax. This is the first place where end-users, who are normally not experts in $\mathcal{DL}$, need sufficient tool support to finish this task. Usability and robustness of the software tools are of utmost importance for the adoption of the proposed formal approach. During the extension of CISO, automatic model consistency checking is performed in the background by the reasoners in a transparent way. End-users work interactively with the reasoner to define the scenario on a coarse level. Any issues discovered by the reasoners are reported via the user interface to the end-users in real-time. At the end of this phase, a logically consistent coarse description of the scenario is stored in the scenario database. Threat models, CI models, mitigation actions, decision makers etc. are automatically represented in a structured way, which makes it possible to further computer processing, like visualising the storylines and integration into reports. In this workflow, all three roles can work simultaneously. Domain experts do not need to wait for the completion of the coarse scenario description. At any time point, domain experts and system developers can check the involved threats and CI through a collaborative platform, which is part of the tool support discussed in Sect. 4.2.

4.2 Software Tool Support

Software tool support is critical to make the proposed approach feasible for a wide variety of users who are not familiar with $\mathcal{DL}$. It is also a deciding factor to improve productivity of scenario development without sacrificing the correctness and soundness of the generated model. The software architecture (see Fig. 3) contains three different components facilitating the development of crisis scenarios for CIP:

- **Scenario Editor** is a graphical software tool providing easy-to-use features to extend CISO. The complete scenario is formally represented as a $\mathcal{DL}$ knowledge base with concepts, properties, and instances. The user interface is tailored for end-users and domain experts. This is the main interface for the users to develop the scenario and materialise it into the database.
- **Scenario Analyser** provides automatic consistency checking and reasoning support for the scenario development. Its core is a $\mathcal{DL}$ reasoner that runs under the hood and provides sophisticated services for checking the scenario model. It provides well-defined interfaces for efficient interplay with Scenario Editor. Models generated by users inside of Scenario Editor are pushed to Scenario Analyser for consistency checking. Any logical inconsistency will be pushed back to Scenario Editor and presented to the users.
- **Real-time Communication Infrastructure** is a Internet-based platform for real-time collaborative working. It is the technical basis for the communication of the whole tool suite. Secured communication channel is chosen to prevent any human-in-the-middle attacks. Real-time capability is one of the

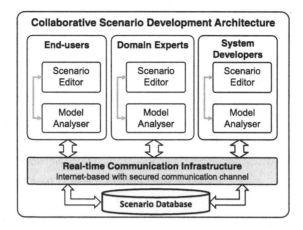

Fig. 3. Architecture of collaborative scenario development

key features to improve system usability. It also provides a transparent interface to communicate with the backend scenario database with transactional support.

This tool suite is able to export flat files with complete scenario data. Besides, scenarios can also be uploaded into the scenario database for further interaction with federated simulation environments.

5   Example Scenario - Train Derailment

In this section, an example CIP scenario - train derailment - is presented using the proposed method. It is original presented in the CIPRNet project [4] as a fictitious scenario. The traditional method is used there to develop and describe the scenario - iterative face-to-face communications via text documents, diagrams and data sheets.

With CISO we want to re-develop it as follows. First we need to create a new knowledge based derived from CISO. As described in Sect. 3, the major task of developing a scenario is to extend the concept CIPScenario by providing all essential elements like threats, decision makers, CI models, etc. The first step is creating the necessary scenario-specific elements:

CargoTrainDerailment(cargoDerailmentInEmmerich).

NationalDecisionMaker(germanCrisisManager).

NationalDecisionMaker(dutchCrisisManager).

Storyline(derailmentStoryline).

containsEvent(derailmentStoryline, derailment).

containsEvent(derailmentStoryline, fireAndExplosion).

containsEvent(derailmentStoryline, chemicalLeak).

Together with the pre-defined elements in CISO, the new scenario can be defined as follows:

$$Thing(derailmentScenario).$$
$$useConseqAnalysisCriterion(derailmentScenario, criterionEU).$$
$$hasThreat(derailmentScenario, cargoDerailmentInEmmerich).$$
$$hasStoryline(derailmentScenario, derailmentStoryline).$$
$$involvesCI(derailmentScenario, railwayModelDeutscheBahn).$$
$$involvesCI(derailmentScenario, transmissionNetworkModel).$$
$$involvesCI(derailmentScenario, baseStations).$$
$$...$$
$$involvesDecisionMaker(derailmentScenario, germanCrisisManager).$$
$$hasContextInformation(derailmentScenario, strongWind).$$
$$containsMitigationAction(derailmentScenario, setupDetour).$$
$$hasResource(derailmentScenario, fireBrigade).$$

This new scenario is defined as an instance of Thing instead of CIPScenario. The reason is that we want to use the reasoner to check the consistency of the definition. If it is consistent it will be of type CIPScenario. If this is not the case, users will get feedbacks from the reasoner. In other words, the goal is:

$$CIPScenario(derailmentScenario).$$

6   Related Work

Scenarios are widely used in different areas like military applications, operational research, etc. The Military Scenario Description Language (MSDL) [17] is an XML-based language for developing military scenarios in an unambiguous way. It provides a common vocabulary and XML-based schema for exchanging scenario data in a networked environment for military use cases. The Coalition Battle Management Language (C-BML) [18] is another standard approved by the Simulation Interoperability Standards Organization in 2014. It is a dedicated language for describing military scenarios focusing on expressing and exchanging plans, orders, requests, and reports across command and control (C2) systems [18]. C-BML provides the information about who, what, when, where, why and a plan contains orders, requests and reports. Both standards provide a common vocabulary for specific domains. They lack however the formal foundations and cannot benefit from the state-of-the-art reasoners for automatic consistency checking and reasoning.

Domain-specific ontologies exist for CIP research with federated simulations [19]. An ontological framework to model CI and interdependencies is proposed within the DIESIS project [19]. It introduces three ontologies: IONT - Infrastructure Ontology, WONT - World Ontology, and FONT - Federation

Ontology for dependency modelling. It is however not sufficient to formalise a complete crisis scenario with the essential elements described in Sect. 2. Similar approach is proposed in [9] for the interoperability of different domain-specific simulators. This approach focuses on the ontology mediation of different simulator ontologies, while ontological support for scenario development is not mentioned. Another ontological modelling for CI is proposed in [10], which focuses on CI model for simulation with automatic reasoning support. However scenario elements like mitigation actions, contextual information mentioned in Sect. 2 are not covered. In addition, DL-based knowledge base for emergency plan is proposed in [3], which however has little support for the modelling CI. Several guidelines [2,5] have also been established for crisis exercises. These can be integrated into the proposed framework for scenario validation.

7 Conclusion

Crisis scenarios play a central role in modelling and simulation based CIP research. Existing approaches for crisis scenario development are more or less ad-hoc without formal support. This is a big obstacle to improve interchangeability, reusability and consistency of crisis scenarios for CIP. In this paper a novel knowledge-driven approach is proposed to address this issue by providing a formal knowledge base in $\mathcal{DL}$ with expressivity $\mathcal{ALEQ}$ and well-defined workflows with sufficient software support. The major objective of this approach is to provide a formal foundation for building large-scale semantic rich crisis scenarios to promote CIP research. End-users, domain experts and system developers can collaborate with each other - with sufficient software tool support - to develop crisis scenarios in a more efficient and effective manner. One of the long-term goals of this knowledge-driven approach is to build a European-wide scenario database with rich semantics, i.e. enabling consistency checking, automatic reasoning, etc. To achieve this, the software tools still need to be further developed and improved to meet the requirements of different end-users. One of the major challenges in simulation-based CIP research is the automatic generation of CI models for domain-specific simulators. This is one limitation of the proposed approach - it still cannot generate these models automatically. However with the envisioned future European-wide scenario database, this issue can be partially addressed by analysing and correlating threats and CI models in the database. Another major limitation of the proposed approach is that users are expected to have basic knowledge about $\mathcal{DL}$. This is for most end-users and domain experts not the case. We try to tackle this limitation by providing easy-to-use software tools with all the theoretical background embedded.

Acknowledgements. This research leading to these results was funded by the European Commission within the Seventh Framework Programme project CIPRNet (grant agreement N° 312450) and PREDICT (grant agreement N° 607697). The authors thank all of the project partners for many constructive discussions and useful suggestions.

References

1. Baader, F., Calvanese, D., McGuinness, D.L., Nardi, D., Patel-Schneider, P.F. (eds.): The Description Logic Handbook: Theory, Implementation, and Applications. Cambridge University Press, Cambridge (2003)
2. BBK: Guideline for Strategic Crisis Management Exercises. Technical report, Federal Office of Civil Protection and Disaster Assistance (2011)
3. Cunxiang, D., Wenjun, W., Peng, Y.: Dl-based the knowledge description of emergency plan systems and its application. In: Third International Conference on Multimedia and Ubiquitous Engineering, MUE 2009, pp. 364–368, June 2009
4. EU FP7 CIPRNet Project: D6.2 Application Scenario. Technical report, CIPRNet (2014)
5. European Commission: COMMISSION STAFF WORKING PAPER - Risk Assessment and Mapping Guidelines for Disaster Management. Technical report (2010)
6. European Commission: COMMISSION STAFF WORKING DOCUMENT - Overview of natural and man-made disaster risks in the EU. Technical report (2014)
7. European Council: COUNCIL DIRECTIVE 2008/114/EC of 8 on the identification and designation of European critical infrastructures and the assessment of the need to improve their protection. Technical report, Official Journal of the European Union, (L 345/75) (2008)
8. Groeve, T.D.: Overview of Disaster Risks that the EU faces. Technical report European Commission - Joint Research Centre (2013)
9. Grolinger, K., Capretz, M.A.M., Shypanski, A., Gill, G.S.: Federated critical infrastructure simulators: towards ontologies for support of collaboration. In: Proceedings of the 24th Canadian Conference on Electrical and Computer Engineering. pp. 1503–1506 (2011)
10. Grolinger, K., Capretz, M.A., Marti, J.R., Srivastava, K.D.: Ontology-based representation of simulation models (2012)
11. Horrocks, I., Motik, B., Wang, Z.: The hermit owl reasoner. In: Horrocks, I., Yatskevich, M., Jiménez-Ruiz, E. (eds.) ORE. CEUR Workshop Proceedings, vol. 858 (2012). http://ceur-ws.org/CEUR-WS.org
12. IRRIIS: The EU IRRIIS Research Project (2006). http://www.irriis.org
13. Joint Research Center: EXITO - the EXercise event Injection TOolkit (2015). http://sta.jrc.ec.europa.eu/index.php/cip-home/75-exito/314-exito
14. Luiijf, E., Nieuwenhuijs, A.: Extensible threat taxonomy for critical infrastructures. IJCIS 4(4), 409–417 (2008)
15. Rome, E., Langeslag, P., Usov, A.: Federated modelling and simulation for critical infrastructure protection. Networks of Networks: The Last Frontier of Complexity. Understanding Complex Systems, pp. 225–253. Springer, Switzerland (2014)
16. Sirin, E., Parsia, B., Grau, B.C., Kalyanpur, A., Katz, Y.: Pellet: a practical owl-dl reasoner. J. Web Sem. 5(2), 51–53 (2007)
17. Standard for Military Scenario Definition Language (MSDL) (2008)
18. Standard for Coalition Battle Management Language (C-BML) Phase 1 (2014)
19. Usov, A., Beyel, C., Rome, E., Beyer, U., Castorini, E., Palazzari, P., Tofani, A.: The DIESIS approach to semantically interoperable federated critical infrastructure simulation. In: Advances in System Simulation (SIMUL), pp. 121–128. IEEE (2010)
20. World Economic Forum: Global Risks 2015, 10th edn. Technical report (2015)

Modelling, Simulation and Analysis Approaches

Recovering Structural Controllability on Erdős-Rényi Graphs in the Presence of Compromised Nodes

Bader Alwasel[1,3] and Stephen D. Wolthusen[1,2(✉)]

[1] School of Mathematics and Information Security, Royal Holloway,
University of London, TW20 0EX Egham, UK
Bader.Alwasel.2012@live.rhul.ac.uk, stephen.wolthusen@rhul.ac.uk
[2] Norwegian Information Security Laboratory, Faculty of Computer Science,
Gjøvik University College, Gjøvik, Norway
[3] Community College of Unaizah, Qassim University,
Buraydah, Kingdom of Saudi Arabia

Abstract. Large-scale distributed control systems such as those encountered in electric power networks or industrial control systems must be assumed to be vulnerable to attacks in which adversaries can take over control at least part of the control network by compromising a subset of nodes. We investigate *Structural Controllability* properties of the control graph in *Linear Time-Invariant systems* (LTI), addressing the question of how to efficiently re-construct a control graph as far as possible in the presence of such compromised nodes. We study the case of sparse Erdős-Rényi Graphs with directed control edges and seek to provide an approximation of an efficient reconstructed control graph while minimising control graph diameter. The approach is based on a BLOCK DECOMPOSITION of a directed graph, allowing to identify cut-vertices and cut-edge. This results in faster re-construction of *Power Dominating Set* (PDS) structure, and ultimately the re-gaining of control for operators of control systems by applying three phases.

Keywords: Structural controllability · Control systems resilience · POWER DOMINATING SET

1 Introduction

Controllability and observability form core concepts in the study of control systems and networks, as it determines the ability to monitor or force the state of a system. As the computational complexity of determining Kalman controllability makes this problematic for time-critical large networks such as electric power networks, more general properties are of particular interest. The problem of Structural Controllability originally defined by Lin [1] offers such a graph-theoretical interpretation of controllability, which is particularly suitable for studying sets of nodes able to control an entire system as represented by a control graph

© Springer International Publishing Switzerland 2016
E. Rome et al. (Eds.): CRITIS 2015, LNCS 9578, pp. 105–119, 2016.
DOI: 10.1007/978-3-319-33331-1_9

(the reader is referred to [1–3]); the identification of minimum Driver Nodes (*DN*) via maximum matchings was proposed by Liu *et al.* [2] as a powerful mechanism, but also offering full control over the network for possible attackers seeking to take over or disrupt these relations. Both attackers and defenders can hence identify nodes of particular interest, thereby strongly motivating the development of algorithms for identifying such sets of *DN*, particularly after an attack or reconfiguration of the underlying network. This offers a strong motivation to study the ability of such systems to recover from deliberate attacks. Informally, controllability requires that a desired configuration can be forced from an arbitrary configuration in a finite number of steps; for a time-dependent linear dynamical system:

$$\dot{x}(t) = \mathbf{A}x(t) + \mathbf{B}u(t), \qquad x(t_0) = x_0 \tag{1}$$

with $x(t) = (x_1(t), \ldots, x_n(t))^T$ the current state of a system with n nodes at time t, a $n \times n$ adjacency matrix $\mathbf{A}$ representing the network topology of interactions among nodes, and $\mathbf{B}$ the $n \times m$ *input* matrix $(m \leq n)$, identifying the set of nodes controlled by a time-dependent *input vector* $u(t) = (u_1(t), \ldots, u_m(t))$ which forces the desired state. The system in Eq. 1 is *controllable* if and only if rank$[\mathbf{B}, \mathbf{AB}, \mathbf{A}^2\mathbf{B}, \ldots, \mathbf{A}^{n-1}\mathbf{B}] = n$ (*Kalman rank criterion*), giving the mathematical condition for controllability, where the rank of the controllability matrix provides the dimension of the controllable subspace of the system (A, B). As verifying the criterion is prohibitively expensive [2,3], efficient ways to achieve structural controllability of LTI systems has been extensively studied in recent years, also regarding robustness [4–6].

In this paper, we study Structural Controllability via the POWER DOMINATING SET (PDS) problem introduced by Haynes [7] for studying power networks; following the literature we also rely on the LTI formulation despite known limitations, for more details we refer the reader to [8–11]. We therefore propose an algorithm for solving PDS in directed Erdős-Rényi graphs in the presence of compromised nodes. For this we assume that given directed PDS for the original graph is constructed by our previous algorithm [12] in terms of the valid colouring. The approach in this paper is relying on a BLOCK DECOMPOSITION of a directed graph, allowing to re-construct a digraph G to a Block-Cut vertex Tree in terms of the valid colouring (Sect. 5), via dividing the algorithm into three phases (Sect. 6), allowing faster re-construction of PDS structure in the presence of compromised nodes while minimising control graph diameter.

2 Preliminary Definitions and Notation

Erdős-Rényi (ER) is a model for generating random graphs. Let a graph $G = (V, E)$, generated by ER, represents a control network *e.g.* for a power network where a vertex represents an electrical or control node (a substation bus where transmission lines, loads, and generators are connected) and an edge may represent a transmission line or a communication link joining two electrical nodes. A vertex u is called an out-neighbour of a vertex v if there is a directed edge from v to u in G. Similarly, u is called an in-neighbour of v if the directed edge (u, v) is present. The degree of a vertex v is denoted by $d(v)$. The number of out-neighbours of v is called the out-degree of v and is denoted by $d^+(v)$, the in-degree $d^-(v)$ is defined as the number in-degree of v (i.e., out-edge and in-edge respectively). A directed edge (v, u) pointing from vertex v to u is said to be incident from v and incident to u. Red edges in the valid colouring is denoted by $(e^r$ or $E_r)$, and blue edges by $(e^b$ or $E_b)$. Note that we denote a digraph G as G_r with only red edges. We define a Block including a compromised node as a compromised Block B^c.

3   Background and Related Work

Electric power companies must be maintained continuously to monitor their systems state as defined by a set of state variables. The purpose of the (PDS) problem study was to place as few Phase Measurement Units (PMUs), which measure the state variables in electric power system, as possible at some locations in order to monitoring an electric power system. Since the cost of PMU devices is rather high, the ability to minimise their number is highly desirable while observing the entire system [7]. The problem of locating a smallest set of PMUs is a graph theory problem introduced by Haynes et al. as a model for studying electric power networks and as an extension to the well-known Dominating Set (DS) problem, which is one of the classic decision problems [7–9]. Non-trivial control systems and controlled networks are necessarily sparse, and direct control of all nodes in such a network is not feasible as direct edges to these would typically result in too high costs as well as an out-degree of the controller node that would be difficult to realise in larger networks. Instead, the general case to be considered is for control to be indirect. However, as control systems will seek to minimise parameters such as latency, the formulation for PDS by Haynes *et al.* [7] extended the classic DOMINATING SET (DS) problem to seek a minimal POWER DOMINATING SET where the covering rule is the same as in DS with a propagation rule. Here we consider a straightforward extension to directed graphs in Definition 1.

Definition 1 (Directed PDS). *Let G be a directed graph. Given a set of vertices $S \subseteq V(G)$, the set of vertices power-dominated by S, denoted by $P(S)$, is obtained as:*

D1 *If a vertex v is in S, then v and all of its out-neighbours are in $P(S)$;*
D2 *(Propagation) if a vertex v is in $P(S)$, one of its out-neighbours denoted by w is not in $P(S)$, and all other out-neighbours of v are in $P(S)$, then w is inserted into $P(S)$.*

One problem immediately arising from vertex removal is the *reconstruction* and recovery of control while having a minimal power dominating set. However, even the basic minimal DS problem is known to be **NP**-complete with a polynomial-time approximation factor of $\Theta(\log n)$ as shown by Feige [13], the power domination problem is known to be **NP**-complete for general graphs even when reduced to certain classes of graphs, such as bipartite, planar, circle, split and chordal graphs [7,10], with approximation algorithms were given by Aazami and Stilp [14]; several studies have been undertaken showing polynomial time algorithms for the power domination problem for different graph classes as summarised in [10] such as block (undirected) graphs [8]. Parameterised results were given in [9]. In addition, Guo *et al.* [10] proposed a valid orientations for optimally solving PDS (over undirected graphs) on graphs of bounded tree-width. Subsequently, Aazami and Stilp [14] reformulated *Directed PDS* (DPDS) as valid colourings of edges and proposed a DP algorithm for DPDS where the underlying undirected graph has bounded tree-width. In earlier work, we proposed a reconstruction algorithm for the partition elements of (directed) control graphs of bounded tree width embedded in Erdős-Rényi random graphs arising after attacks [12]. Recently we have proposed a novel algorithm based on re-using as much as possible of a remaining PDS structure offering controllability after an event or attack leading to the partitioning of the original control network [15]. This DFS-based approach yields improved average-case complexity over previous and related work.

3.1   The Colouring Algorithm for Directed PDS

We reformulated PDS structure of directed graph in terms of valid colouring proposed in [12] (similar to the formulation by [10,14] to obtain DPDS). Our approach applies to a digraph such that the underlying undirected graph has bounded tree-width.

Definition 2 (Colouring of a Directed Graph). *A colouring of a directed graph $G = (V, E)$ is colouring the edges in G into red and blue edges such that $G = (V, E_r \cup E_b)$ where E_r and E_b are the set of red and blue edges, respectively.*

Definition 3 (PDS of Valid Colouring). *We refer to a vertex v in the set of PDS (i.e., $v \in PDS$) of the valid colouring of a digraph $G = (V, E)$ if and only if:*

1. *It has no in-edge in G, where $v \in G : d^-(v) = 0$*
2. *It has no in-red edges in $E(G_r)$, where $v \in G : d^-_{E_r}(v) = 0$*

Definition 4 (Dependency Path (P) in Valid Colouring of DPDS). *A dependency path in a valid colouring of a digraph G, is a sequence of red edges $P = v_1, e_1^r, v_2, e_2^r, \ldots, e_{i-1}^r, v_i$ that starts from vertex $v_1 \in PDS$ and ends at a vertex v_i of $\boldsymbol{P}$ such that $\boldsymbol{P}$ has no a red edge incident from v_i to v_1 (i.e., no directed cycle). However, dependency cycle in a directed graph is a sequence of directed edges whose underlying undirected graph forms a cycle such that all edges in a cycle are coloured by red.*

Definition 5 (The Valid Colouring). *A colouring of a directed graph $G = (V, E)$ is a partition of the edges in G into red and blue edges, such that a **valid** colouring $\Phi = (V, E_r \cup E_b)$ of a digraph $G = (V, E)$ is a colouring of G with the following properties:*

1. *An origin of the colouring of a digraph in G is satisfying the following:*
   (a) *There may exist a domination vertex, denoted by V_D, with out-degree at least 2 and no in-degree in $E(G)$, has at least 2 red out-edges:*

   $$\exists v \in V(G) : \Big(\big(d_G^-(v) = 0\big) \wedge \big(d_G^+(v) \geq 2\big)\Big) \Longrightarrow d_{G_r}^+(v) \geq 2$$

   (b) *There may exist a simple vertex, denoted by V_S, with no in-degree or at least one blue in-edge and at most out-degree of exactly one, has at most 1 red out-edge:*

   $$\exists v \in V(G) : \Big(\big(d_G^-(v) = 0\big) \vee \big(d_{E_b}^-(v) \geq 1\big)\Big) \wedge \big(d_G^+(v) \leq 1\big) \Longrightarrow d_{G_r}^+(v) \leq 1$$

2. *For all other vertices covered by the red edges in $G_r = (V, E_r) \setminus \{V_D, V_S\}$, $\forall v \in G : d_{E_r}^-(v) \leq 1$ and $\forall v \in G : d_{E_r}^-(v) = 1 \Longrightarrow d_{E_r}^+(v) \leq 1$ holds.*
3. *G has no dependency cycle and no two antiparallel edges are coloured red.*

Note that a vertex with $d_{E_r}^-(v) = 0$ in $G = (V, E_r)$ is an origin of Φ

4 Assumptions and Approach

We rely on a number of assumptions:

1. Given a directed graph $G = (V, E)$, constructed as $ER(n, p)$. Any ordered pair of vertices $u, v \in V(G)$ is connected with the edge probability p by a directed edge, such that there is a directed edge $e = \{u, v\} \in E(G)$ from u to v.
2. For the resulting instances of G, we consider the directed graphs that have no self-loops nor parallel edges, but may have two edges with different directions on the same two end vertices (called antiparallel edges) and may have directed cycles.
3. We assume that an instance of directed PDS for G is generated by our previous algorithm in terms of the valid colouring as set forth in [12], where a set of vertices $S \subseteq V(G)$, denoted by $P(S)$, power dominates G if $P(S) = V(G)$.
4. The resulting instances of $G = (V, E)$ is weakly connected such that the underlying undirected subgraph is connected.

We seek to recover the PDS structure in the presence of compromised nodes through:

  i. Decomposing a digraph G into k-separable set of Blocks based on blue and red edges (See Sect. 5):
     a. Finding Edge-Cut Set via considering blue edges.
     b. Identifying cut-vertices giving an equivalent formulation for PDS in directed graphs as shown in [15] via considering red edges.
 ii. Re-using blue edges existing in a compromised Block, allowing to minimise the recovered control graph diameter (See Sub-sect. 6.1), or
iii. To use blue edges that are incident to the compromised Block, allowing rapidly reconstruct the control graph as far as possible (See Sub-sect. 6.2), or
 iv. To identify criteria for the efficient addition of red edges in a compromised Block, (See Sub-sect. 6.3).

5   Reconstructing DPDS via Block Decomposition

A Block Decomposition of a graph B(G), may give equivalent characterisations of trees through identifying cut-vertices which its removal (together with the removal of any incident edges) disconnects a graph, and identifying Blocks of a directed graph where a Block of an undirected graph is a maximal connected subgraph with no cut vertex.

Definition 6 (Cut Vertex). *Let G be a graph with $k(G)$ components. A vertex v of G is called a Cut vertex (**C**) of G if $k(G - v) > k(G)$.*

Definition 7 (A Weakly Red-Connected Component in the Valid Colouring). *Red-Connected Component, denoted by X, is defined as exactly one directed Path (P) weakly connected by red edges (e^r) with no directed cycle $X = \{v_1, e_1^r, v_2, e_2^r, \ldots, e_{i-1}^r, v_i\} = P$ such that for every pair vertices of X, there is an undirected path from v_i to v_1 and a red directed path from v_1 to v_i.*

Definition 8 (A Set of Weakly Red-Connected Components). *In a Block, a set of Red-Connected Components, denoted by S, is defined as a set of directed paths connected by red edges with no directed cycle, such that $S = \{X_1, X_2, \ldots, X_i\}$. We call a set of S that shares the same tail endpoint $v \in PDS$ as a Block, where each Block has at least one Red-Connected Component.*

Definition 9 (A Leaf and Tail of a Weakly Red Connected Component). *A leaf vertex (i.e., a head vertex) is the vertex with no red out-edge, whereas the tail vertex is the vertex with a red in-edge that is incident from $v \in PDS$ to the tail vertex.*

Example 1. See Fig. 1, a Block with $x_{13} \in PDS$ has two RCCs starting from x_{13}, $P_1 = \{x_{14}, x_{17}\}$ and $P_2 = \{x_{15}, x_{16}\}$, where (x_{14}, x_{15}) are the tails of P_1 and P_2 respectively and (x_{16}, x_{17}) are the leaves (heads) of P_1 and P_2 respectively.

Definition 10 (Blue Edge-Cut Set in the Valid Colouring). *Let G be a digraph, constructed by the valid colouring in terms of blue and red edges. A Blue Edge-Cut set, denoted by (Y), of G is a set of blue edges satisfying, see Fig. 3a:*

1. *The removal of all blue edges in Y disconnects G to k-separable set of Blocks such that each Block is connected by red edges.*
2. *The removal of some (but not all) of blue edges in Y does not disconnects G.*

Definition 11 (Cut Vertex in the Valid Colouring). *Let G be a digraph, constructed by the valid colouring in terms of blue and red edges. A vertex $v \in PDS$ of G is called a Cut vertex (**C**) of G if the removal of v with addition of Blue Edge-Cut set (Y) disconnects G to k-separable set of Blocks, see Fig. 3a.*

Definition 12 (Block of Directed PDS in the Valid Colouring). *A Block-Vertex (**B**) of digraph is a maximal connected subgraph by red edges such that a set of Red-Connected Components with no Y that is downstream of a vertex in PDS.*

Definition 13 (Block-Cut Vertex Tree (T^B) of Directed PDS). *Suppose G be a digraph, constructed by the valid colouring in terms of blue and red edges. Let B_k be the set of Blocks and C_k be the set of Cut vertices of G. Constructing a graph T^B with vertex set $C_k \cup B_k$ as an ordinary tree regardless of the fact that every Block-vertex is actually subset of vertices of the original graph such that $c_i \in C$ is adjacent to $b_j \in B$ if and only if the Block b_j of G contains the Cut vertex c_i of G.*

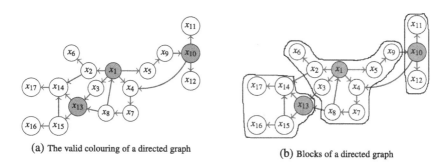

(a) The valid colouring of a directed graph

(b) Blocks of a directed graph

Fig. 1. Re-construction of blocks of a directed graph via red edges (Color fiure online)

Lemma 1 (Construction of Block-Cut Vertex Tree of directed PDS). *Consider Fig. 2, when drawing Block-Cut Vertex Tree (T^B) of Directed PDS, we represent:*

1. *Cut-vertex (which has an equivalent formulation for PDS) by green colour.*
2. *A tree red/blue edge, which describes a relation between a vertex and one of its direct descendants, by a solid line* _____ *satisfying:*
   - i. *Each Cut-vertex has exactly one solid red out-edge,*
   - ii. *Each Cut-vertex may have at most one solid blue in-edge or may have no solid blue in-edge,*
   - iii. *Each Block may have at least one solid blue out-edge incident to C_k, or have no solid blue out-edge.*
   - iv. *Each Block has exactly one solid red in-edge,*
3. *The remaining blue in/out edges are represented by a dashed line* _ _ _ _ _

Example 2. Consider the graph in (Fig. 1) and how is re-constructed as Block-Cut Vertex Tree as shown in (Fig. 2). The Blocks are $B_1 = \{x_2, x_3, x_4, x_5, x_6, x_7, x_8, x_9\}$, $B_2 = \{x_{14}, x_{15}, x_{16}, x_{17}\}$, $B_3 = \{x_{11}, x_{12}\}$; and Cut-vertices which have the equivalent formulation for PDS are $C_1 = \{x_1\}$, $C_2 = \{x_{13}\}$, $C_3 = \{x_{10}\}$. However, according to the Lemma 1 there is only one solid red out-edge incident from $C_k \to B_k$ such $\{(x_1 \to B_1), (x_{13} \to B_2), (x_{10} \to B_3)\}$, or may have at most one solid blue in-edge such $\{x_{10}, x_{13}\}$ or no solid blue in-edge such $\{x_1\}$. Moreover, there may have at least one solid blue out-edge incident from $B_k \to C_k$ such $\{(B_1 \to x_{13}), (B_1 \to x_{10})\}$, or have no solid blue out-edge such $\{B_2, B_3\}$. Note that blue in/out edges have no effect on the Structural Controllability of G as we only consider red edges for obtaining full control of G; however, those blue in/out edges are still existing in G as a part of connectivity and, thus, blue in/out edges (represented by a dashed line) could be used to recover Structural Controllability.

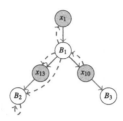

Fig. 2. Construction of Block-Cut Vertex Tree (T^B) of Directed PDS (Color figure online)

Theorem 1. *Given directed PDS of G reconstructing by the valid colouring in terms of red and blue edges, one can construct Block-Cut vertex Tree T^B of directed PDS by identifying Cut-vertices and Blocks of directed PDS.*

Proof. According to the Definition 13, $T^B(G) = C_k \cup B_k$. We show how to obtain (B_k). A Block (B) of directed PDS is identified by applying the Definition 10, where the removal of a Blue Edge-Cut set will disconnect G into a set of Red-Connected Components (S) that are downstream of $v \in PDS$ as in the Definition 8 (i.e., a maximal connected subgraph by red edges), Fig. 3a. Therefore, each S is as Block. Now we define C_k. According to the constraints in the Definition 5, each vertex in the valid colouring has at most one red in-edge except a vertex $u \in PDS$ that may have at least one blue in-edge $e_b(w, u) \in Y$ such that the removal $e_b(w, u)$ will disconnect G (see green vertices in Fig. 3a), hence, u is a Cut-vertex. By way of contradiction, let assume that not all of Blue Edge-Cut set are omitted, see Fig. 3b. Thus, there may exist some Blocks that are still connected to G via blue edges in S which contradicts the Definitions 10 and 12.

We formulate the relationship between T^B and PDS together with Theorem 1:

Theorem 2. *Given a Block-Cut vertex Tree of directed PDS (T^B) of G, constructed by the valid colouring, a Cut-vertex (C) is said to be PDS if and only if:*

1. *The removal of all blue edges in Y disconnects G to k-separable set of Blocks connecting by red edges.*
2. *There is no dependency cycle in each Block.*

(a) Removal of Blue Edge-Cut set   (b) Removal of **some** Blue Edge-Cut set

Fig. 3. Case enumeration for the removal of Blue Edge-Cut set (Color figure online)

Proof. 1. **Condition (1):**

Consider the Fig. 3, we prove that the set of PDS will be changed in case of not all of Y are omitted. By applying the propagation rule as defined in Definition 1; the blue edge (x_8, x_{13}) should be coloured to a red edge in order to control $\{x_{13}, x_{15}, x_{16}\}$ in sequence. However, x_{13} will no longer be PDS, thus, x_{14} should be controlled by x_2 that will be in PDS in order to control $\{x_6, x_{14}\}$ simultaneously. Hence, the set of PDS has changed to become $\{x_1, x_{10}, x_2\}$.

2. **Condition (2):**

We show by way of contradiction that there is no dependency cycle in T^B. let $u \to v$ denotes a vertex v is covered after u; assume $X = u_1, u_2, \ldots, u_m$ is a dependency cycle such that all red edges in X are in the same direction and $u_1 \in PDS$ has a red in-edge incident from u_m. Therefore, the red edge (u_i, u_{i+1}) implies that $u_i \to u_{i+1}$ for all $i = 1, 2, \ldots, m - 1$; thus we get $u_1 \to u_2 \to \cdots \to u_m$, but this contradicts with the covering rules as the head u_m has a red edge incident to u_1 implying $u_m \to u_1$.

6   The Process of Recovering Structural Controllability

The algorithm is divided into three phases for recovering Structural Controllability in the presence of compromised nodes and minimising control graph diameter. As a low diameter of a control network is desirable, it might minimise delays in a network and speed up communication in a network design. We consider (in order of priority) the blue edges that are inside a compromised Block itself, or that are incident to a compromised Block, and/or adding edges inside a compromised Block. We recall that each Block has at least one RCC, where $X = \{v_1, e_1^r, \ldots, e_{i-1}^r, v_i\}$ or a set of RCCs, where $S = \{X_1, X_2, \ldots, X_i\}$. The tail vertex of X is denoted by $t(v)$ and the head vertex of X by $h(v)$. A sequence of vertices downstream of a compromised node in X is denoted by W. A compromised node may be $v \in PDS$ or $v \notin PDS$, thus, there are two cases of recovering Structural Controllability via internal blue edges of a Block.

6.1   First Phase: Recovering via Internal Blue Edges of a Compromised Block

We seek to take the advantage of existing blue edges inside a compromised Block to repair the Structural Controllability and minimise the diameter of a graph.

Because of the lack of number of blue edges that is existing inside a Block, it is necessary to consider the external blue edges that are incident to a Block. However, if both approaches are not helpful, then the addition of red edges inside a compromised Block is required.

A: The Case of a Compromised Node Is in PDS:

Lemma 2. *Assume that a Block has a compromised node $v \in PDS$ and there exists internal blue edges, then a blue edge can be coloured to red edge if it satisfies:*

1. *If there is a blue edge incident from each $h_i(v)$ to each $t_{i+1}(v)$ then $t_i(v)$ that has no in-edge should be PDS in a Block, see Fig. 4a, or*
2. *If there is a blue edge incident from any $t_i(v)$ to each $t_{i+1}(v)$ then $t_i(v)$ that has no in-edge should be PDS in a Block, see Fig. 4b, or*
3. *If there is a blue edge incident from any $t_i(v)$ to exactly one (or all) $t_{i+1}(v)$ and/or a blue edge incident from $h_i(v)$ to the remaining $t(v)$ that is not covered yet then $t_i(v)$ that has no in-edge should be PDS in a Block, Fig. 4c, otherwise,*
4. *Applying any previous condition without placing PDS and go to the second phase.*

B: The Case of a Compromised Node Is NOT in PDS:

Lemma 3. *Assume that a Block has a compromised $v \notin PDS$ and internal blue edges, then a blue edge is coloured to red if there is a blue edge incident from $h_i(v) \in X_i$ to $t_i(v) \in W_i$, or from $u \in PDS$ to $t_i(v) \in W_i$ see Fig. 4d; otherwise go to the next phase.*

6.2 Second Phase: Recovering via External Blue Edges of a Block

If compromised nodes are still not controlled, then we recover Structural Controllability via the external blue edges of a Block (B^{ex}), that incident to a compromised Block (B^c).

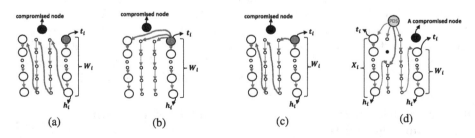

(a)   (b)   (c)   (d)

Fig. 4. Recovering compromised nodes via internal blue edges in a block (Color figure online)

Algorithm 1. Recovering via internal blue edges of a Block

---

1 **if** *A compromised node $v \in PDS$ and a Block has internal blue edges* **then**
2   **if** *the number of S in a Block > 1* **then**
3   **if** *there is e_b incident from each $h_i(v)$ to each $t_{i+1}(v)$* **then**
4 | Colouring $e_b \to e_r$ and $d^- t_i(v) = 0$ is PDS in B^c
5   **else if** *If there is e_b incident from any $t_i(v)$ to each $t_{i+1}(v)$* **then**
6 | Colouring $e_b \to e_r$ and $d^- t_i(v) = 0$ is PDS in B^c
7   **else if** *satisfies the constraint (3) in the definition (2)* **then**
8 | Colouring $e_b \to e_r$ and $d^- t_i(v) = 0$ is PDS in B^c
9   **else**
10 | Apply any previous condition without placing PDS and go to the next phase.
11   **else if** *the number of S is exactly one* **then**
12 | $t_i(v) \in W$ is PDS in B^c
13 **else if** *A compromised node $v \notin PDS$ and a Block has internal blue edges* **then**
14 | Applying the constraint in lemma (3)

Lemma 4 (Colouring an External Blue Edge to Red Edge). *Let assume that a Block has a compromised node either $v \in PDS$ or $v \notin PDS$ and blue edges incident from B^{ex} to B^c, then a blue edge can be coloured to red edge if it satisfies, see Fig. 5:*

1. *There is a blue edge incident from $v \in PDS$ in B^{ex} to $t_i(v) \in W_i$ in B^c, and/or*
2. *There is a blue edge incident from $h_i(v) \in X_i$ in B^{ex} to $t_i(v) \in W_i$ in B^c.*

Algorithm 2. Recovering via external blue edges of a Block

---

1 **if** *exists compromised nodes that are not covered yet in the Algorithm (1)* **then**
2   **if** *there is e_b incident from $B^{ex}(v) \in PDS$ to $t_i(v) \in W_i$ in B^c* **then**
3 | Colouring $e_b \to e_r$
4   **else if** *there is e_b incident from $h_i(v) \in X_i$ in B^{ex} to $t_i(v) \in W_i$ in B^c* **then**
5 | Colouring $e_b \to e_r$
6   **else**
7 | compromised nodes are still not covered yet, then apply the algorithm 3

6.3 Third Phase: Recovering Structural Controllability via Adding Edges

Because of the lack of blue edges that reside in B^c or are incident from B^{ex}, moreover, each red edge are already in use to control other vertices, we identify the criteria of adding red edges inside a compromised Block.

Lemma 5 (The Addition of Red Edge). *Suppose that a Block has a compromised node and there are no blue edges whether to reside in B^c or to be*

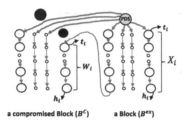

Fig. 5. Recovering compromised nodes either $(v \in PDS)$ or $(v \notin PDS)$ via external blue edges of a block (Color figure online)

incident from B^{ex} to B^c, then each W_i should be controlled by a red edge such that, see Fig. 6:

a. *if a compromised $v \in PDS$ then a red edge is added from any $t_i(v)$ to each $t_{i+1}(v)$ and $d^- t_i(v) = 0$ or $d_{er}^- t_i(v) = 0$ should be PDS in a Block, or*
b. *if a compromised $v \notin PDS$ then a red is added from $v \in PDS$ to $t_i(v) \in W_i$, or from $h_i \in X_i$ to $t_i(v) \in W_i$, see Fig. 6b.*

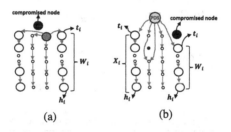

Fig. 6. Recovering compromised nodes $(v \in PDS)$ or $(v \notin PDS)$ via adding red edges (Color figure online)

Algorithm 3. Recovering via adding red edges inside a compromised Block

---

1 **if** *exists compromised nodes that are not covered yet in the Algorithms (1) and (2)* **then**
2   **if** *a compromised node $v \in PDS$* **then**
3   Adding a red edge from any $t_i(v)$ to each $t_{i+1}(v)$;
4   Placing $d^- t_i(v) = 0$ or $d_{er}^- t_i(v) = 0$ is PDS in B^c
5   **else**
6   Adding e^r from $v \in PDS$ to each $t_i(v) \in W_i$ or from $h_i \in X_i$ to $t_i(v) \in W_i$

The motivation of the algorithm is not only reconstruction of the structure of PDS in the presence of compromised nodes but also the ability to minimise their number while observing the entire system.

Lemma 6. *Given a directed PDS of G, reconstructing in terms of the valid colouring. Let G has a compromised node. The cardinality of PDS achieved by the proposed algorithm remains the same as (or less than) the number of given PDS.*

Proof. We prove that the number of PDS after applying the proposed algorithm is less than given PDS. By way of contradiction, let assume that a compromised Block has $v, u \in PDS$, and only v is compromised node; then all the RCCs, denoted by S_v, that were connected to v should be now controlled, see Fig. 5. By applying the three phases proposed, S_v is power dominated if and only if:

a. There is a blue edge incident from $u \in PDS$ to the tails of S_v, and/or
b. There is a blue edge incident from the heads of RCCs of u to the tails of S_v,and/or
c. By adding red edges from u to the tails of S_v.

Hence, the cardinality of PDS will become one (i.e., $u \in PDS$), which is a contradiction to the assumption. Let prove the equality of PDS. The same argument is applied; assume a Block has $u \in PDS$ and $v \notin PDS$ is compromised, thus, the vertices downstream of v, denoted by w_i, should be controlled, see Fig. 4d. By applying the same constraints above, w_i is power dominated with the same of number of PDS, so the lemma is proved.

Note that in case of $v \in PDS$ is compromised, then all the neighbours of v should be power dominated, meaning each RCC that were connected to v should have at most one red in-edge by applying the three phase propose. Hence, we prove the next lemma.

Lemma 7. *Given power dominating set $S \subseteq V$ in a digraph G, the number of dependency paths of $v \in S$ is exactly equal to the number of neighbours of v.*

Proof. Assume that a Block has only one vertex $v \in PDS$ that controls all vertices in a Block. By applying the first role (D1) for v, all the neighbours of v are controlled by red edges incident from v. By way of contradiction, suppose that the Block has w which is a neighbour of v that is not controlled by v (i.e., $e_b = vw$), then either:

a. w should be controlled by $u \in PDS$ in other Block which contradicts the assumption that a Block has only one vertex in PDS that controls all vertices in a Block, or
b. w is a vertex in PDS, which also contradicts the assumption, or
c. w has a red edge incident from $x \notin PDS$ in the Block of v by applying the second role D2, thus, w is not a neighbour of v. This is a contradiction, so the lemma is proved.

Together with Theorems 1 and 2, we immediately obtain our main result:

Lemma 8. *Given directed PDS of G, one can repair Structural Controllability of G in the presence of compromised nodes by reconstructing G as a Block-Cut vertex Tree in terms of the valid colouring.*

6.4   Time Complexity

Lemma 9. *Given directed PDS of G, one can solve Structural Controllability of G in the presence of compromised nodes in $O(nc^W)$ time for a constant c.*

Proof. The time complexity is classified based on three phases. The total running time of the Algorithm 1 is to utilise blue edges existing in B^c, hence in the worst case, the most time-consuming part is to determine blue edges that are incident to each tail of W_i in B^c in case of $v \in PDS$ where there is (4^W) states. For the average case, it considers only the path W_i that was leftover of a compromised node v in case of $v \notin PDS$ where there is $(2^{(W-1)})$ states such that there are at most $\{2^{(W-1)}.4^W\}$ states in the algorithm, where W denotes the number of dependency paths that are downstream of a compromised node. Thus, the most running time of the Algorithm 1 is $O(nc^W)$. However, the most running time of the Algorithm 2 in the average case of a compromised $v \in PDS$ or $v \notin PDS$ is $O(nc^W)$, such that either $B^{ex}(v)$ or $X_i \in B^{ex}$ has an blue in-egde incident to W_i in B^c, where there are at most $\{2^W.2^{(W-1)}\}$ states. On the other hand, the best case is to execute the Algorithm 3 such that if a compromised $v \in PDS$ then a red edge is added from any $t_i(v)$ to each $t_{i+1}(v)$ or if a compromised $v \notin PDS$ then a red is added from $v \in PDS$ to $t_i(v) \in W_i$, such that the running time is $O(nc^W)$, where there are at most $\{2^{(W-1)}.1^W\}$ states.

7   Conclusion

Structural Controllability is a highly interesting concept for understanding vulnerabilities to attack in critical infrastructures. This, however, requires the ability to recover controllability as fast as possible since adversaries may repeatedly attack. This paper proposed a novel algorithm to re-construct a control graph as far as possible in the presence of compromised nodes. The approach is based on a BLOCK DECOMPOSITION of a digraph, allowing to re-construct PDS structure by applying three phases. Future work will study the effects of rewiring edges on Structural Controllability properties of directed Erdős-Rényi graphs, while keeping the total number of edges unchanged.

References

1. Lin, C.T.: Structural Controllability. IEEE Trans. Autom. Control **19**(3), 201–208 (1974)
2. Liu, Y.Y., Slotine, J.J., Barabási, A.L.: Controllability of Complex Networks. Nature **473**, 167–173 (2011)
3. Wang, W.X., Ni, X., Lai, Y.C., Grebogi, C.: Optimizing controllability of complex networks by minimum structural perturbations. Phys. Rev. E **85**(2), 026–115 (2012)
4. Pu, C.L., Pei, W.J., Michaelson, A.: Robustness analysis of network controllability. Phys. A **391**(18), 4420–4425 (2012)

5. Pósfai, M., Liu, Y.Y., Slotine, J.J., Barabási, A.L.: Effect of correlations on network controllability. Nature Sci. Rep. **3**(1067), 1–7 (2013)
6. Nacher, J.C., Akutsu, T.: Structural controllability of unidirectional bipartite networks. Nature Sci. Rep. **3**(1647), 1–7 (2013)
7. Haynes, T.W., Hedetniemi, S.M., Hedetniemi, S.T., Henning, M.A.: Domination in graphs applied to electric power networks. SIAM J. discrete Math. **15**(4), 519–529 (2002)
8. Xu, G., Kang, L., Shan, E., Zhao, M.: Power domination in block graphs. Theoret. Comput. Sci. **1–3**, 299–305 (2006)
9. Kneis, J., Mölle, D., Richter, S., Rossmanith, P.: Parameterized power domination complexity. Inf. Process. Lett. **98**(4), 145–149 (2006)
10. Guo, J., Niedermeier, R., Raible, D.: Improved algorithms and complexity results for power domination in graphs. Algorithmica **52**(2), 177–202 (2008)
11. Alwasel, B., Wolthusen, S.: Structural controllability analysis via embedding power dominating set approximation in Erdős-Rényi Graphs. In: the proceedings of the 29th IEEE International Conference on Advanced Information Networking and Applications (AINA-2015), Gwangju, Korea, IEEE Press (2015)
12. Alwasel, B., Wolthusen, S.: Reconstruction of structural controllability over Erdős-Rényi graphs via power dominating sets. In: Proceedings of the 9th Cyber and Information Security Research Conference (CSIRC 2014), Oak Ridge, TN, USA, ACM Press, April 2014
13. Feige, U.: A threshold of ln n for approximating set cover. J. ACM **45**(4), 634–652 (1998)
14. Aazami, A., Stilp, K.: Approximation algorithms and hardness for domination with propagation. SIAM J. Discrete Math. **23**(3), 1382–1399 (2009)
15. Alwasel, Bader, Wolthusen, Stephen D.: Recovering structural controllability on Erdos-Rènyi graphs via partial control structure re-use. In: Panayiotou, Christos G., et al. (eds.) CRITIS 2014. LNCS, vol. 8985, pp. 293–307. Springer, Heidelberg (2016). doi:10.1007/978-3-319-31664-2_30

Vulnerability Against Internet Disruptions – A Graph-Based Perspective

Annika Baumann[(⊠)] and Benjamin Fabian

Institute of Information Systems,
Humboldt-Universität zu Berlin, Berlin, Germany
{annika.baumann,bfabian}@wiwi.hu-berlin.de

Abstract. The Internet of today permeates societies and markets as a critical infrastructure. Dramatic network incidents have already happened in history with strong negative economic impacts. Therefore, assessing the vulnerability of Internet connections against failures, accidents and malicious attacks is an important field of high practical relevance. Based on a large integrated dataset describing the Internet as a complex graph, this paper develops a multi-dimensional Connectivity Risk Score that, to our knowledge, constitutes the first proposal for a topological connectivity-risk indicator of single Autonomous Systems, the organizational units of the Internet backbone. This score encompasses a variety of topological robustness metrics and can help risk managers to assess the vulnerability of their organizations even beyond network perimeters. Such analyses can be conducted in a user-friendly way with the help of CORIA, a newly developed software framework for connectivity risk analysis. Our approach can serve as an important element in an encompassing strategy to assess and improve companies' connectivity to the Internet.

Keywords: Vulnerability · Internet robustness · Internet topology · Graph mining · Risk score

1 Introduction

The importance of the Internet as today's communication and information medium is undisputed. It has revolutionized worldwide communication, made it cost efficient and fast and created countless of new or refined business models. There are numerous businesses in the world whose core competencies rely completely on the Internet. Based on these considerations, it becomes apparent that a limited or disrupted Internet connectivity can lead to significant financial losses for businesses and even economies. A study of the IT systems integrator CDW revealed that network disruptions caused $1.7 billion in financial losses in 2010 [1]. This is an indicator of how crucial the Internet is for many business activities today.

In this paper, we aim to develop an analysis method and score that can help risk managers to assess the potential vulnerability of their organizations even beyond their own area of control, i.e., beyond their network perimeters. Here the question arises how robust their Internet connectivity is regarding failures, accidents and malicious attacks. How difficult is it to tear certain parts of their network neighborhood down? This article

© Springer International Publishing Switzerland 2016
E. Rome et al. (Eds.): CRITIS 2015, LNCS 9578, pp. 120–131, 2016.
DOI: 10.1007/978-3-319-33331-1_10

will examine this problem by first developing a global graph of the Internet based on a combination of several recent data sources. This graph will serve as a basis for robustness analyses focusing on the local vulnerability of single autonomous systems (ASs). From a high-level vantage point, an AS can be considered as an "atomic unit" of the Internet backbone, constituting a single administrative domain that is under the control of a particular organization, such as a company or public institution. Many companies in several industries own a dedicated AS [2], while for others the AS of their Internet service provider can be investigated.

From a topological point of view, connectivity risk can be characterized by being a potential victim of a random failure or a targeted attack. This leads to a certain duality: On the one hand, ASs that are not well-connected to the Internet are most at risk with respect to failures. On the other hand, those ASs, which are indeed well-connected and therefore contribute most to communication ability and efficiency of the entire network, represent an attractive target for attacks aimed at weakening the global Internet. In order to make a statement about which ASs will fit into these two risk categories from a topological viewpoint, a proposal for a multi-dimensional score is developed in this paper that we call Connectivity Risk Score (CRS). This score is based upon a combination of selected and normalized topological metrics. Normalization ensures the comparability across ASs and network graph instances. Moreover, the CRS also reflects that the Internet topology is highly complex and the connectivity status of a certain AS depends on various factors.

The paper is structured as follows: First, related literature in the area of Internet resilience will be presented. Afterwards, the relevant methodology used in this paper will be described. Then, the development and evaluation of the CRS will be discussed. This score and all of the aggregated metrics can be accessed in a user-friendly way by security analysts via our newly developed CORIA analysis software that is presented in the subsequent section. The final section will summarize our contributions and results, discuss limitations as well as comment on future work.

2   Related Work

An important design feature of the Internet is its robustness. The term *resilience* can be seen as synonym and can be described as the ability of a certain system to return to a normal condition after external impacts. The *robustness* of the Internet is therefore "the ability of the network to provide and maintain an acceptable level of service in the face of various faults and challenges to normal operation" [26, p. 2]. The approach presented in the current article extends established reliability analysis of online services, such as Tseng and Wu [3] who focus on the reliability of critical servers, by analyses of connectivity based on the Internet graph.

Several researchers investigated the question of how to assess Internet robustness, but so far the main focus was placed on a global perspective [4]. In an early work, Albert et al. [5] analyzed the attack and failure tolerance of the Internet at the AS level based on both the classical *Erdös–Rényi* (ER) model and a scale-free graph model for the Internet. Dolev et al. [6] additionally considered economically driven restrictions of data exchange over the Internet backbone, i.e., policy-driven routing. Wu et al. [7] examined the router robustness of the Internet in case of node removal, also taking policy restrictions into account. Xiao et al. [8] focused on the attack tolerance of the Internet under the assumption that the possession of complete and global information about the Internet graph is an unrealistic assumption. Finally, Deng et al. [9] considered the so-called *k-fault tolerance* of the Internet on the AS level which is the reachability of a pair of nodes in the network after the removal of k nodes.

More recent literature examines Internet resilience in a more specialized way. For example, Zhao et al. [10] analyze the effect of removing the so-called *k-core* nodes from the Internet AS-level graph, i.e., the most important nodes which have at least degree k. Using a simulation based approach, Çetinkaya et al. [11] propose a framework for better understanding the robustness of networks such as the Internet for future improvements. Shirazi et al. [12] examine the resilience of anonymous communication networks such as Tor and propose a new metric for measuring robustness. Moreover, some projects already exist which examine the idea of combining different metrics to estimate the resilience of a network from a theoretical point of view (see for example [29, 30]) where our approach will add significant results from a practical perspective.

3 Methodology

In order to obtain an extensive and recent dataset, we use a combination of three different main sources for Internet connectivity data: *Border Gateway Protocol* (BGP) routing tables, *traceroute* measurements and *Internet Routing Registry* (IRR) data.

In case of BGP routing tables, data provided by CAIDA's AS Rank project are used [13] comprising a 5-day-period (06/01–06/05/2012). In addition, a research group of the University of California in Los Angeles (UCLA) provides another dataset [14]. Choosing the closest time period with available data files from 05/24/12 to 05/28/12, this dataset contains 159,383 unique AS paths. The traceroute-based Macroscopic Topology Project of CAIDA uses Archipelago (Ark) as a measurement tool [15]. All data files fitting into the appropriate time period (either the same as in case of CAIDA AS Rank or the most similar available) were downloaded from their website and preprocessed using only direct links between two ASs. After merging of the data, 57,922 unique AS paths are provided by Ark. In addition, Internet Routing Registry (IRR) data is also used in this paper. For this purpose, the data files of all available 34 IRRs were downloaded from their website [16]. Based on the method mentioned by Siganos and Faloutsos [17] as well as Zhang et al. [18], the necessary AS path information was selected as a part of the *aut-num* object class. To gain reliable data only dyadic relationships were included in the dataset and those that were updated at last in 2012[1].The final IRR dataset consists of 47,348 unique AS paths.

---

[1] An exception is the RIPE IRR. This registry is considered as the most accurate and current one [18]. Therefore, from the RIPE registry all entries last changed in 2011 and 2012 have been included in this dataset.

All the individual datasets of CAIDA AS Rank, UCLA, Ark and IRR were then merged into one single file for the final dataset used in this paper resulting in 44,397 nodes and 199,073 edges.

4 Connectivity Risk Score (CRS)

4.1 Selection of Topological Metrics

To develop a comprehensive risk score, a literature survey was conducted examining existing metrics specifically used for assessing Internet robustness. Overall, 37 metrics could be identified[2]. Most of these metrics provide just a very general statement about the connectedness of an AS. Because of this, the CRS combines several metrics into a single measure to take advantage of multiple metrics and outweigh their disadvantages. Therefore in the next step, a number of requirements were defined which needed to be fulfilled by the metrics in order to be selected for the CRS. The initial properties that we required for the selection of metrics were:

1. A statement about the connectivity to the network for a single AS should be derived from it (not the entire graph, not aggregated AS groups).
2. The metric should have two distinct value ranges in order to distinguish the attractiveness for an attack and the susceptibility to failures.

Therefore, metrics that provide a statement solely for the global topology or AS groups were not selected (i.e., assortativity coefficient, symmetry ratio, (joint) degree distribution, average neighbor connectivity, eigenvalue-based metrics as well as global average metrics such as average degree, average clustering coefficient or diameter). Overall, six out of the initial 37 metrics remain which meet the requirements and are therefore used for the CRS: degree [DEG], average neighbor degree [AND], iterated average neighbor degree (two-hop neighborhood of a node) [IAND], betweenness centrality [BC], shortest path length [SPL] and eccentricity [ECC]. Some of these metrics are calculated based on the whole network structure (e.g., betweenness centrality) meaning that changing arbitrary nodes in the network might have an influence on the characteristics of that node. Those quasi-local metrics are still rather important for capturing the topological connectivity of a single AS since it cannot be seen as an isolated unit but is interconnected with a huge, interrelated network structure. For a more detailed description of these metrics see, e.g., [19, 20]. All of these metrics were calculated for the AS-level graph with the help of the graph analysis software NetworkX [21] and average results for them are presented in Table 1.

Correlation of the CRS candidate metrics based on the AS data set is shown in Table 2. None of the metrics are very highly correlated except for degree and betweenness centrality where there is still no perfect correlation, however. Based on these results, we conclude that the selection of metrics for the CRS is useful and non redundant.

---

[2] The complete list of identified metrics is available from the authors upon request.

Table 1. Average results of metrics for AS data set (not normalized)

	DEG	AND	IAND	BC	SPL	ECC
Average	8.9679	703.29	154.44	0.0001	3.5585	7.8302
Median	2.0000	315.00	95.573	0.0000	3.5056	8.0000
Max	4330.0	4330.0	4330.0	0.1300	7.8300	11.000
Min	1.0000	1.1400	1.1700	0.0000	2.1100	6.0000
Average Norm.	0.0018	0.1464	0.0350	0.0004	0.7470	0.6340
Median Norm.	0.0002	0.0641	0.0218	0.0000	0.7563	0.6000
Standard Deviation	60.385	901.43	202.03	0.0013	0.4425	0.5800

Table 2. Correlation of normalized metrics on AS data set

	DEG	AND	IAND	BC	SPL	ECC
Degree [DEG]	1.00					
Average Neighbor Degree [AND]	−0.05	1.00				
Iterated Average Neighbor Degree [IAND]	−0.07	−0.38	1.00			
Betweenness Centrality [BC]	0.85	−0.03	−0.03	1.00		
Shortest Path Length [SPL]	0.20	0.55	−0.33	0.10	1.00	
Eccentricity [ECC]	0.15	0.44	−0.25	0.07	0.74	1.00

4.2 Normalization Process and Weighting of the Metrics

Because the results of the different metrics vary and also feature individual value ranges, they need to be normalized in order to calculate a composite score. For the metrics degree and betweenness centrality we used min-max normalization which maps the original range to the interval between [0,1]. In case of the metrics eccentricity and shortest path length – because here low values are desirable in terms of connectedness to the network – we used the max-min normalization.

For the (iterated) average neighbor degree we applied the z-normalization, which generates a normally distributed dataset with a new mean of zero and a variance of one due to possible distortions caused by high or low degree neighboring nodes. In order to consider the fact that nodes with only few neighbors tend to have a higher probability of having a median equal to the average neighbor degree, the number of neighbors was additionally taken into account. The resulting equation for the normalized (iterated) average neighbor degree of node i is as follows:

$$[I]AND_{corrected,i} = [I]AND_i + \left(\left(\frac{Median_i - [I]AND_i}{\sigma_i} \right) \cdot (\# \, of \, Neighbors_i)^{-1} \right) \cdot [I]AND_i \quad (1)$$

The up-voted and down-voted results for the (iterated) average neighbor degree were then finally normalized with the help of min-max normalization.

Furthermore, it is not reasonable to consider all metrics as equally important because their impact on the connection status of an AS might vary significantly. For the final CRS all metrics were weighted by a particular value. It was determined that the weights should sum up to one. The degree and the betweenness centrality were equally weighted and considered to be most important. Furthermore, the network environment one hop away from a node was considered to be more important for the robustness of a node than the network environment at subsequent hops due to the further distance from a node. Therefore, the average neighbor degree and the iterated neighbor degree were handled as less important and therefore weighted increasingly less. Because of the relatedness of the shortest path length and the eccentricity, the combination of both was weighted with the same amount as the degree and the betweenness centrality. There-fore, each of both distance-based metrics has a weighting of 0.125. This leads to the final weightings of 0.25 for the degree and the betweenness centrality, 0.125 for the shortest path length and the eccentricity, 0.15 for the average neighbor degree and 0.1 for the iterated average neighbor degree. The final score ranges between zero and one hundred percent.

4.3   Application of the CRS

Once the results for the selected metrics of the CRS are calculated, ranges need to be established that indicate critical areas for interpretation. The theoretical range of the CRS is between 100 % and 0 %, while the effective values, based on the dataset used, range between 74.58 % at the maximum and 0.01 % at the minimum. There are two numerical subranges that indicate those ASs that are most at risk. If the CRS is plotted against the risk of an AS in terms of robustness, a theoretical U-shaped curve is the result (see Fig. 1, left), which can be regarded as exemplary representation used to visually communicate the idea of the CRS.

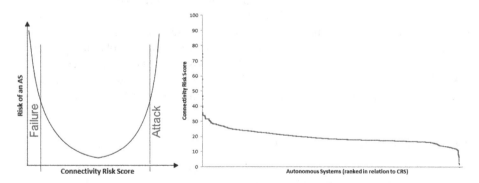

Fig. 1. Critical areas for ASs (left) and distribution of CRS values (right)

It is assumed that an AS is not at risk if it is neither vulnerable to random failures nor an attractive target for global attacks. This is associated with the following interpretation of the CRS: a small CRS value indicates a vulnerability to random errors. In the worst case, ASs that appear at the bottom of a CRS ranking list have a small degree and low (iterated) average neighbor degree. Their path options are quite limited. Furthermore, their betweenness centrality would in general be quite small, meaning that there are no or only few shortest paths passing through that node. Eccentricity and shortest path length can be expected to be high, indicating that these ASs are probably located somewhere at the edge of the network. Therefore, ASs with a low CRS value are badly connected to the network and insignificant for its communication ability, which makes them prone to random errors, but not attractive attack targets. On the other hand, a high CRS value is an indicator of high attractiveness for targeted attacks. In particular, ASs with a high degree as well as a high (iterated) average neighbor degree have a high CRS. Their path options are quite versatile. Both distance-based metrics are low. Those ASs are located at important communication points of the network, which can also often lead to a high betweenness centrality because many shortest paths are passing through those kinds of nodes. In summary, ASs with a high CRS value are well connected to the network and form an important communication backbone. This makes them highly attractive for deliberate attacks targeted at nodes whose removal would hurt the entire network most.

The distribution of the CRS values based on the empirical AS dataset is shown in Fig. 1, right. Each data point shows a specific AS and its corresponding value of the CRS. There are many ASs with a low and few with a high CRS value. Only four of them reach a threshold of 50 % while two of them are extreme outliers having values of 74.58 % and 72.36 %. The average CRS value for all ASs is around 19.86 %. This again shows that there are many ASs having a low value, while the majority of them is located somewhere between 30 % and 10 %. This is an indicator that even today the global robustness of the Internet graph has a lot of potential for improvement.

A desirable global distribution of the CRS would involve a quite homogeneous accumulation of ASs in a certain score area to reduce the impact of attacks. This means that all ASs would be equally important for the communication ability of the network and the elimination of a selected AS would not have such a dramatic effect as it is the case now, e.g., more similar to the Erdös–Rényi model [5]. At the same time, the CRS values should be as high as possible. A general increase of the CRS values for every ASs would be beneficial and would enhance the robustness of the global Internet graph by reducing the impact of random errors. We emphasize that the CRS serves as a first risk indicator to assess the vulnerability of single ASs but should be complemented in risk management practice by a more detailed examination of each particular AS.

4.4   Selective Validation of the CRS

In order to validate the usefulness of our CRS, we selected two poorly connected ASs with a low score and visualized their nearby graph environment (see Fig. 2). Bold numbers represent the associated AS number, expressions in brackets specify the underlying organization; if an additional number is given, it refers to the degree of the nodes at the end of the network segment. The illustration makes it obvious that AS 636 and AS 45,076 are indeed badly connected to the Internet topology according to our dataset as was indicated by the CRS. For example, if any one of the subsequent one-degree nodes fail, these nodes will be affected as well and get completely disconnected from the rest of the network. Therefore, their connectivity depends not only on their own characteristics but also on those of the following ASs. In case of AS 45,076 the breakdown of any single node out of five (including the node itself) will affect this AS most severely. If only the degree metric were used, these ASs would not have scored worse than many other nodes with degree 1 and their particular vulnerability could have been easily overlooked.

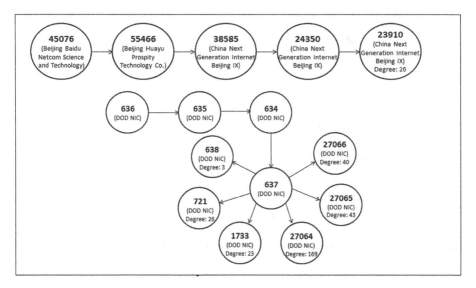

Fig. 2. Two examples of badly connected ASs

5 Connectivity Risk Analyzer (CORIA)

Based on the theoretical foundations presented in the earlier sections, we developed a web-based software framework that supports security analysts and consultants in assessing the connectivity risks of a particular organization. This *Connectivity Risk Analyzer* (CORIA) can be accessed via web browser. The analyst can search for individual AS and display the results of all connectivity metrics and the CRS discussed in this article. Moreover, statistical analyses of the entire AS datasets are possible and ASs can be ranked according to any of the metrics.

The high-level system architecture consists of a backend, the storage area as well as the frontend. The backend is responsible for importing AS data and calculating metrics and scores. It is implemented in the Python programming language and utilizes the network analysis framework NetworkX [21]. The calculation time of base metrics for the AS dataset used in this article are displayed in Table 3. All measurements were obtained in a virtual machine that was equipped with one CPU core running at 3 GHz and 4 GB of memory.

These results indicate that CORIA could cope with frequent updates of the underlying data set, which is one important direction for future improvements. The storage tier makes the results of the backend calculations persistent and enriches them with general information about each AS for later display via the frontend. It can also store interim results of calculations. For speed and flexibility, the storage tier is implemented using the Redis key-value store [22]. User requests via a web browser are served by the frontend tier which is based on established web technology. It is implemented as a combination of a Ruby application based on the Sinatra framework [23] and HTML views based on the Twitter Bootstrap library [24]. An example user view is shown in Fig. 3.

Table 3. Calculation runtimes for the AS data set

Metric	Duration [s]	Duration [m]	Percentage of duration
DEG	0.468	0.01	0.000817 %
AND	1.307	0.02	0.0022 %
IAND	631.865	10.53	1.10 %
BC	40226.493	670.44	70.26 %
SPL	7553.916	125.9	13.19 %
ECC	7456.873	124.28	13.02 %
Total	57250.629	954.18	100 %

CORIA is designed with flexibility in mind: new or updated AS datasets can be loaded into the software whenever required. Further or refined metrics can be added with ease and can be flexibly combined into several different aggregated scores.

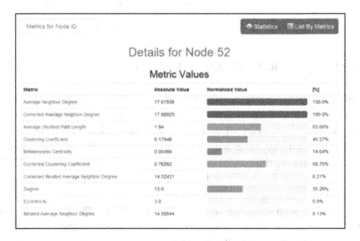

Fig. 3. Example user view in CORIA (AS screen)

6 Summary, Limitations and Future Work

To the best of our knowledge, our proposed CRS marks the first attempt to measure the vulnerability of single ASs with regard to random failures and targeted attacks. The CRS takes several connectivity-based aspects into account and is therefore multi-dimensional (degree, average neighbor degree, iterated average neighbor degree, betweenness centrality, shortest path length, eccentricity). Considering these various dimensions helps to cope with the high complexity of the AS-level graph. In summary, the lower the CRS value, the more prone a specific AS is to random failures. The higher the CRS value, the more attractive a specific AS is for an attack. A desirable global state could involve a quite homogeneous accumulation of ASs in a certain high CRS value area.

Our article is subject to typical limitations of our research area that we aim to address in future work. Because there is a general lack of complete information regarding the Internet topology, our dataset is still incomplete. Also the dataset used in this work can be seen as only a first exemplarily starting point of investigation since it represents solely the AS level, is still incomplete in terms of included ASs as well as corresponding paths, and it originates from 2012. Furthermore, our data might contain some incorrect edges because its reliability strongly depends on the quality of the data sources used, e.g., the insertion of traceroute data whose alias resolution process is still not mature. Furthermore, policy-driven routing as well as traffic flow aspects are not considered so far but we plan to include this aspect in future work due to the possible current overestimation of viable connections in the Internet graph. Possible existing internal connections between ASs belonging to the same organization may not be visible in the public dataset. This might lead to imprecise risk assessment results based on the CRS only due to the underestimation of connectedness of the concerned ASs. However, an internal risk manager could take the CRS as a starting point of investigation and then verify the actual private connections of his or her organization.

In future work we also aim to further refine the CRS by developing an extended score which would take into account the homogeneity of ASs or rather their similarity of attractiveness in terms of being an attack target. In addition, we want to include an assessment of how hard it is to cut a certain AS off. It might also be valuable to utilize additional input for an extension of this score by using third-party knowledge. This could be achieved with the help of expert and stakeholder interviews.

Furthermore, statistical correlations between the current metrics and future metrics on different datasets should be investigated. Based on this, the weights could be adjusted accordingly in order to reduce internal correlations, improving the balance of the various metrics used in the score. Moreover, the score could then more reliably be transferred to other complex networks with different properties than the Internet AS graph. Therefore, we also plan to integrate further metrics. As research has shown, the effects of quasi-local metrics such as the spectrum of the graph, e.g., as in case of the spread of virus diffusions [27] which might be influenced by rather global metrics such as the assortativity coefficient [28], show again the deep interconnection of the network where the general structure has an immense influence on characteristics of single nodes. Therefore in future research these effects of global metrics should not be underestimated and be taken into account.

We also aim to further validate the CRS and related newly developed scores. This could, for example, be conducted through several case studies such as in the application field of cloud computing [31], an analysis of historical events of failure, a complementary IP-based analysis or insider knowledge of contracts between ISPs. Furthermore, we plan to enhance the web-based connectivity-risk analyzer CORIA with new features such as integrating further publicly available information on each AS and the possibility to manually add internal connections that may not be visible in the public data. Furthermore, each future evolution of the CRS and the underlying data set will be easily implemented in CORIA because it was designed for flexibility and extensibility. Another promising direction is adoption of methods from network reliability estimation, such as proposed by [25] for failures of cloud computing nodes, to our AS-level context. Not least, there is an important area of research on how to improve the connectivity of single organizations in a way that is technically and economically feasible. Since connectivity of an organization A does not only depend on the degree and local edges of A, one of the challenges involves how to motivate other organizations B and C to create links that primarily benefit A. Here, we aim to develop practical approaches based on game theory and economic mechanism design.

References

1. CDW. Billions Lost due to IT Network Outages in 2010: Survey (2011). http://www.eweek. com/c/a/Enterprise-Networking/Billions-Lost-Due-to-IT-Network-Outages-in-2010-Survey-559569. Accessed 30 Apr 2015
2. Baumann, A., Fabian, B.: Who runs the internet? Classifying autonomous systems into industries. In: Proceedings of the 10th International Conference on Web Information Systems and Technologies (WEBIST), Barcelona, Spain (2014)
3. Tseng, J.C., Wu, C.-H.: An expert system approach to improving stability and reliability of web service. Expert Syst. Appl. **33**(2), 379–388 (2007)
4. Baumann, A., Fabian, B.: How robust is the internet? – Insights from graph analysis. In: Lopez, J., Ray, I., Crispo, B. (eds.) CRiSIS 2014. LNCS, vol. 8924, pp. 247–254. Springer, Heidelberg (2015)
5. Albert, R., Jeong, H., Barabási, A.-L.: Error and attack tolerance of complex networks. Nature **406**, 378–382 (2000)
6. Dolev, D., Jamin, S., Mokryn, O., Shavitt, Y.: Internet resiliency to attacks and failures under BGP policy routing. Comput. Netw. **50**(16), 3183–3196 (2006)
7. Wu, J., Zhang, Y., Morley Mao, Z., Shin, K.G.: Internet routing resilience to failures: analysis and implications. In: Proceedings of 2007 ACM CoNEXT Conference (CoNEXT 2007), New York, NY, USA (2007)
8. Xiao, S., Xiao, G., Cheng, T.H.: Tolerance of intentional attacks in complex communication networks. IEEE Commun. Mag. **46**(1), 146–152 (2008)
9. Deng, W., Karaliopoulos, M., Mühlbauer, W., Zhu, P., Lu, X., Plattner, B.: k-fault tolerance of the internet AS graph. Comput. Netw. **55**(10), 2492–2503 (2011)
10. Zhao, J., Wu, J., Chen, M., Fang, Z., Xu, K.: K-core-preferred attack to the internet: is it more malicious than degree attack? In: Wang, J., Xiong, H., Ishikawa, Y., Xu, J., Zhou, J. (eds.) WAIM 2013. LNCS, vol. 7923, pp. 717–728. Springer, Heidelberg (2013)
11. Çetinkaya, E.K., Broyles, D., Dandekar, A., Srinivasan, S., Sterbenz, J.P.: Modelling communication network challenges for future internet resilience, survivability, and disruption tolerance: a simulation-based approach. Telecommun. Syst. **52**(2), 751–766 (2013)
12. Shirazi, F., Diaz, C., Mullan, C., Wright, J., Buchmann, J.: Towards measuring resilience in anonymous communication networks. In: Proceedings of 6th Hot Topics in Privacy Enhancing Technologies (HotPETs 2013) (2013)
13. CAIDA AS Rank (2014). AS Ranking. http://as-rank.caida.org/. Accessed 30 Apr 2015
14. UCLA (2014). http://irl.cs.ucla.edu/. Accessed 30 Apr 2015

15. CAIDA Ark (2014). Archipelago Measurement Infrastructure. http://www.caida.org/projects/ark/. Accessed 30 Apr 2015
16. IRR.net (2014). Internet Routing Registry. http://www.irr.net/. Accessed 30 Apr 2015
17. Siganos, G., Faloutsos, M.: Detection of BGP routing misbehavior against cyber-terrorism. In: Proceedings of the 2005 IEEE Military Communications Conference (MILCOM 2005), pp. 923–929 (2005)
18. Zhang, B., Liu, R., Massey, D., Zhang, L.: Collecting the internet AS-level topology. ACM SIGCOMM Comput. Commun. Rev. 35(1), 53–61 (2005)
19. Mahadevan, P., Krioukov, D., Fomenkov, M., Huffaker, B., Dimitropoulos, X., Claffy, K., Vahdat, A.: The internet AS-level topology: three data sources and one definitive metric. ACM SIGCOMM Comput. Commun. Rev. (CCR) 36(1), 17–26 (2006)
20. Manzano, M., Calle, E., Harle, D.: Quantitative and qualitative network robustness analysis under different multiple failure scenarios. In: Proceedings of the 3rd International Congress on Ultra Modern Telecommunications and Control Systems and Workshops, pp. 1–7 (2011)
21. NetworkX (2014). http://networkx.lanl.gov/. Accessed 30 Apr 2015
22. Redis (2014). http://redis.io/. Accessed 30 Apr 2015
23. Sinatra (2014). http://www.sinatrarb.com/intro.html. Accessed 30 Apr 2015
24. Twitter Bootstrap (2014). Twitter Bootstrap Library. http://getbootstrap.com/about/. Accessed 30 Apr 2015
25. Lin, Y.-K., Chang, P.-C.: Maintenance reliability estimation for a cloud computing network with nodes failure. Expert Syst. Appl. 38(11), 14185–14189 (2011)
26. Sterbenz, J.P.G., Hutchison, D., Çetinkaya, E.K., Jabbar, A., Rohrer, J.P., Schöller, M., Smith, P.: Resilience and survivability in communication networks: strategies, principles, and survey of disciplines. Comput. Netw. 54(8), 1245–1265 (2010)
27. Wang, Y., Chakrabarti, D., Wang, C., Faloutsos, C.: Epidemic spreading in real networks: an eigenvalue viewpoint. In: International Symposium on Reliable Distributed Systems, pp. 25–34 (2003)
28. D'Agostino, G., Scala, A., Zlatić, V., Caldarelli, G.: Robustness and assortativity for diffusion-like processes in scale-free networks. EPL (Europhysics Letters) 97(6), 68006 (2012)
29. Van Mieghem, P., Doerr, C., Wang, H., Hernandez, J.M., Hutchison, D., Karaliopoulos, M., Kooij, R.E.: A framework for computing topological network robustness. Delft University of Technology (2010)
30. ResumeNet (2011). http://www.resumenet.eu/. Accessed 14 Aug 2015
31. Fabian, B., Baumann, A., Lackner, J.: Topological analysis of cloud service connectivity. Comput. Ind. Eng. 88, 151–165 (2015)

A Statechart-Based Anomaly Detection Model for Multi-Threaded SCADA Systems

Amit Kleinmann[✉] and Avishai Wool

Tel-Aviv University, 69978 Tel-aviv, Israel
amitkl@post.tau.ac.il, yash@eng.tau.ac.il

Abstract. SCADA traffic between the Human Machine Interface (HMI) and the Programmable Logic Controller (PLC) is known to be highly periodic. However, it is sometimes multiplexed, due to asynchronous scheduling. Modeling the network traffic patterns of multiplexed SCADA streams using Deterministic Finite Automata (DFA) for anomaly detection typically produces a very large DFA, and a high false-alarm rate. In this paper we introduce a new modeling approach that addresses this gap. Our *Statechart DFA* modeling includes multiple DFAs, one per cyclic pattern, together with a DFA-selector that de-multiplexes the incoming traffic into sub-channels and sends them to their respective DFAs. We evaluated our solution on traces from a production SCADA system using the Siemens S7-0x72 protocol. We also stress-tested our solution on a collection of synthetically-generated traces. In all but the most extreme scenarios the *Statechart* model drastically reduced both the false-alarm rate and the learned model size in comparison with the naive single-DFA model.

1 Introduction

1.1 Background

SCADA systems are used for monitoring and controlling numerous Industrial Control Systems (ICS). In particular, SCADA systems are used in critical infrastructure assets such as chemical plants, electric power generation, transmission and distribution systems, water distribution networks, and waste water treatment facilities. SCADA systems have a strategic significance due to the potentially serious consequences of a fault or malfunction.

SCADA systems typically incorporate sensors and actuators that are controlled by Programmable Logic Controllers (PLCs), and which are themselves managed by a Human Machine Interface (HMI). PLCs are computer-based devices that were originally designed to perform the logic functions executed by electrical hardware (relays, switches, and mechanical timer/counters). PLCs have evolved into controllers with the capability of controlling the complex processes used for discrete control in discrete manufacturing.

This work was supported in part by a grant from the Israeli Ministry of Science and Technology.

© Springer International Publishing Switzerland 2016
E. Rome et al. (Eds.): CRITIS 2015, LNCS 9578, pp. 132–144, 2016.
DOI: 10.1007/978-3-319-33331-1_11

SCADA systems were originally designed for serial communications, and were built on the premise that all the operating entities would be legitimate, properly installed, perform the intended logic and follow the protocol. Thus, many SCADA systems have almost no measures for defending against deliberate attacks. Specifically, SCADA network components do not verify the identity and permissions of other components with which they interact (i.e., no authentication and authorization mechanisms); they do not verify message content and legitimacy (i.e., no data integrity checks); and all the data sent over the network is in plaintext (i.e., no encryption to preserve confidentiality). Therefore, deploying an Intrusion Detection Systems (IDS) in a SCADA network is an important defensive measure.

1.2   Related Work

Byres et al. [5] describe different attack trees on SCADA systems based on the Modbus/TCP protocol. They found that compromising the slave (PLC) or the master (HMI) has the most severe potential impact on the SCADA system. For instance, an attacker that gains access to the SCADA system could identify as the HMI and change data values in the PLC. Alternately, an attacker can perform a Man In The Middle attack between a PLC and HMI and "feed" the HMI with misleading data, allegedly coming from the exploited PLC.

Carcano et al. describe a system with a pipe in which flows high pressure steam [12]. The pressure is regulated by two valves. An attacker capable of sending packets to the PLCs can force one valve to complete closure, and force the other to open. Each of these SCADA commands is perfectly legal when considered individually, however when sent in a certain order they bring the system to a critical state. Marsh [18] presents an attack scenario where a system-wide water hammer effect is caused simply by opening or closing major control valves too rapidly. This can result in a large number of simultaneous main breaks. The Stuxnet malware [11,17] implemented a similar attack by changing centrifuge operating parameters in a pattern that damaged the equipment - while sending normal status messages to the HMI to hide the fact that an attack is under way.

Fundamentally all these attacks work by injecting messages into the communication stream—possibly legitimate messages—on an attacker-selected pattern and schedule. Hence a good anomaly detection system needs to model not only the messages in isolation but also their sequence and timing.

A survey of techniques related to learning and detection of anomalies in critical control systems can be found in [2].

While most of the current commercial network intrusion detection systems (NIDS) are signature-based, i.e., they recognize an attack when it matches a previously defined signature, Anomaly-based Network Intrusion Detection Systems (IDS) "are based on the belief that an intruder's behavior will be noticeably different from that of a legitimate user" [19].

Different kinds of Anomaly Intrusion Detection models have been suggested for SCADA systems. Yang et al. [26] used an Auto Associative Kernel Regression (AAKR) model coupled with the Statistical Probability Ratio Test (SPRT) and applied them on a SCADA system looking for matching patterns. The model used numerous indicators representing network traffic and hardware-operating statistics to predict the 'normal' behavior. Several recent studies [3,7] suggest anomaly-based detection for SCADA systems which are based on Markov chains. However, Ye et al. [27] showed that although the detection accuracy of this technique is high, the number of False Positive values is also high, as it is sensitive to noise. Hadiosmanovic et al. [14] used the logs generated by the control application running on the HMI to detect anomalous patterns of user actions on process control application.

Nai Fovino et al. [12] have presented a state-based intrusion detection system for SCADA systems. Their approach uses detailed knowledge of the industrial process' control to generate a system virtual image. The virtual image represents the PLCs of a monitored system, with all their memory registers, coils, inputs and outputs. The virtual image is updated using a periodic active synchronization procedure and via a feed generated by the intrusion detection system (i.e., known intrusion signatures).

Model-based anomaly detection for SCADA systems, and specifically for Modbus traffic, was introduced by Cheung et al. [8]. They designed a multi-algorithm intrusion detection appliance for Modbus/TCP with pattern anomaly recognition, Bayesian analysis of TCP headers and stateful protocol monitoring, complemented with customized Snort rules [21]. In subsequent work, Valdes and Cheung [23] incorporated adaptive statistical learning methods into the system to detect for communication patterns among hosts and traffic patterns in individual flows. Later Briesemeister et al. [4] integrated these intrusion detection technologies into the EMERALD event correlation framework [20].

Sommer and Paxson [22] discuss the surprising imbalance between the extensive amount of research on machine learning-based anomaly detection pursued in the academic intrusion detection community, versus the lack of operational deployments of such systems. One of the reasons for that, by the authors, is that the machine learning anomaly detection systems are lacking the ability to bypass the "semantic gap": The system "understands" that an abnormal activity has occurred, but it cannot produce a message that will elaborate, helping the operator differentiate between an abnormal activity and an attack.

Erez and Wool [10] developed an anomaly detection system that detects irregular changes in SCADA control registers' values. The system is based on an automatic classifier that identifies several classes of PLC registers (Sensor registers, Counter registers and Constant registers). Parameterized behavior models were built for each class. In its learning phase, the system instantiates the model for each register. During the enforcement phase the system detects deviations from the model.

Goldenberg and Wool [13] developed a model-based approach (the GW model) for Network Intrusion Detection based on the normal traffic pattern in Modbus SCADA Networks.

Subsequently, Kleinmann and Wool [16] demonstrated that a similar methodology is successful also in SCADA systems running the Siemens S7 protocol.

Caselli et al. [6] proposed a methodology to model sequences of SCADA protocol messages as Discrete Time Markov Chains (DTMCs). They built a state machine whose states model possible messages, and whose transitions model a "followed-by" relation. Based on data from three different Dutch utilities the authors found that only 35 %–75 % of the possible transitions in the DTMC were observed. This strengthens the observations of [13,16] of a substantial sequentiality in the SCADA communications. However, unlike [13,16] they did not observe clear cyclic message patterns. The authors hypothesized that the difficulties in finding clear sequences is due to the presence of several threads in the HMI's operating system that multiplex requests on the same TCP stream. Each independently scheduled thread is responsible for certain intervals of registers.

1.3   Contributions

DFA-based models have been shown to be extremely effective in modeling the network traffic patterns of SCADA systems [13,16], thus allowing the creation of anomaly-detection systems with low false-alarm rates. However, the existing DFA-based models can be improved in some scenarios.

In this paper we address two such scenarios: the first scenario is the one identified in [6]: the HMI is multi-threaded, each thread independently scans a separate set of control registers, and each thread has its own scan frequency. The second scenario occurs when the SCADA protocol allows the HMI to "subscribe" to a certain register range, after which the PLC asynchronously sends a stream of notifications with the values of the subscribed registers. The commonality between the scenarios is that the network traffic is not the result of a single cyclic pattern: it is the result of several multiplexed cyclic patterns. The multiplexing is due to the asynchronous scheduling of the threads inside the HMI, or to the asynchronous scheduling of PLC-driven notifications. Attempting to model a multiplexed stream by a single DFA typically produces a very large DFA (it's cycle length can be the least-common-multiple of the individual cycle lengths), and also a high false-alarm rate because of the variations in the scheduling of the independent threads.

Our solution to both scenarios is the same: instead of modeling the traffic of an HMI-PLC channel by a single DFA, we model it as a *Statechart* of multiple DFAs, one per cyclic pattern, with a DFA-selector that de-multiplexes the incoming stream of symbols (messages) into sub-channels and sends them to their respective DFAs. Our design supports simple cases, in which each sub-channel has a unique set of symbols—and also the complex cases in which the patterns overlap and some symbols belong to multiple sub-channels.

We evaluated our solution on traces from a production SCADA system using the latest variant of the proprietary Siemens S7 protocol, so called S7-0x72. Unlike the standard S7-0x32 protocol, which is fairly well understood, little is published about the new variant. Based on recent advances in the development of an open-source Wireshark dissector for this variant, we were able to model S7-0x72 in the *Statechart* framework, including its subscribe/notify capability. A naive single-DFA model caused a false-alarm rate of 13–14 % on our traces, while the *Statechart* model reduced the false-alarm rate by two orders of magnitude, down to at most 0.11 %. A separate contribution is our description of the S7-0x72 protocol, with its complex message formats and advanced semantics.

We also stress-tested our solution on a collection of synthetically-generated traces, with intentionally difficult scenarios multiplexing up to 4 periodic patterns and with up to 56 % symbol overlap between patterns. In all but the most extreme scenarios the *Statechart* model drastically reduced both the false-alarm rate and the model size in comparison with the naive single-DFA model.

2   The DFA-based Model for Modbus

The GW model [13] was developed and tested on Modbus traffic. Modbus is a simple request-response protocol widely used in SCADA networks. A Modbus HMI sends a request to a Modbus PLC. The request includes a function code specifying the service, and the address range of data items. Modbus functions include reading values from coils (bit-size entities) or registers (16-bit entities), writing values to coils and registers, and performing diagnostics. After the PLC processes the request, it sends a response back to the HMI.

In the GW model, the key assumption is that traffic is *periodic*, therefore, each HMI-PLC channel is modeled by a Mealy Deterministic Finite Automaton (DFA). The DFA for Modbus has the following characteristics: (a) A symbol is defined as a concatenation of the message type, function code, and address range, totaling 33-bits; (b) A state is defined for each message in the periodic traffic pattern.

The GW model suggests a network anomaly detection system that comprises two stages: A learning stage, and an enforcement stage. In the learning stage a fixed number of messages is captured, the pattern length is revealed, and a DFA is built for each HMI-PLC channel. The learning assumes that the sniffed traffic is benign. In the enforcement stage, traffic is monitored for each channel (according to its DFA), and proper events are triggered.

Based on traffic captured from a production Modbus system, Goldenberg and Wool discovered that over 97 % of Modbus traffic is well modeled by a single DFA per HMI-PLC channel. However they also discovered a phenomenon that challenges the DFA-based approach: In addition to a frequent scan cycle that occurs multiple time per second, they found a second periodic pattern with a 15-minute cycle. Attempting to model both cycles by a single DFA produces a very large, unwieldy model: Its normal pattern consists of hundreds of repetitions of the fast scan cycle followed by one repetition of the slow cycle. Such a pattern is also inaccurate since the slow cycle does not always interrupt the fast cycle at the same point, and while the slow pattern is active, symbols from both patterns are interleaved.

3   A Statechart-Based Solution

Our first observation is that, as hypothesized by Caselli et al. [6] modern HMIs employ thread-based architecture (e.g., this is how the Afcon's Pulse HMI [1] is built): While each thread is responsible for certain tasks (e.g., controlling access to a range of registers on a PLC), the threads run concurrently with different scheduling frequencies, and share the same network connections. Hence, to accurately model the traffic produced by such an HMI (with the PLC's responses), we should use a formalism that is more descriptive than a basic DFA. Our choice is to base our model on the concept of a Statechart [15]: the periodic traffic pattern driven by each thread in the HMI is modeled by its own DFA within the *Statechart*. Each DFA is built using the learning stage of the GW model. The *Statechart* also contains a DFA-selector to switch between DFAs.

3.1   The Statechart Enforcement Phase

During the enforcement stage, each DFA in the *Statechart* maintains its own state, from which it transitions based on the observed symbols (messages).

The DFA-selector's role is to send the input symbol s to the appropriate DFA. To do so it relies on a symbol-to-DFA mapping ϕ: $\phi(s)$ denotes the set of DFAs that have symbol s in their pattern. If each pattern has a unique set of symbols then ϕ is 1-1. However, in the general case, a symbol may appear in multiple patterns and ϕ is one-to-many. Upon receiving a symbol s the DFA-selector uses the following algorithm:

- If $\phi(s) = \varnothing$ the DFA-selector reports an "Unknown" symbol.
- If $\phi(s) = \{D\}$, i.e., the symbol is a unique symbol of a single DFA D, then s is sent to D, which handles it using its own transition function.
- Else, if $|\phi(s)| > 1$, the selected DFA is the member of $\phi(s)$ for which the absolute difference between the current time and the *predicted arrival time of s* is minimal.

In order to implement this policy:

- During the DFA learning stage of the GW model, for each state r in the DFA's pattern we calculate the average time difference to its immediate successor in the cyclic pattern (along the "Normal" transition). We denote this Time to Next State by $TNS(r)$.
- During the enforcement phase, each DFA D retains the time-stamp $T_{last}(D)$ of the last symbol that was processed by it (in addition to the identifier of the current state).

The predicted arrival time $T_{pred}(s, D)$ of a symbol s for a DFA $D \in \phi(s)$ which is currently at state q, is calculated as follows:

1. Identify the tentative state q' that DFA D transitions to from state q upon symbol s. Note that q' is not necessarily the immediate successor of q in the pattern—the transition from q to q' may be a "Miss" or a "Retransmission".
2. Let $P(q, q')$ denote the path of DFA states starting at q and ending at q' along the "Normal" transitions (not including q'). Then $T_{pred}(s, D) = T_{last}(D) + \sum_{r \in P(q,q')} TNS(r)$: The predicted arrival time is the sum of inter-symbol delays along the "Normal" path between q and the tentative transition-to state q' added to the time-stamp of the last symbol processed by DFA D.

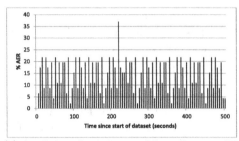

Dataset #	1	2
Duration	560 Sec.	2632 Sec.
TCP Packets	15875	67585
S7 Packets	4600	23553
AER	9.19	9.16

Dataset #	1		2	
DFA type	Naiv	Schrt	Naiv	Schrt
Model size	62	3	12	3
False alrm %	14.54	0.11	12.98	0

(a) Applying the naive model on dataset #1. (b) Results of applying both models

Fig. 1. Detected abnormal symbols after applying the models on the S7 datasets.

3.2 The Statechart Learning Phase

The goal of the learning phase is to construct the *Statechart* for a specific HMI-PLC channel, given a captured stream symbols from the channel. For this we need to create the symbol-to-DFA mapping ϕ, for the use of the DFA selector, and we need to create the individual DFAs themselves. A key component in this learning phase is the Goldenberg and Wool learning algorithm, that accepts a periodic stream of symbols and creates a single DFA that best models that stream. Thus our *Statechart* learning phase is done as follows:

1. Split the channel's input stream into multiple sub-channels.
2. For each sub-channel use the GW learning algorithm to create a DFA.
3. Create the DFA-selector's mapping ϕ from the sub-channel DFAs.

The sub-channel splitting (step 1) can be implemented in different ways, depending on the available semantic knowledge. The easy case is when we know how many sub-channels can exist, each sub-channel has a unique set of symbols, and there is a filter criterion to recognize them. In this case the splitting algorithm works as a simple demultiplexer: for every input symbol it activates the filter criterion and sends the symbol to the (single) sub-channel based on the filter outcome. The difficult case is when we don't know in advance how many sub-channels exist, and the sub-channels potentially have overlapping symbols.

In the S7-0x72 traces we observed the easy case: the channel consisted of 2 sub-channels, one for request and response messages, and the other for notification messages. Since the message types are in the packet meta-data it is easy to split the input stream. Similarly, Goldenberg and Wool [13] reported that in their Modbus traces the slow and fast cycles had distinct symbols.

However, it seems that in the Modbus data set analyzed by Caselli et al. [6] the number of sub-channels is not clear in advance, and sub-channel symbols may be overlapping. Since this data set was not available to us we chose to stress-test the capabilities of our *Statechart* approach in this scenario using synthetic data (see Sect. 5.2).

4   The S7-0x72 Protocol

The S7 PLC Platform. The Siemens SIMATIC S7 product line is estimated to have over 30 % of the worldwide PLC market [9]. It includes both standard PLC models (S7-200, S7-300 and S7-400), and new generation PLCs (S7-1200 and S7-1500). Siemens has its own HMI software for its SIMATIC products called STEP7 and uses its own S7 communication protocol, over TCP port 102.

Two different protocol flavours are implemented by SIMATIC S7 products: The standard SIMATIC S7 PLCs implement a legacy S7 flavor, identified by the value 0x32, while the new generation PLCs implement a very different S7 flavor identified by 0x72. Among other changes, the newer S7-0x72 protocol also supports security features.

The standard S7-0x32 protocol is quite well understood, and a standard Wireshark dissector is available for it. The newer S7-0x72 protocol is not yet fully described in open literature. There is, however, a Wireshark dissector for it which is still in beta status [24].

A unique feature of the S7-0x72 protocol is its optional subscription model (in addition to the traditional request-response pattern). The HMI can send a special "subscribe" message, referring to certain control variables, to a PLC. Subsequently the PLC sends back a periodic stream of "notification" messages with the values of the subscribed variables. The challenge that this subscription model poses to a DFA-based anomaly detection system is that the notification messages are sent asynchronously, and are not part of the HMI-driven request-response pattern.

Experimenting with the S7-0x72 Data. Due to the proprietary nature and potential sensitivity of SCADA operations, real SCADA network data is rarely released to researchers. An important aspect of this work is that we were able to collect and analyze traces from a production S7 network running the S7-0x72 protocol from a control network of a solar power plant. In these traces we observed a single channel between the HMI and a Siemens S7-1500 PLC. We observed both the request-response and the unique subscribe/notification communication patterns. An overview of the S7 datasets can be found in Fig. 1b. During our recordings the infrastructure was running normally without any intervention of operators.

The message format and protocol semantics described here are based on the reverse engineering work of Wiens [24]. Somewhat surprisingly the S7-0x72 message formats are very different from those of the older S7-0x32 protocol, even though the overall protocol semantics are quite similar. An S7 0x72 packet is composed of the following parts:

- Header: 'magic ID' byte with a value of 0x72, a PDU type (one byte) and the length of the data part.
- Data part: includes meta data fields describing the data, data values, and an optional integrity part that is supported only by the newest S7-1500 PLCs (it contains two bytes representing an ID, one byte for the digest length and

a 32 byte message digest, which is apparently a cryptographic hash or MAC, details are yet unknown).

– Trailer: utilized to enable fragmentation.

Unlike the packet structure of the S7-0x32 protocol, nearly every field inside the S7-0x72 data part may be composed of recursively defined data structures. Further, elementary components such as numeric values are encoded using the variable-length quantity (VLQ) encoding [25], a universal code that uses an arbitrary number of binary octets. The precise S7-0x72 packet structure depends on the type of the command and the information it is instructed to carry. The beta Wireshark dissector [24] is able to parse the structure of over 30 different S7-0x72 commands.

To use the GW model we need to hash the meta-data fields of a SCADA packet into a symbol while ignoring the actual data values. In order to model the S7-0x72 packets we relied on the deep understanding embedded in the Wireshark dissector [24] to identify the structural meta-data components in the packets (command codes and arguments, register types and reference ids, etc.). In total we extracted 11–17 meta-data fields, comprising of 17–26 bytes, out of typical S7-0x72 packets, which were hashed into 64-bit symbols.

Figure 1a shows the false alarm rate over time of the naive DFA model applied to S7 dataset #1. Figure 1b summarizes the results on the two S7 traces, comparing the Naive and Statechart models. We can see that the naive DFA model has high false-alarm rates: 14.54 % and 12.98 %. The *Statechart* model successfully reduced the false-alarm rate by two orders of magnitude, down to at most 0.11 %. The table shows that the model sizes dropped from the incorrect sizes of 62 and 12 by the naive DFA model down to the correct size of 3 (a request-response pattern of 2 symbols and a notification pattern of 1).

Table 1. Overview of the sets of sequences used to generate the synthetic datasets

ID	Length	Uniq.	Period	ID	Length	Uniq.	Period	ID	Length	Uniq.	Period
1	6	6	300	7	10	8	300	11	10	8	250
	4	4	950		8	7	350		4	2	650
2	6	6	300		10	9	400		6	4	1100
	4	4	950	8	10	8	300		8	7	420
3	6	4	300		8	7	850	12	6	4	250
	4	1	400		10	9	1300		4	4	350
4	6	4	300	9	10	7	300		10	9	550
	4	2	950		8	4	350		8	7	420
5	10	9	300		10	8	400	13	10	9	300
	4	2	600	10	6	3	300		4	2	600
	4	3	200		4	2	350		4	2	200
6	10	7	300		6	2	400		6	3	350
	10	7	950								
	10	7	2000								

5   Stress Testing with Synthetic Data

5.1   Generation of Synthetic Data

In order to test our model in different scenarios, we implemented a multi-threaded generator, where each of the threads simulates an HMI thread transmitting a cyclic pattern of SCADA commands. Each simulated thread has a pattern P of symbols, and a frequency f. Every f msec the thread wakes up and emits the pattern P as a burst, at a 1-msec-per-symbol rate, and returns to sleep. The thread's true timing has a jitter caused by the OS scheduling decisions. Further, when multiple threads are active concurrently then their emitted symbols are arbitrarily serialized.

We generated 13 scenarios, varying the number of patterns, the number of unique symbols per pattern, and their frequency. Table 1 shows the parameters of the scenarios that were used in our simulations. For the purpose of our evaluation and analysis we defined the following metrics:

- The *Symbol Uniqueness* of a channel = $\sum_{i=1}^{n} U_i / \sum_{i=1}^{n} L_i$, where L_i is the length of the cyclic pattern of sub-channel i and U_i is the number of symbols unique to that sub-channel.
- A channel's *Time Overlap* is the percentage of 1-msec time slots at which multiple packets where scheduled to be sent over the communication link during the time of the trace.
- The *model size* of a DFA is its number of states, and the model size of a statechart is the sum of the model sizes of its DFAs.

5.2   Experiments with the Synthetic Data

We started our evaluation by running the DFA described by Goldenberg and Wool, which we henceforth call the "naive-DFA". We ran the model's learning stage on the synthetic datasets with a maximum pattern length of 100 symbols

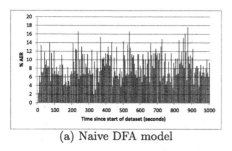

(a) Naive DFA model

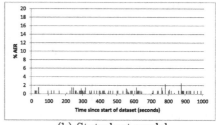

(b) Statechart model

Fig. 2. The false-alarm rate of the two models on synthetic dataset #11. Each time frame on the X axis represents 5 s. The Y axis shows the false alarm frequency as a percentage of the Average Event Rate (AER) for each time period.

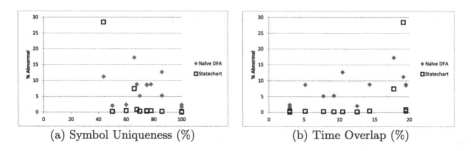

(a) Symbol Uniqueness (%)   (b) Time Overlap (%)

Fig. 3. The false alarm rates as a function of the Symbol Uniqueness and Time Overlap over the synthetic datasets.

and a validation window of 400 (100 · 4) symbols. Then we ran the enforcement stage on the full datasets using the learned patterns.

When we applied the naive DFA model on the synthetic datasets it learned model sizes that are on average 3.5 times longer than the statechart model sizes for the same traces. Moreover, the *Statechart* model produced a much lower false-alarm rate on the same datasets. E.g, Fig. 2 illustrates the results of applying the two models on dataset #11.

Figure 3 shows that the *Statechart* managed to model the benign traffic successfully with very low false-alarm rate: up to 0.9% in nearly all our intentionally complex scenarios. The two exception cases are of datasets #10 (the worst result) and #13 (2nd worst result) that have very low symbol uniqueness (44 % and 67% respectively, compared to an average of 77% for the successful cases) and a high time overlap (19.13% and 17.74% respectively—approximately twice the average of the successful cases of 9.76%). In other words, only when around half of the symbols are not unique to a single pattern, *and* there is significant time overlap between patterns, does the *Statechart* model's performance deteriorate. In the more realistic scenarios, when symbol uniqueness is high or when the time overlap is low, the model performs extremely well.

6   Conclusions

In this paper we developed and applied the *Statechart DFA* model, which is designed specifically for anomaly detection in SCADA networks. This model has three promising characteristics. First, it exhibits very low false positive rates despite its high sensitivity. Second, it is extremely efficient: it has a compact representation, it keeps minimal state during the enforcement phase, and can easily work at line-speed for real-time anomaly detection. Third, its inherent modular architecture makes it scalable for protecting highly multiplexed SCADA streams. Our experiments demonstrate that the *Statechart DFA* anomaly detection model handles multiplexed SCADA traffic patterns very well.

References

1. Afcon Technologies: Pulse HMI Software (2015). Accessed 6 May 2015
2. Alcaraz, C., Cazorla, L., Fernández, G.: Context-awareness using anomaly-based detectors for smart grid domains. In: Proceedings of the 9th International Conference on Risks, and Security of Internet and Systems (CRISIS), Trento, Italy, September 2014
3. Atassi, A., Elhajj, I.H., Chehab, A., Kayssi, A.: The State of the Art in Intrusion Prevention and Detection, Auerbach Publications. In: Intrusion Detection for SCADA Systems, pp. 211–230. Auerbach Publications, January 2014
4. Briesemeister, L., Cheung, S., Lindqvist, U., Valdes, A.: Detection, correlation, and visualization of attacks against critical infrastructure systems. In: 8th International Conference on Privacy Security and Trust (PST), pp. 17–19 (2010)
5. Byres, E.J., Franz, M., Miller, D.: The use of attack trees in assessing vulnerabilities in SCADA systems. In: Proceedings of the International Infrastructure Survivability Workshop (2004)
6. Caselli, M., Zambon, E., Kargl, F.: Sequence-aware intrusion detection in industrial control systems. In: Proceedings of the 1st ACM Workshop on Cyber-Physical System Security, pp. 13–24. ACM, New York (2015)
7. Chen, C.-M., Hsiao, H.-W., Yang, P.-Y., Ya-Hui, O.: Defending malicious attacks in cyber physical systems. In: IEEE 1st International Conference on Cyber-Physical Systems, Networks, and Applications (CPSNA), pp. 13–18, August 2013
8. Cheung, S., Dutertre, B., Fong, M., Lindqvist, U., Skinner, K., Valdes, A.: Using model-based intrusion detection for SCADA networks. In: Proceedings of the SCADA Security Scientific Symposium, pp. 127–134 (2007)
9. Electrical Engineering Blog: The top most used PLC systems around the world. Electrical installation & energy efficiency, May 2013. http://engineering.electrical-equipment.org/electrical-distribution/the-top-most-used-plc-systems-around-the-world.html
10. Erez, N., Wool, A.: Control variable classification, modeling and anomaly detection in Modbus/TCP SCADA networks. In: 9th Annual IFIP Working Group 11.10 International Conference on Critical Infrastructure Protection, Washington, DC, USA, March 2015
11. Falliere, N., Murchu, L.O., Chien, E.: W32. stuxnet dossier. White Paper, Symantec Corporation, Security Response (2011)
12. Fovino, I.N., Carcano, A., De Lacheze Murel, T., Trombetta, A., Masera, M.: Modbus/DNP3 state-based intrusion detection system. In: 24th IEEE International Conference on Advanced Information Networking and Applications (AINA), pp. 729–736. IEEE (2010)
13. Goldenberg, N., Wool, A.: Accurate modeling of modbus/tcp for intrusion detection in SCADA systems. Int. J. Crit. Infrastruct. Prot. 6(2), 63–75 (2013)
14. Hadziosmanovic, D., Bolzoni, D., Hartel, P.H., Etalle, S.: MELISSA: towards automated detection of undesirable user actions in critical infrastructures. In: Proceedings of the European Conference on Computer Network Defense, EC2ND 2011, Gothenburg, Sweden, pp. 41–48, USA, IEEE Computer Society, September 2011
15. Harel, D.: Statecharts: a visual formalism for complex systems. Sci. Comput. Program. 8(3), 231–274 (1987)
16. Kleinmann, A., Wool, A.: Accurate modeling of the siemens S7 SCADA protocol for intrusion detection and digital forensic. JDFSL 9(2), 37–50 (2014)

17. Langner, R.: Stuxnet: dissecting a cyberwarfare weapon. IEEE Secur. Priv. **9**(3), 49–51 (2011)
18. Marsh, R.T.: Critical foundations: protecting america's infrastructures - the report of the president's commission on critical infrastructure protection. Technical report, October 1997
19. Mukherjee, B., Heberlein, L.T., Levitt, K.N.: Network intrusion detection. IEEE Network **8**(3), 26–41 (1994)
20. Porras, P.A., Neumann, P.G.: EMERALD: event monitoring enabling responses to anomalous live disturbances. In: 1997 National Information Systems Security Conference, October 1997
21. Roesch, M.: Snort - lightweight intrusion detection for networks. In: Proceedings of the 13th USENIX Conference on System Administration, LISA 1999, pp. 229–238. USENIX Association, Berkeley (1999)
22. Sommer, R., Paxson, V.: Outside the closed world: on using machine learning for network intrusion detection. In: 2010 IEEE Symposium on Security and Privacy (SP), pp. 305–316, May 2010
23. Valdes, A., Cheung, S.: Communication pattern anomaly detection in process control systems. In: IEEE Conference on Technologies for Homeland Security (HST), pp. 22–29. IEEE (2009)
24. Wiens, T.: S7comm wireshark dissector plugin, January 2014. http://sourceforge.net/projects/s7commwireshark
25. Wikipedia: Variable-length quantity – Wikipedia, the free encyclopedia, (2015). Accessed 5 May 2015
26. Yang, D., Usynin, A., Hines, J.W.: Anomaly-based intrusion detection for SCADA systems. In: 5th Int International Topical Meeting on Nuclear Plant Instrumentation, Control and Human Machine Interface Technologies, pp. 12–16 (2006)
27. Ye, N., Zhang, Y., Borror, C.M.: Robustness of the markov-chain model for cyber-attack detection. IEEE Trans. Reliab. **53**(1), 116–123 (2004)

Electric Grid Protection and Resilience

Controllability Assessment for Cascade Effects in ICT-enabled Power Grids

Georgios Theodoridis[✉], Luca Galbusera, and Georgios Giannopoulos

Institute for the Protection and Security of the Citizen,
European Commission Joint Research Centre (JRC),
Via Fermi 2749, 21027 Ispra (VA), Italy
{georgios.theodoridis,luca.galbusera,
georgios.giannopoulos}@jrc.ec.europa.eu
https://ec.europa.eu/jrc/

Abstract. Despite the available monitor and control functionalities, the timely reconfiguration of the modern power grids is not always feasible, due to the inherent inertia of the power elements. Therefore, especially in the case of abrupt phenomena (e.g. loss of power lines), the power grids tend to suffer from severe cascade effects, since the triggering failure is usually followed by successive overloads. Additionally, the grid's efficient reaction is further restrained by the performance of the underlying ICT system, i.e. delays in the reception of the monitor/control information. The present paper introduces a novel framework for assessing the controllability of ICT-enabled power grids. Assuming structural failures, the proposed methodology quantifies the system's ability to be readjusted in a way that ceases the progressing damage and re-establishes operation within the grid's physical constraints. The controllability is identified as a function of the overall system's power and ICT characteristics, without considering any specific control strategy.

Keywords: Power grid · ICT · Controllability · Cascade

1 Introduction

Electric power availability is a pivotal prerequisite in the modern era. In this respect, great emphasis has been laid on the field of SCOPF (Security Constrained Optimal Power Flow) [2,12], in order to guarantee the grid's resilience against contingencies taking into account the wide set of techno-economic restrictions. The objective is to explore the reconfiguration of the grid's operating point after a substantial incidental anomaly (e.g. line failure) within the acceptable parameter space [13]. The complexity of such an analysis increases significantly when the transient phenomena are covered and the specific control strategies are considered [18].

In parallel, due to the obvious merits that stem from the incorporation of automation into the power production and delivery process, the research effort has been lately drawn on the study and development of the Smart Energy Grids

© European Union, 2016
E. Rome et al. (Eds.): CRITIS 2015, LNCS 9578, pp. 147–158, 2016.
DOI: 10.1007/978-3-319-33331-1_12

(SEG), i.e. ICT-enabled power grids that allow for the grid's real-time monitoring and control [7]. Significant part of this research regards the complications and the hazards that are introduced into the SEG operation by the interdependencies of the collaborating subsystems [9,14], taking particularly into account the inherent vulnerabilities (e.g. cyber attacks) [8,16] and potential deficiencies (e.g. transmission delays/failures) [3,10,15] of the underlying communication network.

As a consequence, it is of primary importance to define both conceptually and numerically an adequate metric for the resilience of the grid's control [4,11,17]. Within this framework, the present paper proposes a novel methodology for assessing the controllability of ICT-enabled power grids. Assuming structural failures, the proposed methodology quantifies the system's ability to be readjusted in a way that ceases the propagating cascade and re-establishes operation within the grid's physical constraints. The controllability is identified as a function of the overall system's power and ICT characteristics, without considering any specific control strategy.

The rest of the paper is organized as follows. In Sect. 2 the problem to be addressed is described and in Sect. 3 the necessary formulation of the power grid is provided. Section 4 introduces the proposed methodology for the definition of the grid's controllability along with the corresponding metric for its numerical assessment. Section 5 presents the results of a case study and in Sect. 6 the final conclusions are drawn.

2   Problem Definition: Cascade Phenomena in Smart Power Grids

The cascade effect is considered as one of the greatest dangers against the resilience of the power grids. In general, the term cascade effect in the case of the power grids describes the sequence of infrastructural or operational failures and malfunctions that may follow an initial triggering failure at the power production/transfer system. The triggering event is usually caused by the combination of both internal and external anomalous conditions that are extreme enough to render insufficient the implemented preventive measures. On the contrary, the resulting cascade can also evolve only due to the inner dynamics of the power system itself without the catalytic effect of any coexisting external factors.

The most common cause of a power grid cascade is the loss of a power line, which can take place either due to a problem of the equipment at the line's endings (e.g. transformers) or due to damage of the line itself (e.g. tree fall). Numerous such cases have been recorded worldwide and they are usually related to inadequate maintenance, operation close to the infrastructure's limits and accidental events. Under such circumstances, the power flow that had been so far serviced by the failing line is immediately re-routed, according to the inherent physics of the electrical system (laws of electrical current flow), through alternative paths of the remaining grid imposing additional burden to the newly traversed lines.

In case any of the lines is overloaded beyond its capacity by the increased power flow, the line is cut out by the local protection switches, depriving the grid of even more power transfer capacity. Thus, an extensive chain of power line failures is initiated, since the continuously shrinking grid has to cater for the augmenting power flow excess that is left unserviced from the tripped power lines. Because of this iterative amplification, the cascade escalates with an exponential-like rate until the disconnected generation is high enough so as the remaining power that is exchanged among the power nodes to be sustainable by the surviving grid.

Let $t_0 \in \mathbb{R}^+$ be the time instance that the triggering event occurs. Then $\forall t \in [0, t_0)$, i.e. during the grid's normal operation,

$$F_e(t) \leq C_e, \ \forall e \in \mathcal{E}(t) \tag{1}$$

where $\mathcal{E}(t)$ is the set of the operational lines at time t, $F_e(t)$ is the value of the power traversing any line $e \in \mathcal{E}(t)$, and C_e is the line's maximum acceptable power flow (capacity). Respectively, the cascade will eventually stop at the time instance $t_s \in (t_0, \infty)$ when the power flow at the remaining lines will have been eventually restored at acceptable levels.

Thus, regardless of the exact control objectives and strategy, the controllability of the energy grid against cascade effects is defined as its ability to comply with (1) for a $t_s > t_0$, taking into account the functional restrictions of its comprising elements, i.e. the power elements' reconfigurability and tolerance. For the SEGs, apart from the adaptability of the core electrical grid, the ICT performance must be also considered for the estimation of the system's controllability, since the response of the power elements to the mitigation actions is inhibited by the network delays that are introduced to the reception of the control signals.

For the exact quantification of the controllability notion, it should be taken into account that the cut out of power lines during the cascade has threefold consequences. Firstly, the power equipment is jeopardised due to the produced arcs. Secondly, putting the lines again into operation is a cumbersome and time-consuming procedure, which can be executed only after the stabilisation of the grid, and whose complexity depends on the number of lines to be restored. Thirdly, despite the broad penetration of Distributed Energy Resources (DER), the points of major power generation and consumption are in general not collocated. Therefore, as the grid's power transfer capability decreases along with the cascade, load shedding is also required so as to compensate for the missing power provision. Thus, the smart grid's controllability can be assessed on the basis of the number of tripped power lines before the cascade's propagation is intercepted, i.e. $|\mathcal{E}(t_0)| - |\mathcal{E}(t_s)|$, where $|\cdot|$ is the cardinality of the set.

Despite he particular precautions that are taken by the power grid operators, the probability of appearance of cascade phenomena is far from being considered negligible. For instance, the TSOs (Transmission System Operators) apply the *N-1 redundancy* as a fundamental rule for the design of the high-voltage power transmission grids, so as to guarantee their stable and reliable operation even if a power line is rendered non-operational due to an incident. Nevertheless, significant power cascade effects still occur, due to a combination of coincidental anomalies, e.g. line disconnection for maintenance, compromise of the *N-1* rule for market reasons etc. [2].

3 Formulation of the Energy Grid

Smart power grids derive essentially from the integration of three interoperable subsystems: (i) the mere energy grid; (ii) the control system; and (iii) the ICT network. This session, describes the main attributes of the electricity grid and their formulation with respect to its controllability against cascade effects.

3.1 Power Nodes

The electricity grid is represented as a directed graph $\mathcal{S}(t) = \{\mathcal{N}, \mathcal{E}(t)\}$, where $t \in \mathbb{R}_0^+$. The graph's vertices ($\mathcal{N}$) stand for the grid's power nodes (e.g. generations, consumptions, transformers), while the graph's edges ($\mathcal{E}(t)$) correspond to the grid's power lines, which allow the power exchange among the power nodes. The topology of the electrical grid ($\mathcal{S}(t)$) at each time instance is fully described by a directional arc-node incidence matrix $M(t)$ of size $|\mathcal{N}| \times |\mathcal{E}(t)|$, where -1 and $+1$ denote the line's starting and ending node respectively.

For each node $n \in \mathcal{N}$, the instantaneous generation $G_n(t)$ and load $L_n(t)$ are defined, with $G_n(t) \in [G_n^{MIN}, G_n^{MAX}]$ and $L_n(t) \in [L_n^{MIN}, L_n^{MAX}]$. These absolute boundaries are estimated by the node's specifications, external conditions (e.g. weather conditions for Renewable Energy Resources) as well as its configuration with respect to the grid. For example, assuming that the node's total generation dispatch and load shedding is possible, $G_n^{MIN} = L_n^{MIN} = 0$.

For an electrical system to be considered operational, it must be at a power equilibrium, i.e. at every time instance $t \in \mathbb{R}_0^+$ the aggregate power production must be equal to the aggregate demand. Otherwise, frequency droops or excesses appear, which can cause malfunctions at the consumption side as well as the disconnection of the thermal rotor-based generators. The power balance condition for $\mathcal{S}(t)$, $\forall t \in \mathbb{R}_0^+$ is expressed as

$$\sum_{n \in \mathcal{N}} G_n(t) = \sum_{n \in \mathcal{N}} L_n(t) \tag{2}$$

In order to quantify the power nodes' ability to respond to any reconfiguration requests, the variables G_n^{inc}, G_n^{dec}, L_n^{inc}, and L_n^{dec} are introduced, which represent the increase/decrease rate of the generation and load for every node n. These variables practically model the fact that, due to technical restrictions (e.g. inertia of the big thermal power plants) and on grounds of the power grid's stability (e.g. minimisation of the transient phenomena), the reconfiguration of the nodes' power levels is neither possible nor advisable to be executed immediately, but a smooth convergence to the control values is necessary.

Hence, for a given time window $\tau \geq 0$, the actual operational constraints of the electrical nodes are calculated by

$$G_n^{min}(t,\tau) = max\{G_n^{MIN}, G_n(t) - G_n^{dec} \cdot \tau\}$$
$$G_n^{max}(t,\tau) = min\{G_n^{MAX}, G_n(t) + G_n^{inc} \cdot \tau\} \tag{3}$$
$$L_n^{min}(t,\tau) = min\{L_n^{MIN}, L_n(t) - L_n^{dec} \cdot \tau\}$$
$$L_n^{max}(t,\tau) = min\{L_n^{MAX}, L_n(t) + L_n^{inc} \cdot \tau\}$$

The minimum and maximum achievable generation and load at each node is a time varying function of the available response time (τ), the node's reference operating point (t), its absolute constraints, and its reconfiguration rates. All the above attributes of the power nodes, i.e. G_n^{MAX}, G_n^{MIN}, G_n^{inc}, G_n^{dec}, L_n^{MAX}, L_n^{MIN}, L_n^{inc}, L_n^{dec}, are in general time-varying, since, except for the nodes' inherent characteristics, they are also dependent on various factors both internal and external to the power grid. Nevertheless, for the relatively short duration of the cascade they can be safely considered as constant. This is also the case for the instantaneous generation and load, $G_n(t)$ and $L_n(t)$. Their variations during the cascade do not result from alterations on the demand, but they are only caused by the regulation of generation and load that is carried out for mitigating the cascade. Thus, the values of normal operation after the cascade are considered equal to the ones before the triggering event, i.e. $G_n(t_0^-)$ and $L_n(t_0^-)$.

The aforementioned features of the power nodes can be estimated by utilising historical data consolidated with the knowledge of the grid's configuration and specifications [1,5].

3.2 Power Lines

The set $\mathcal{E}(t)$ represents the transmission lines of the grid operating at time t. Every edge ends at two different nodes and any pair of nodes is only connected with a single edge. Moreover, each edge is oriented, so as to define the power flow direction. In contrast to $\mathcal{N}$ which is constant, $\mathcal{E}(t)$ is time-varying, since a power line can be rendered non-operational (open-circuit) due to an overload tripping. The initial set of edges $(\mathcal{E}(0))$ is the overall set of available transmission lines and the power grid at this nominal state $(\mathcal{S}(t), \forall t \in [0, t_0))$ is a *connected* graph, i.e. a single power island.

$$\mathcal{E}(t) = \mathcal{E}(0), \ \forall t \in [0, t_0) \tag{4}$$
$$\mathcal{E}(t) \subseteq \mathcal{E}(0), \ \forall t \in [t_0, \infty)$$

Any alterations to the initial set $\mathcal{E}(0)$ are the result of lines' failures. No establishment of new transmission lines or recovery of previously failing ones is considered. Thus,

$$\mathcal{E}(t_2) \subseteq \mathcal{E}(t_1), \ \forall t_2 > t_1 \in [t_0, \infty) \tag{5}$$

For the calculation of the power flows, the *DC Power-Flow Model* is applied, since the details of the transient phenomena do not need to be scrutinised and the emphasis is laid on the macroscopical evolution of the events. Hence, assuming a single-island grid that is described by the arc-node incidence matrix $M(t)$, the value of the power flowing through each line can be calculated as a function of the nodes' injection power from

$$F(t) = W^{-1}(-M'(t)) \left(\bar{M}(t) W^{-1} \bar{M}'(t) \right)^{-1} \bar{P}(t) \tag{6}$$

where $F(t)$ is the vector of the lines' power flow, $P(t) = G(t) - L(t)$ is the vector of the nodes' algebraic injection power, and $\bar{}$ indicates that one and the same arbitrary row is removed from all matrices, so as the system of equations to have a single solution under the power balance condition (2). Furthermore, W is the reactance matrix, i.e. a $|\mathcal{E}(t)| \times |\mathcal{E}(t)|$ diagonal matrix, whose elements of the main diagonal are equal to the reactance of the respective transmission line. Equation (6) can only be applied if and only if the power balance condition expressed in (2) is satisfied.

Although $\mathcal{S}(t)$, $\forall t \in [0, t_0)$ is a single-island electrical grid, any line failure may result in its splitting into multiple islands, whose number, composition and connectivity varies in time. Hence, any island i composed at time t is associated to the graph $\mathcal{S}_i(t) = \{\mathcal{N}_i, \mathcal{E}_i(t)\}$, where $\mathcal{N}_i \subseteq \mathcal{N}$ and $\mathcal{E}_i(t) \subseteq \mathcal{E}(t)$, with $|\mathcal{N}_i| \geq 1$ and $|\mathcal{E}_i(t)| \geq 0$. Thus, Eqs. (2) and (6) are in general applied per island:

$$\sum_{n \in \mathcal{N}_i} G_n(t) = \sum_{n \in \mathcal{N}_i} L_n(t) \tag{7}$$

$$F_i(t) = W_i^{-1} \bar{M}'_i(t) \left(\bar{M}_i(t) W_i^{-1} \bar{M}'_i(t) \right)^{-1} \bar{P}_i(t) \tag{8}$$

Remark 1. A power equilibrium is feasible for island i, if

$$\sum_{n \in \mathcal{N}_i} G_n^{max} \geq \sum_{n \in \mathcal{N}_i} L_n^{min} \qquad \sum_{n \in \mathcal{N}_i} G_n^{min} \leq \sum_{n \in \mathcal{N}_i} L_n^{max} \tag{9}$$

As mentioned in Sect. 2, every power line $e \in \mathcal{E}(0)$ is characterized by a maximum sustainable power (capacity) $C_e > 0$, which is equal to the threshold of the line's trip switch and it is statically determined according to the specifications of the line's elements, i.e. the ending transformers and the cabling. Any increase in the flowing power above this limitation causes the disconnection of the line after time $T_e > 0$. This non-zero latency T_e describes the inherent inertia of the electrical current as well as the tolerance of the trip switches, and it will be referred to as the line's tolerance time. The value of T_e can be retrieved by the grid operators [6].

4   Controllability

The control system can either consist of a single controller or it can be implemented as a constellation of multiple cooperating physical control entities.

For ease of reference, the control system will be hereafter referred to as *controller*, without implying any specific control architecture.

The controller repeatedly calculates and applies the most efficient operating point for the electrical grid, in order to increase its performance with respect to the varying conditions of the overall system. To this end, a wide range of often competing optimisation criteria are taken into account. Under normal grid operation, the controller regulates the reallocation of the available power resources for efficiently covering the altering demand, in a way that does not compromises the power grid's resilience. Moreover, under conditions of infrastructural/equipment failures or unpredicted operational anomalies, the controller is responsible for the implementation of the mitigation measures.

Nevertheless, the hereby introduced definition of the power grid's controllability is agnostic of the specific control strategy and depends only on the structural properties of the power grid and the operational constraints of both the power grid and the underlying ICT network.

Following the analysis of Sects. 2 and 3, let $S(t_0^-) = \{\mathcal{N}, \mathcal{E}(t_0^-)\}$ be the graph of a single-island power grid just before the time instance t_0 when the power line $e^{tr} \in \mathcal{E}(t_0^-)$ that triggers the cascade accidentally fails. Before t_0, the grid is in power balance, i.e.

$$\sum_{n \in \mathcal{N}} G_n(t_0^-) = \sum_{n \in \mathcal{N}} L_n(t_0^-) \tag{10}$$

and the power flow at each line $e \in \mathcal{E}(t_0^-)$ is computed by

$$F(t_0^-) = W^{-1}(-M'(t)) \left(\bar{M}(t_0^-)W^{-1}\bar{M}'(t_0^-)\right)^{-1} \bar{P}(t_0^-) \tag{11}$$

with

$$F_e(t_0^-) \leq C_e, \ \forall e \in \mathcal{E}(t_0^-) \tag{12}$$

After the failure of any number of power lines, the power flows are redistributed following the new less connected topology of the grid, i.e. $\mathcal{E}(t) \subset \mathcal{E}(t_0^-)$, and they are calculated by (6). Thus, the subset of overloaded power lines at any moment $t \in (t_0, \infty)$ is defined by

$$\mathcal{E}^O(t) = \left\{e \in \mathcal{E}(t) : F_e(t) > C_e\right\}, \ \forall t \in (t_0, \infty) \tag{13}$$

where $\mathcal{E}(t)$ is the subset of power lines still operating at time t. If $\mathcal{E}^D(t)$ is the subset of the lines that have already been disconnected until time t (including also the initially failing line), then $\mathcal{E}(t_0^-) = \mathcal{E}(t) \cup \mathcal{E}^D(t), \forall t \in (t_0, \infty)$. Leveraging the computation of $\mathcal{E}^O(t)$ in (13), the next power line that is expected to fail ($e^{nf}(t)$) can be also calculated as the overloaded power line with the minimum time left until it is tripped

$$e^{nf}(t) = \left\{e \in \mathcal{E}^O(t) : \tau_{e^{nf}(t)} = min\{T_e - v_e(t), \forall e \in \mathcal{E}^O(t)\}\right\} \tag{14}$$

where t is the moment that the estimation is carried out, T_e is the lines' tolerance time, $v_e(t)$ is the time that each line is already in overload, and the difference $\tau_e(t) = T_e - v_e(t)$ is the time left before line e gets disconnected.

In this respect, the set of overloaded lines after the triggering failure is calculated from (6) and (13) for $t = t_0^+$ and $\mathcal{E}(t_0^+) = \mathcal{E}(t_0^-) - e^{tr}$. Eventually the second line to fail is computed from

$$e^{nf}(t_0^+) = \left\{ e \in \mathcal{E}^O(t_0^+) : \tau_{e^{nf}(t_0^+)} = min\{T_e, \forall e \in \mathcal{E}^O(t_0^+)\} \right\} \qquad (15)$$

since $v_e(t_0^+) = 0, \forall e \in \mathcal{E}^O(t_0^+)$.

Therefore, in order the cascade to be halted, the power generation must be adequately reallocated within a time window equal to $\tau_{e^{nf}(t_0^+)}$, i.e. before the first line $(e^{nf}(t_0^+))$ is tripped. In general, according to the formulation of Sects. 2 and 3, the $(k+1)^{th}$ line disconnection will be avoided if and only if there is a time instance $t \in (t_k, t_k + \tau_{e^{nf}(t_k^+)})$ such that: (i) the power flows are maintained below the lines' capacity

$$F_e(t_k^+) \leq C_e, \ \forall e \in \mathcal{E}(t_k^+) \qquad (16)$$

(ii) the power nodes' operational limitations described in (3) are satisfied

$$G_n^{min}(t_0^-, \tau_{e^{nf}(t_k^+)} - d_n(t_0^-)) \leq G_n(t) \leq G_n^{max}(t_0^-, \tau_{e^{nf}(t_k^+)} - d_n(t_0^-)), \ \forall n \in \mathcal{N} \qquad (17)$$

$$L_n^{min}(t_0^-, \tau_{e^{nf}(t_k^+)} - d_n(t_0^-)) \leq L_n(t) \leq L_n^{max}(t_0^-, \tau_{e^{nf}(t_k^+)} - d_n(t_0^+)), \ \forall n \in \mathcal{N}$$

and (iii) the power equilibrium is established

$$\sum_{n \in \mathcal{N}_i} G_n(t) = \sum_{n \in \mathcal{N}_i} L_n(t), \ \forall i \in \mathcal{I}(t_k^+) \qquad (18)$$

where t_k is the time instance that the kth line tripping after the initial triggering failure $(k \in \mathbb{N}_0^+)$ occurs, $\tau_{e^{nf}(t_k^+)}$ is the remaining time until the next line after the kth one to be cut out (time between the kth and $(k+1)^{th}$ line damage), and $\mathcal{I}(t_k^+)$ is the set of islands (possibly more than one) that the graph $\mathcal{S}(t_k^+) = \{\mathcal{N}, \mathcal{E}(t_k^+)\}$ consists of.

The term $d_n(t_0^-) > 0$ in (17) introduces the delay that is imposed by the ICT network on the communication between the controller and the power node n, i.e. the necessary time for the node's reconfiguration orders to be received. Its value is the one measured before the burst of the cascade. The higher is the ICT delay the broader is the gap between the identification of the problem and the moment that the control directives start being deployed. This hindrance is common for any control scheme regardless of its exact content. If the ICT latency is longer than the allowable response time $(\tau_{e^{nf}(t_k^+)} - d_n(t_k^+) < 0)$, the node remains at its previous condition and (17) is applied for $\tau_{e^{nf}(t_k^+)} - d_n(t_k^+) = 0$.

Moreover, in (17) the reference operating point, as described in (3), is always taken equal to the grid's state before the start of the cascade (t_0^-). This way, the analysis considers the best-case scenario that the system reacts directly to the kth line tripping, without taking into account the intermediate reconfigurations for mitigating the previous $k - 1$ line disconnections.

The combined inequalities-equation system of (16) – (18) describes the suggested controllability conditions for the smart power grid. If these conditions are met for $k = 0$, the cascade is totally avoided. Otherwise, the sequential disconnection of power lines takes place as presented in Sect. 2. The conditions (16) – (18) are examined recursively after every new tripping until a solution is found for $t \in (t_K, t_K + \tau_{enf(t_K^+)})$, where K is the total number of lines that are disconnected along the evolution of the cascade before the grid is stabilised, i.e. $k = \{0, 1, \ldots, K\}$.

Within this framework, a new metric is introduced for quantitatively assessing the controllability of the power grid against cascade effects. Let Q be the number of lines that would be tripped due to overload after the triggering line failure if no reconfiguration of the grid was possible. By definition, Q is calculated with the same iterative procedure that is followed above for the calculation of K, with the only difference that (17) is implemented for $\tau_{enf(t_k^+)} - d_n(t_k^+) = 0$. Then, the controllability of the smart energy grid against the cascade that is caused by the accidental failure of power line $e \in \mathcal{E}(t_0^-)$ is

$$B(e) = \frac{Q(e) - K(e)}{Q(e)}, \ e \in \mathcal{E}(t_0^-) \tag{19}$$

Given that $K = \{0, 1, \ldots, Q\}$, the range of values for B is $[0, 1]$.

As it is noted in (19), the above calculations regard the triggering failure of a specific power line. Thus, they must be applied for each one of the grid's power lines, in order a generic conclusion for the grid's controllability to be reached. The smart power grid is considered *strictly controllable* if and only if $B(e) = 1, \ \forall e \in \mathcal{E}(t_0^-)$. In any other case, the smart power grid is identified as *loosely controllable*, and its controllability is quantified as the mean of the controllability value for all the possible triggering line failures

$$B = \frac{\sum\limits_{e \in \mathcal{E}(t_0^-)} B(e)}{|\mathcal{E}(t_0^-)|} \tag{20}$$

Practically, the Eqs. (16) – (18) offer the connection between the fields of power and time that is necessary for quantifying the conceptual context of the controllability notion.

5   Case Study

The proposed methodology for the quantification of the smart energy grid's controllability is applied on the IEEE 14-Bus Test System, which is depicted in Fig. 1. The purpose of this case study is to analyse the implementation of the suggested controllability definition on a realistic power grid and evaluate its efficiency to capture the grid's attributes and dynamics.

For the nodes' generation and load before the cascade, i.e. $G_n(t_0^-)$ and $L_n(t_0^-)$, the indicative operational values provided by the IEEE 14-Bus Test

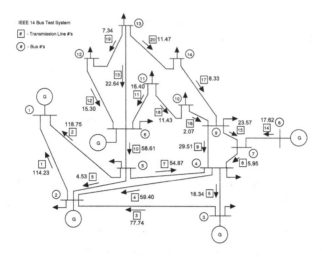

Fig. 1. The IEEE 14-Bus Test System.

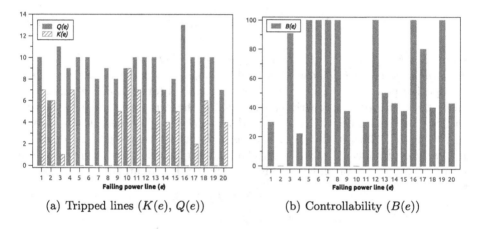

(a) Tripped lines $(K(e),\,Q(e))$ (b) Controllability $(B(e))$

Fig. 2. Controllability on IEEE 14-Bus Test System

System are considered. Moreover, next to the line's index in Fig. 1, the line's power flow under normal conditions has also been added, as computed by (11). The purpose is to facilitate the investigation of the potential cross-correlation between the power transferred by each line and the controllability of the smart energy grid in case of this line's failure. The values are in *power units* (*p.u.*).

The variables G_n^{MAX} and L_n^{MAX} are considered equal to 110 % of their nominal values $(G_n(t_0^-)$ and $L_n(t_0^-))$, while $G_n^{MIN} = L_n^{MIN} = 0$, $\forall n \in \mathcal{N}$. The values of G_n^{inc}, G_n^{dec}, L_n^{inc}, and L_n^{dec} follow a narrow normal distribution with mean equal to $0.1 \cdot G_n(t_0^-)$ and $0.1 \cdot L_n(t_0^-)$ respectively, where the values are expressed in *p.u./t.u.*, with t.u. standing for *time units*. The lines' tolerance time T_e is estimated by a narrow normal distribution with a mean of 10 t.u.

The results are summarised in Fig. 2, where the values of K and Q are presented for all the possible triggering failure scenarios. Studying in Fig. 2(a) the behaviour of the grid without any mitigation response (Q), it is observed that the propagation of the cascade under such circumstances is rather extensive, since half of the grid's lines are expected to be tripped. On the contrary, from Fig. 2(b) it is deduced that in several failure scenarios the cascade effect can be significantly alleviated. Based on the same figure, the grid's controllability appears to be dependent on the trigger line's importance in terms of transferred power. However, no strict correlation can be identified, since high values of B are measured also in cases that the triggering event regards a line with low power flow.

6   Conclusions

This paper has proposed a novel methodology for the quantitative assessment of the controllability of smart energy grids, laying particular emphasis on the grid's ability to timely react against the cascade effects that result from accidental power line failures. To this end, there have been defined the necessary conditions that must be satisfied in order the cascade to be ceased. Moreover, a corresponding metric for evaluating the response capability of the grid under such circumstances has been introduced. It must be underlined that the suggested controllability assessment framework is completely agnostic of the exact control details and only the structural characteristics and the operational limitations of the energy grid are taken into account. Additionally, by identifying the impact of the communication delay on the grid's inertia, it allows for incorporating the performance of the ICT network in the controllability criteria. This way the gap between the power and time analysis is successfully bridged and the behaviour of the SEG can be explored as an overall system. Eventually, the proposed controllability definition can be leveraged for investigating the impact of the whole range of the power and ICT features on the resilience of the power grid, so as to facilitate the identification of the most suitable preventive and reactive measures on per case basis.

References

1. Balaguer, I., Lei, Q., Yang, S., Supatti, U., Peng, F.Z.: Control for grid connected and intentional islanding operations of distributed power generation. IEEE Trans. Ind. Electron. **58**(1), 147–157 (2011)
2. Capitanescu, F., Martinez Ramos, J.L., Panciatici, P., Kirschen, D., Marano Marcolini, A., Platbrood, L., Wehenkel, L.: State-of-the-art, challenges, and future trends in security constrained optimal power flow. Electr. Power Syst. Res. **81**(8), 1731–1741 (2011)
3. Chaudhuri, B., Majumder, R., Pal, B.: Wide-area measurement-based stabilizing control of power system considering signal transmission delay. IEEE Trans. Power Syst. **19**(4), 1971–1979 (2004)

4. Clauset, A., Tanner, H.G., Abdallah, C.T., Byrne, R.H.: Controlling across complex networks: emerging links between networks and control. In: Loiseau, J.J., Michiels, W., Niculescu, S.-I., Sipahi, R. (eds.) Topics in Time Delay Systems. LNCIS, vol. 388, pp. 329–347. Springer, Heidelberg (2009)

5. Delille, G., Francois, B., Malarange, G.: Dynamic frequency control support by energy storage to reduce the impact of wind and solar generation on isolated power system's inertia. IEEE Trans. Sustain. Energ. 3(4), 931–939 (2012)

6. Delourme, B., Lasnier, A., Lefevbre, H., Simeant, G.: Minimizing the cost of generation redispatching taking into account remedial actions. In: CIGRE Conference, France (2006)

7. Fang, X., Misra, S., Xue, G., Yang, D.: Smart grid - the new and improved power grid: A survey. IEEE Commun. Surv. Tutorials 14(4), 944–980 (2012)

8. Kundur, D., Feng, X., Liu, S., Zourntos, T., Butler-Purry, K.: Towards a framework for cyber attack impact analysis of the electric smart grid. In: 2010 First IEEE International Conference on Smart Grid Communications (SmartGridComm), pp. 244–249, October 2010

9. Laprie, J.C., Kanoun, K., Kaaniche, M.: Modelling interdependencies between the electricity and information infrastructures. In: Proceedings of International Conference on Computer Safety, Reliability Security (2007)

10. Li, H., Shi, Y.: Network-based predictive control for constrained nonlinear systems with two-channel packet dropouts. IEEE Trans. Ind. Electron. 61(3), 1574–1582 (2014)

11. Momoh, J.: Smart grid design for efficient and flexible power networks operation and control. In: Power Systems Conference and Exposition, 2009. PSCE 2009, pp. 1–8. IEEE/PES, March 2009

12. Monticelli, A., Pereira, M., Granville, S.: Security-constrained optimal power flow with post-contingency corrective rescheduling. IEEE Trans. Power Syst. 2(1), 175–180 (1987)

13. Pizano-Martianez, A., Fuerte-Esquivel, C., Ruiz-Vega, D.: Global transient stability-constrained optimal power flow using an omib reference trajectory. IEEE Trans. Power Syst. 25(1), 392–403 (2010)

14. Rinaldi, S., Peerenboom, J., Kelly, T.: Identifying, understanding, and analyzing critical infrastructure interdependencies. IEEE Control Syst. 21(6), 11–25 (2001)

15. Shafiee, Q., Stefanovic, C., Dragicevic, T., Popovski, P., Vasquez, J., Guerrero, J.: Robust networked control scheme for distributed secondary control of islanded microgrids. IEEE Trans. Ind. Electron. 61(10), 5363–5374 (2014)

16. Sridhar, S., Hahn, A., Govindarasu, M.: Cyber-physical system security for the electric power grid. Proc. IEEE 100(1), 210–224 (2012)

17. Vugrin, E.D., Camphouse, R.C.: Infrastructure resilience assessment through control design. Int. J. Crit. Infrastruct. 7(3), 243–260 (2011)

18. Zarate-Minano, R., Van Cutsem, T., Milano, F., Conejo, A.: Securing transient stability using time-domain simulations within an optimal power flow. IEEE Trans. Power Syst. 25(1), 243–253 (2010)

Case Study: Information Flow Resilience of a Retail Company with Regard to the Electricity Scenarios of the Sicherheitsverbundsübung Schweiz (Swiss Security Network Exercise) SVU 2014

Patrick O. Leu[1](✉) and Daniel Peter[2](✉)

[1] Head of POS Infrastructure and Systems,
Migros Genossenschaftbund, Zürich, Switzerland
pleu@pleu.ch
[2] Lucerne School of Business, University of Applied Sciences,
Lucerne, Switzerland
daniel.peter@hslu.ch

Abstract. The Sicherheitsverbundsübung Schweiz 2014 tested the availability of critical infrastructures. The present case study examines the extent to which one of the largest retailers in Switzerland will be able to continue operations under this scenario. Various interviews, simulations and process categorizations were undertaken to this end. The findings clearly demonstrate that with a short-term black-out, damages incurred by the retailers focused on here quickly exceed the 100 million Swiss franc mark. Meanwhile, a longer power shortage situation would probably be an existential threat. Under these preconditions, it becomes obvious that the security of the food supply for the Swiss population via organised channels will not be guaranteed. The problem analysis clearly conveys that awareness as to critical infrastructures has far from reached decision maker level and that the resilience of processes has been weakened further due to strategic decisions.

Keywords: Resilience · IT security · Continuity management · Power blackout · Retail business · Process Assessment Model · COBIT 5 · Business Continuity Management (BCM) · IT Service Continuity Management (ITSCM) · Business impact analysis

1 Introduction

The availability of critical infrastructures such as the communications and energy infrastructures is of vital importance both for society and for the economy [1]. Next to threat scenarios arising from (terrorist) attacks on critical infrastructures, there is also an exposure to natural perils (a. o. storms, floods, avalanches, severe winters). A third hazard group is based on human or technical error [2].

Communication and energy infrastructures are distributed over huge areas and frequently very insufficiently protected against the risks mentioned above. Smaller events, for

© Springer International Publishing Switzerland 2016
E. Rome et al. (Eds.): CRITIS 2015, LNCS 9578, pp. 159–170, 2016.
DOI: 10.1007/978-3-319-33331-1_13

instance an excavator cutting through a power cable, mainly only have a local and temporary impact. In addition, companies are quite able to protect themselves against the effects of such events by employing suitable measures (e.g. emergency power generators).

While it is quite possible for crisis committees to manage any isolated events and/or events which are clearly geographically limited, the challenges clearly increase if several large-scale events occur at the same time, or if there is an event affecting a whole country. The Sicherheitsverbundsübung 2014 (SVU 14) simulated several large-scale events and had them occur in a serial and parallel manner [3, 4]. In particular, the SVU 14 describes scenarios such as drought, power cut, power shortage situations, cold spells and a pandemic. It was the aim of the exercise to check the effectiveness of preparatory measures, and to examine the co-operation between authorities, sectors and organisations during such scenarios [3].

On 27th June 2012, the Swiss Federal Council published the "Nationale Strategie zum Schutz kritischer Infrastrukturen" strategy paper (on the "National Strategy for the Protection of Critical Infrastructures") [5]. It describes the recording of critical infrastructures ("CI") in a classified register. The categorization is ordered by sectors and sub-sectors here (see Table 1).

The criticality of the sub-sectors is split into three groups and represents the relative importance in a normal hazard situation. Criticality can change depending on the event and the need for action arising from this. A derivation of the criticality to individual items in the sub-sector across the board is not possible.

In addition, the strategy paper states 15 measures split into two fields of action. The cross-CI field of action [5, p. 7726 et seqq.] safeguards a co-ordinated approach, which is meant to improve the robustness of society, economy and state against breakdowns in critical infrastructures. The second field of action [5, p. 7731 et seqq.] addresses specialist authorities and the operators of critical infrastructures. One measure is meant to check the self-protection or robustness of the critical infrastructure respectively, and to improve and thus increase them if necessary. To support the approach, the Bundesamt für Bevölkerungsschutz BABS (Federal Office of Civil Protection) has published a guide [6].

2   "SVU 14" Scenario

The hazard and threat scenario constructed for SVU 14[1] basically comprises of a countrywide pandemic and a country-wide power shortage situation [7]. A cyber attack onto the power industry in September leads to a power shortage situation. Consumers are asked to reduce their power consumption. Because there is only insufficient compliance with this request, the Bundesrat implements the "Verordnung über die Elektrizitätsbewirtschaftung (VEB, Provisions for electricity management)"[2] in accordance with art. 28 of Federal Law. This describes how to manage electric energy which is only available in limited quantities.

---

[1] In contrast to a hazard, a threat requires intent. The cyber attack intentionally leads to a power shortage situation. The pandemic however is a hazard.

[2] The "VEB" is available in draft form. The definitive version will be published by the Federal Council in a shortage situation.

Despite everything, the power grid in the western parts of Europe collapses for 48 h. Once it is possible to start up and stabilize the power grid, it will only be available with a severely limited output of a maximum 70 % for another 8 to 12 weeks [3]. This power shortage situation tries to keep the grid stable with the help of restrictions applied to power supplied. Quantitative restrictions and reduction models are used as tools for stabilization. At the same time the VEB is implemented, the Eidgenössische

Table 1. List of critical infrastructures by sectors and sub-sectors [5: 7719]

Sectors	Sub-Sectors		
	regular criticality	high criticality	extreme criticality
Authorities	Diplomatic missions and head offices of international organisations	Parliament, government, judiciary, public administration	
	Research and education		
	Cultural assets		
Energy		Natural gas supply	Crude oil supply
			Power supply
Disposal		Waste	
		Sewage	
Finances		Insurance	Banks
Health	Laboratories	Medical care and hospitals	
Industry	Engineering, electrical and metal industries	Chemical and drugs industry	
	Sub-Sectors		
Sectors	regular criticality	high criticality	extreme criticality
Information and communication		Media	Information technologies
		Postal service	Telecommunications
Food		Food supply	Water supply
Public safety	Army	police, fire brigade, ambulance service	
	Civil defence		
Transport	Shipping	Air	Rail
			Roads

Departement für Wirtschaft, Bildung und Forschung (WBF, Federal Department for Economy, Education and Research) implements the "Vollzugsverordnung für die Kontingentierung und Netzabschaltung" (Executive Statute for quantitative restrictions and grid disconnection) [7].

- **Quantitative Restrictions:** Industrial buyers with an annual electricity requirement of > 100,000 kW/h have the option of maintaining a sustainable power supply by reducing their electricity consumption to 70 % of their reference consumption (same month of the previous year). This is under the specific condition that there is a direct feed, and that the electricity purchased can be metered remotely [7].
- **33 % reduction model** means 8 h of power, then 4 h without power. **50 % reduction model** means 4 h of power, then 4 h without power. The period over which power is available will be changed over after a week, so that it is not always the same time that no power is available [7].

At the same time the power shortage situation occurs, a pandemic erupts across Switzerland, peaking in November [2]. About a quarter of the population is affected. Smaller peripheral events which despite their size have quite a significant influence on the power shortage situation scenario are a cold spell preceded by a drought. The former leads to an above-average demand for energy, the latter to below-average reservoir filling levels [2].

Below we will examine what impact the power cut and power shortage situation will have on processes inside the retailer's branch businesses. The retail companies and processes examined are typical for the company and critical with regard to the importance of country-wide supplies. Special attention is to be paid to the effects of transferring sales - currently organised in a decentralized manner - to a centralized solution.

3   Object of Analysis

The retail company analysed was founded in 1925 and is among one of the largest food suppliers in Switzerland. In the year 2014, the company generated a turnover in excess of 10 billion Swiss franc (some 10 billion Euro) in the supermarket and consumer market sector. Corresponding to an overall Swiss market share of some 40 %, this means the company is co-responsible for the well-being of the Swiss population to a significant degree. In addition, its group of companies also operates in the energy, finance and industry sectors with more than 50 companies. Historic, mainly politically motivated events lead to the company having a 45 % rate of in-house production compared to turnovers generated - a high, above-average proportion which is atypical for their industry[3].

---

[3] The authors are not allowed to mention the name of the examined organisation.

4 Methodical Approach

To procure the data and information required, we undertook various interviews with experts inside and outside the company [8]. Amongst others, these included the Heads of Informatics and of Infrastructure, Process Owners, Divisional Heads and IT Service Continuity Owners from the Informatics sector. With regard to operational aspects, those responsible for security services, logistics and energy supply were available for interviewing. To obtain an external assessment, four electricity grid operators were interviewed. Because sound data communications are just as important to the retail sector as the energy supply itself, we also interviewed exponents of the two largest communications providers.

With regard to external organisations, we interviewed OSTRAL (Swiss organisation for power supply in exceptional situations) and authorities such as the Oberzolldirektion (Customs Head Offices) and the Bundesamt für Bevölkerungsschutz (Federal Office of Civil Protection).

Using these expert interviews [8] and by also analysing secondary materials, we undertook a maturity level analysis of the internal processes. We based this on the recommendation of the guide for the protection of critical infrastructures by the Bundesamt für Bevölkerungsschutz, BABS [9].

During the investigation, we focussed on critical units of the company under evaluation. We therefore selected three companies from the group of companies involved, from the retail and branch network sectors, two companies from the logistics and product management sector as well as a joint subsidiary responsible for central IT services, marketing, central purchasing, logistics and HR. We assessed the organisational and technical measures taken by the CI operator. Within the context of this paper, critical infrastructures (CI) denotes the following:

- Data centre sites essential to the operation of the critical business process.
- Informatics workplace sites essential to the operation of the systems involved in the critical business process (do not necessarily have to be identical to the data centre sites).
- Branch sites necessary for the sales element of the critical business process.
- Logistics sites responsible for the replenishment of supplies in the critical business process.

With regard to organizational evaluation points, we checked up to which maturity level management systems are present in the areas of risk and continuity. The processes are assessed with the aid of a maturity level model. This is based on the process assessment model (PAM) of the COBIT 5 standard (based on ISO/IEC 15504). In particular, continuity management systems such as business continuity management (BCM), IT service continuity management (ITSCM) and crisis and emergency management concepts were evaluated. In connection with preventative measures, we focused on risk, security and protection management processes.

The technical evaluation points aim for the requirements derived from the SVU 14 (power cut and power shortage situation). The most important questions here were:

- Can the site be supplied with electricity using existing technical measures (power generating equipment) for 48 h?
- Are emergency work spaces set up at the site for informatics and operations employees?
- How is access to the building and work spaces safeguarded during these 48 h?
- Can the maximum power consumption be reduced to 70 % of the reference consumption (same month of the previous year) for a period of 8 to 12 weeks at company level?
- Is it possible to maintain operations on the site by using existing technical measures (power generation units), or by procuring such measures for a period of 8 to 12 weeks, with a reduction model (33 % or 50 %)?

The influences of an event on a business as described by SVU 14 are assessed in accordance with the company specifications of the business impact analysis (BIA). There are five grades of damage categories, specifying the extent of the impairment by damages incurred from different angles (from "very low" to "very high"). A time-line with 5 points of measurement (from 4 h to 30 days) also shows how an event can change in the long run. The event is assessed from different angles. Different angles and categories do not have to be related to each other. From a technical angle for instance, a category 3 event does not automatically mean there is a category 3 financial loss. The following angles are assessed:

- Time it takes for the company to recover from the event.
- Lost turnover potentially caused by the event.
- Additional costs potentially caused by the event.
- Damage to the reputation potentially caused to the company.
- Final consumers and how they are affected by the event.
- Business process and how this is impaired by the event.
- IT services disrupted by the event.

5 Simulation and Findings

The basis for the simulation is the SVU 14 scenario. The results of the technical and organizational assessment of the companies checked were integrated into the simulation (see Table 2). The result is a sobering one. Just about one site in Switzerland is able to survive all scenarios across the overall duration and under the aspect of all potential manifestations.

To calculate the monetary consequences, assumptions about turnover generated during this period were available. To assess the impact on processes, final consumers and reputation, specifications from the business impact analysis (BIA) were available (Table 3).

Table 2. Result of scenario applied to sites (addressing the resilience)

Site	Power cut			33% reduction model	50% reduction model
	without reduction model	with 33% reduction model	with 50% reduction model		
Data Centres West	1	1	1	1	1
Data Centres East	1	3	1	1	1
Data Centres East 2	4	4	4	2	2
Data Centre East 3	4	4	4	2	2
Work site East 2	4	4	4	2	4
Work site East 3	4	4	4	2	4
Data centre Central	1	4	2	1	1
Work site Central	4	4	4	2	4
Logistics site East	4	4	4	2	4
Branches	4	4	4	4	4
Information flow	4	4	4	4	4

Table 3. Damage impact assessment in accordance with "power shortage situation" scenario BIA

	4 hours	24 hours	48 hours	7 days	30 days
Lost turnover	1	1	1	3	4
Additional expenditure	1	1	1	2	4
Impact on final consumers	4	4	4	4	4
Impact on business process	4	4	4	4	4
Impact on IT services	4	4	4	4	4
Damage to reputation	1	1	2	4	4

If you consider the power cut with a view to turnover development, the following picture emerges. The bars represent the turnover development in the four retail sectors during a normal week-end in October. The curves however show the picture in case of the "power cut" SVU scenario (see Fig. 1).

Compared to the normal case, the curves are not rising (03/10/2014) because the cut resulted in a failure to replenish supplies, and a considerable amount of fresh and frozen product spoil. There is simply less to buy for final consumers. Fresh and frozen products are probably compensated for by groceries (tins, ready meals, etc.).

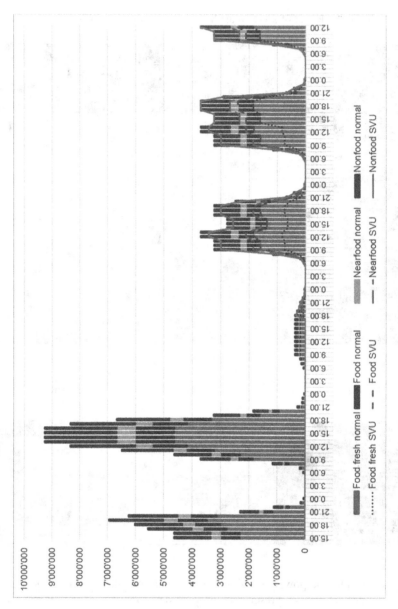

Fig. 1. Power cut scenario - comparison of normal sales vs. SVU scenario sales in CHF

6   Vulnerabilities Identified and Conclusion

All of the companies are prepared for quantitative restrictions either badly or not at all. All companies lack plans for power reductions of 33 % and 50 %. It is widely unknown which internal consumers consume how much energy. Although there is an idea of possible savings potential (for instance cold storage rooms), it was widely unknown in how far savings could be realized in this sector, and what yield these will generate.

A similar picture emerges for the informatics sector: Data centre operators were not able to advise how high a room temperature they were able to run while still being able to run stable system operations.

Strategic connectivity partners are presumably also excluded from the allocation conditions. This assumption however is not currently a secure one.[4] This special position is explained by the impossibility of achieving savings around the 33 % mark, without refraining from partial shut-downs of services and infrastructures perceivable as discriminatory. A prioritization of data connection customers would have to take place analogous to the power suppliers. In an emergency, you will have to do without any consideration of non-discriminatory measures. It is probably better to have CI providers supplied for as long as possible than having to execute a non-discriminatory total switch-off.

If the case arises that electricity generators request their consumers to reduce their power consumption, i.e. quantitative restrictions are applied, there is no company-internal co-ordination process available at the moment. Authorities and associations are probably not currently clear about who to contact in the company, and which responsibilities are covered by a partner contacted this way. It is not clear either how to proceed in such a case inside the group of companies. There is an urgent need for action here.

6.1   Findings on Power Shortage Situation (Reduction Models)

All of the companies are prepared for a reduction model either badly or not at all. There are only few precautions to be found in individual companies from an organizational angle. Measures found are generally sector-specific, often have developed in a situational manner from an event encountered, and have not been co-ordinated in the company overall. Technical measures do work in isolated cases, although this is due to lucky coincidence rather than deliberate intent.

Generally it is to be stated that the company will not work in case a reduction model is applied, in particular due to the strong centralization of informatics services. In case a reduction model is run for longer than seven days, the retailer faces a serious existential threat. Even if power is available locally, nothing can be sold in branches if there is a central IT solution in operation. Since converting to displaying prices on the shelves in 2011, there is no additional information about prices any longer either. It is therefore not possible to use pocket calculators. The current emergency till consisting of mobile data input devices for the supply replenishment procedure will shortly no longer be in existence. A centralized facility will be commissioned in the near future.

With a decentralized till architecture, an hour a day should be sufficient to safeguard sales and supply replenishment processes. Loyalty schemes or electronic payment transactions are excluded here. The communication between data centres and logistical sites can also be maintained with just a few hours a day. As the reduction model has to

---

[4] 20 January 2015.

be worked out by every grid operator individually for their respective regions, there is a very slim chance that a Ticino branch remains in direct contact with one of the two data centres during this phase - which could stretch over several weeks.

An emergency program by the logistics companies safeguards smooth goods deliveries without follow-up orders by branches over 48 h. After a week, deviations will however become so severe that they have nothing much in common with actual needs locally. Existing internal emergency scenarios do not take into account a total failure across Switzerland. They are based on the assumption that suppliers still function.

The connectivity partners questioned reckon that a reliable and continuous communications link during a reduction model phase is nigh on impossible. The reason can be found in the uncoordinated power supply or one which is allocated by sectors and cannot be coordinated. In accordance with Cablecom statements, the type of connection of a site might play a role in deciding whether a connection (from branch to data centre) could also be possible without continuous power. Here, glass fibre-based connections are probably more resistant than copper-based cables, as a glass fibre connection is able to carry data across longer distances unamplified. However, this is only hypothetical. It is impossible to provide a qualification across the board. Even if this applies from a technological angle, every individual case, and in this case every cable, has to be checked first. Cloud-related network services such as MPLS where an exact location of data streams is impossible, further impede the implementation of measures.

Industrial companies will not be able to run any production jobs with a 50 % reduction model. These statements were heard quite frequently during our interviews in industry-related circles. Verification is not part of this paper.

6.2   Conclusion

A power cut does not present any or only minimal problems for the sites checked. However, processes will no longer run. Branches will have to make large staffing efforts. They will suffer financial turnover losses because all branches will have to be closed, but will be able to cope with the consequences of spoiled products in the fresh produce sector. An event in Italy 2003 presented retailers with losses of some 120 million Euro [10, p. 2]. For the company assessed, some 130 million Swiss franc were estimated. If you project this taking into consideration their market share of some 40 %, a total loss of some 320 million Swiss franc across Switzerland would result.

There is an existential threat by the reduction model in connection with a centralized till solution architecture. As continuous communication is no longer safeguarded, branches will not be able to keep selling. With the 33 % reduction model, chances are slightly higher than with the 50 % reduction model, because individual sites and sectors will have power for longer. Due to the different segmentation and different switching times (power on, power off, power on), it is possible that communication pathways can still be maintained with branches close to data centres.

Research confirms that only a handful of companies will be able to bypass even the less severe power cut scenario. The other companies will be out of action either immediately, or will have to struggle against the effects with high manual efforts. For the other sites, it is recommended to run an orderly shut-down of all systems immediately after the cut starts to prevent worse from happening, because there are insufficient emergency power infrastructures.

None of the companies is prepared for the more severe scenario of a power shortage situation. None of them has preventative (for quantitative restrictions) or reactive (for cyclical power switch-offs) measures to hand. Measures found are only ever sector-specific (informatics only, logistics only, etc.), and have often been developed in a situational manner from an event encountered, and have not been co-ordinated in the company overall. Technical measures do work in isolated cases, although this is due to lucky coincidence rather than deliberate intent. In all companies, measures are taken to the best of their knowledge, instead in accordance with tactical or strategic specifications by the company management, the reason being that such approaches are simply lacking. Specifications from a business impact analysis (BIA) were nowhere in existence. If they were, they were largely obsolete (some of the BIA documents were seven years old). In consequence, precautions, although well-meaning and very effective in part, were nei-ther co-ordinated with any business strategy nor other sectors within the company.

As a national company, you need to be able to co-ordinate the necessary preven-tative measures across the whole company. Structural bodies to do so, for instance appropriate co-ordination offices, were lacking. In case of emergency, i.e. if one of the scenarios arises, any company-external party does not know who to report to. This lack of knowledge clearly showed during interviews. Numerous names of people to be contacted in an emergency were mentioned. Whether it is then clear who is responsible internally for the one issue or the other, is difficult to assess, not to mention the availability of these individuals in case an event occurs.

The most important measure is to prevent cyclical power switch-offs by all avail-able means. This can be achieved with effective power saving measures. For a better alignment of precautions, it is urgently recommended to request all companies to provide company management specifications. Work spaces must be available for any power cut scenario, where specialists have emergency power-fed work spaces available to them should an event occur. In case cyclical power switch-offs would need to be pushed through despite all efforts, the retailers' survival not least depends on auton-omous branch stores. This in particular is being revoked in Switzerland at the moment due to centralization efforts.

References

1. Tagesanzeiger. 31 Attacken auf Schweizer Wasserkraftwerke. Tagesanzeiger. Retrieved 8 February 2015
2. EATON Corporation: Blackout Tracker; Jahresraport 2014 Deutschland, Österreich, Schweiz; Acherrn (2015)
3. Swiss Conferation: Sicherheitsverbundsübung 2014 (SVU 14) http://www.vbs.admin.ch/internet/vbs/de/home/themen/security/svu14/uebersicht.html (2015). Retrieved 14 June 2015
4. Häfliger, M.: Bund und alle Kantone üben nationale Notlage. http://www.nzz.ch/schweiz/tausende-in-sicherheits-verbundsuebung-2014-involviert-bund-und-alle-kantone-ueben-nationale-notlage-1.18413147, 28 October 2014. Retrieved 14 June 2015

5. Swiss Conferation: Nationale Strategie zum Schutz kritischer Infrastrukturen. https://www. admin.ch/opc/de/federal-gazette/2012/7715.pdf (2012). Retrieved 14 June 2015
6. Bundesamt für Bevölkerungsschutz. Leitfaden Schutz kritischer Infrastrukturen– Entwurf. Berne, 5 November 2014
7. Bundesamt für Bevölkersungschutz. Sicherheitsverbundsübung 2014 (SVU 2014) – Allgemeine Lage – Für Module Notlage. Berne, 1 September 2014
8. Helferich, C.: Die Qualität qualitativer Daten: Manual für die Durchführung qualitativer Interviews. Wiesbaden (2004)
9. Bundesamt für Bevölkerungsschutz: Leitfaden Schutz kritischer Infrastrukturen (2015) http://www.bevoelkerungsschutz.admin.ch/internet/bs/de/home/themen/ski/leitfaden. parsysrelated1.85483.DownloadFile.tmp/leitfadenski2015de.pdf. Retrieved 14 June 2015
10. Bundesamt für Bevölkerungsschutz: Nationale Gefährungsanalyse - Gefährdungsdossier – Ausfall Stromversorgung (2013). http://www.bevoelkerungsschutz.admin.ch/internet/bs/de/ home/themen/gefaehrdungen-risiken/-nat__gefaehr-dungs-anlayse/gefaehrdungsdossier. html. Retrieved 14 June 2015

RESA: A Robust and Efficient Secure Aggregation Scheme in Smart Grids

Zhiyuan Sui$^{(\boxtimes)}$, Michael Niedermeier, and Hermann de Meer

University of Passau, Innstr. 43, 94032 Passau, Germany
suizhiyu@fim.uni-passau.de, {michael.niedermeier,demeer}@uni-passau.de

Abstract. In this paper, we indicate the increasing interests in providing network security and privacy in Smart Grids, and propose a novel usage data aggregation scheme. The proposed scheme combines multiple cryptosystems to achieve anonymity and multidimensional data aggregation without a trusted third party. In our approach, smart meters transmit usage reports through hop-by-hop communication. If the communication is delayed or fails at one hop, it is possible to reroute the traffic through another hop. Therefore, the robustness of grid communication networks is improved. Additionally, an aggregation tree is constructed in order to optimize the aggregation time. Finally, smart meters utilize a highly efficient hash-based message authentication code to ensure data integrity and identity authentication. Although some existing approaches can achieve similar security features, our scheme has lower computational cost according to performance analysis and experiments.

Keywords: Smart grids · Multidimensional aggregation · Privacy preservation · Robustness · Security · Optimization

1 Introduction

Smart Grids have been gaining more popularity from both academia and industry because of the required grid reliability and potential tremendous benefits they offer to consumers. Smart Grids provide two-way communication between the power provider and consumers. The consumers are equipped with intelligent usage measurement devices, called smart meters, which report usage data to the power provider periodically. According to the collected usage data, power providers define the electricity prices to achieve better monitoring, control and stability of the Smart Grid. The concept of Smart Grids is obviously highly beneficial to the demand management and energy efficiency. However, the challenges concerning cyber attacks also arise with the development of Smart Grids. The communication between the power provider and consumers must be authenticated and secured against modification and forgery. Any of those attacks could be fatal to the electricity grid, and must be detected and treated accordingly. Transmitting trustworthy energy usage reports is an important task, considering the privacy and efficiency challenges in Smart Grids [1,2]. Firstly, privacy is a

© Springer International Publishing Switzerland 2016
E. Rome et al. (Eds.): CRITIS 2015, LNCS 9578, pp. 171–182, 2016.
DOI: 10.1007/978-3-319-33331-1_14

primary concern from the consumers' point of view. The fine-granular energy consumption readings of a smart meter can be used to spy on and expose a victim's behavior. This in turn can lead to personalized advertisements or discrimination against a user who is negatively classified according to his power usage profile. Therefore, the usage data must be protected in Smart Grids. Secondly, the computational resources at the consumers' side are very limited. The consumers need real-time usage instructions from their power providers to behave accordingly [3], otherwise the balance between energy generation and consumption cannot be ensured.

Fine-granular data collection in Smart Grids has raised a large amount of privacy preservation and security questions. The power provider requires aggregated data to forecast consumption of households in the future. According to this scenario, Rongxing et al. [4] propose a privacy preserving usage data aggregation scheme based on the Paillier homomorphic crpytosystem [5]. In this scheme, a trusted party, who has the knowledge of the connection between the ciphertexts and their sources, is responsible for the collection of the usage reports from the smart meters. Compared to traditional symmetric encryption schemes, this scheme improves privacy preservation of the consumers. However, finding a trusted party is a challenging task in itself. Therefore, some anonymous authentication schemes were introduced for Smart Grids. Chia-Mu et al. [6] employ ring signature schemes to protect the profiles. However, the computational cost is increasing with the size of the ring. Liu et al. [7] employ blind signatures to anonymize the consumers' real identities. This scheme however cannot protect consumers' usage data profiles. Zhang et al. [8] construct a self-certified signature scheme and Sui et al. [9] construct an incentive-based anonymous authentication scheme to realize third party free schemes. Those schemes are based on anonymity networks, in which the sources of usage reports are anonymous. This makes it difficult to identify smart meter or communication failures. Li et al. [10,11] roughed out a possible framework for secure information aggregation in Smart Grids. Smart meters transmit the usage data in a hop-by-hop way. The operation center decrypts the aggregated data using its secret key. Therefore, neither a trusted party nor an anonymity network is necessary. However, it does neither describe how to construct the aggregation tree, nor how to ensure aggregation in cases of failure. Moreover, the computation of public key signatures is costly.

In this paper, we improve the system model introduced in [11] and propose a robust and efficient secure aggregation scheme for privacy preservation, named RESA. Inspired by the fact that the locations of smart meters are fixed and stable, the usage data can be aggregated using hop-by-hop communication. For one thing, a highly efficient symmetric encryption algorithm can be employed to guarantee data integrity and identity authentication instead of an asymmetric one. For another, anonymity can be achieved without a trusted party. Apart from that, the contributions of RESA include:

1. Firstly, RESA optimizes the aggregation tree model to minimize the aggregation time and realize the almost real-time power usage report during demand and response time.

2. Secondly, the Elgamal encryption algorithm and Chinese Remainder Theorem are utilized to achieve multidimensional usage data aggregation. The Elgamal encryption algorithm is more efficient than the Paillier cryptosystem [5]. Using the Chinese Remainder Theorem, usage data can be compressed. This reduces the computational cost. Additionally, using the Elgamal encryption algorithm, the usage data can be protected from unauthorized access.
3. Thirdly, RESA employs an efficient symmetric encryption algorithm to authenticate smart meters' identities and protect usage reports against modification. Therefore, RESA can achieve more efficient authentication than previous anonymous authentication schemes [6 − 10].
4. Finally, RESA improves the system security compared with previous work [11], in which the power provider can be informed in time if there is a smart meter failure or communication delay. However, it does not consider the trustworthiness in Smart Grids. RESA employs cheap tamper-resistant black boxes and cryptosystems [12,13] to improve the security of the system.

The remainder of this paper is structured as follows: In Sect. 2, the preliminaries, which are later on required in this paper, are explained in detail. Section 3 illustrates the system model as well as the security requirements in our Smart Grid system, while Sect. 4 describes our proposed scheme that features both anonymity and security. Section 5 discusses the security requirements and compares the computational and communicational performance of our scheme with previous works. Section 6 concludes this paper.

2   Preliminaries

Several important cryptography technologies, which are necessary to understand our work, are listed in this section.

2.1   Chinese Remainder Theorem

In RESA, the Chinese Remainder Theorem is employed to compress the multidimensional data into a single dimensional one. Therefore, the communication overhead is reduced. The Chinese Remainder Theorem is a statement about simultaneous congruences. Randomly choose pairwise co-prime integers $a_1, a_2, ..., a_l$. For any given sequence of integers $d_1, d_2, ..., d_l$, the congruence equations

$$\begin{cases} N = d_1 \bmod a_1 \\ N = d_2 \bmod a_2 \\ \quad ... \\ N = d_l \bmod a_l \end{cases} \quad (1)$$

have the only solution $N = d_1 A_1 A_1^{-1} + ... + d_l A_l A_l^{-1} \bmod A$, where $A = a_1 a_2 ... a_l$, $A = a_j A_j (1 \leq j \leq l)$, $A_j A_j^{-1} = 1 \bmod a_j (1 \leq j \leq l)$.

2.2 Hash-Based Message Authentication Code

Hash-based Message Authentication Code (HMAC) is a short piece of information to authenticate a message. The sender and the receiver communicate with each other by running a key establishment protocol (e.g. Diffie-Hellman protocol [13]) and generate a shared session key K for a predefined cryptographic hash algorithm $\mathcal{H}$ (e.g. SHA-1, MD5 [14]).

1. **Sending:** The sender computes the hash value of message m: HMAC= $\mathcal{H}(K, m)$. After that, the sender sends (m, HMAC) to the receiver.
2. **Verification:** Upon the receipt of the message and the HMAC tag (m, HMAC), the receiver computes HMAC= $\mathcal{H}(K, m)$, HMAC$' = \mathcal{H}(K, m)$ and compares HMAC to HMAC$'$. If they are equal, the HMAC is valid.

2.3 EC-Elgamal Encryption Scheme

The EC-Elgamal encryption scheme [15], which is based on the elliptic curve discrete log assumption, is equivalent to the original Elgamal scheme and can achieve the additive homomorphic properties with less computation overhead than [5]. The EC-Elgalmal encryption scheme is comprised of three algorithms: key generation, encryption and decryption.

1. **Key Generation:** Input a random security parameter κ, output a prime p of size κ. Generate an additive group $\mathbb{G}$ over a finite field $\mathbb{Z}_p^*$, and select a generator P of $\mathbb{G}$. Then, randomly pick $x \in \mathbb{Z}_p^*$ as the secret key. After that, select a mapping pair $\mathcal{M} \leftarrow \mathbb{G}, \mathcal{M}' \leftarrow Z$ used to map values into points on curve. Finally, compute $P_{pub} = \gamma P$ and publish (q, P, P_{pub}) as the public parameters.
2. **Encryption:** Given data d, generate a group element $m = \mathcal{M}(d)$, randomly choose an integer r and output the ciphertext $(c_1 = rP, c_2 = rP_{pub} + m)$.
3. **Decryption:** Given the ciphertext (c_1, c_2), the group element can be decrypted as: $m = (c_2 - xc_1)$ and the corresponding data is $d = \mathcal{M}'(m)$.

3 System Model and Requirements

3.1 System Model

In RESA, we adopt the aggregation tree model [11], where the usage data is transmitted by hop-by-hop communication, as shown in Fig. 1. The system model mainly consists of two entities: the electricity utility (EU) and the smart meter (SM). We assume that each EU communicates with multiple SMs in a concrete area, and the number of SMs is large enough for each SM to cloak its usage data by data aggregation techniques.

1. **SM:** The SM is the energy consumption reporting device present at each consumer's site. But consumers cannot learn or modify the secret knowledge of SMs, which are assumed to be resistant against tampering. The SMs, which form a tree construction regularly, report consumers' encrypted energy usages

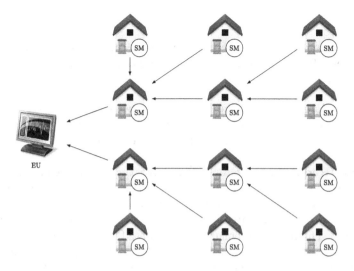

Fig. 1. Network model

to the EU using hop-by-hop communication. Therefore, no one can link the usage report to its source. Once the SM cannot receive the usage data from its neighbor SM in a predefined time, it can determine that the communication needs to be fixed.

2. **EU:** The EU is an infrastructure that is controlled by the power provider and is in charge of the SMs in a concrete area. It collects and analyzes the usage data from SMs periodically, and broadcasts consumption related instructions or electricity prices to customers according to the aggregated data. In our scheme, the EU is assumed as honest but curious. It acts according to the prescribed actions, but is curious to the consumers' energy usage.

3.2 Security Requirements

Because the EU makes decisions according to SMs' usage reports, adversaries might try to send fake usage reports to misinform the EU. Besides the security issues, the adversary might also be interested in consumers' usage profiles. They will try to eavesdrop the communication data or intrude the EU's database to steal data. In our aggregation scheme, the main aim is to ensure trustworthiness of the data from both EU and SMs while ensuring the privacy of legitimate users:

1. **Trustworthiness:** The adversary is not able to modify the consumption reports from SMs, nor the instruction from the EU without authorization (data integrity). The usage reports and the consumption instruction can be determined whether they derive from a legitimate source (authentication).
2. **Privacy Preservation:** The EU cannot learn individual SM's usage data (unconditional anonymity). Even if an adversary eavesdrops the communication among SMs, it cannot get the consumers' usage data without the help of the EU (confidentiality).

3.3 Design Goal

Under the aforementioned system model and security requirements, we design a robust and efficient aggregation scheme, which satisfies the following goals simultaneously:

1. **Optimal Aggregation:** The EU and SMs need almost real-time communication to balance the electricity consumption and generation in the grid. Due to the limited computational resources at the consumers' side, it is necessary to optimize the aggregation time.
2. **Security Requirements:** As stated above, the security requirements should be achieved to resist malicious behaviors, which would lead to fake information injection or consumers' privacy leakage.
3. **Robust Communication:** Missing usage data also leads to misinformation. Security mechanisms can ensure that accepted usage reports are from legitimate sources, but they cannot guarantee that all the legitimate reports can be successfully received. According to the usage report, failing communication and the broken SMs must be identified.

4 Proposed Scheme

The RESA scheme consists of the following procedures: initialization, hop-by-hop aggregation, failure report and secure response protocols. To simplify the description, we assume that each SM M_i only has one child M_{i-1}. It can be easily extended to other tree construction.

In the initialization protocol, the interrelated SMs generate their session keys. After that, the SM reports its energy consumption data regularly (normally every 15 min) using the hop-by-hop aggregation protocol. The SM encrypts the usage data using Elgamal encryption algorithm, compresses it to the usage report from the child and sends it to its parent. During the failure report protocol, if a SM M_i does not receive the usage report from its child M_{i-1}, it will report the communication delay and inform M_{i-1}'s child M_{i-2} and reconstruct the aggregation tree. In the secure response protocol, The EU broadcasts the instructions with the signature to the SMs once it discovers the generated amount of electricity cannot satisfy the requested quantity. Consumers check the timestamp, confirm that the instruction is valid and make their decisions.

4.1 Initialization

Based on the system model in Sect. 3, the EU and SMs execute the following steps to initialize the system.

1. Firstly, each SM is equipped with a tamper-resistant black box [12]. The black box contains a key pair **(SK, PK)**. Any other party has access to the public key **PK**. The secret key **SK** is stored securely within the black box

and is never disclosed or changed, as the black box is assumed to be tamper-resistant. A secure public key signature scheme, including a signing algorithm **sig** and a verification algorithm **ver**, has been selected for a SM with the key pair **(SK, PK)**. Additionally, a hash function $\mathcal{H} \leftarrow \mathbb{Z}_p^*$ will be selected to generate the hash-based message authentication code.

2. Then, the EU selects l random integers $a_1, ..., a_l$, computes $A = \prod_{j=1}^{l} a_j$, $A_1 = A/a_1$, ..., $A_l = A/a_l$ and $A_1^{-1} = 1/A_1 \bmod a_1$, ..., $A_l^{-1} = 1/A_l \bmod a_l$. After that, the EU selects a mapping function pair $(\mathcal{M} \leftarrow \mathbb{G}, \mathcal{M}' \leftarrow Z)$ and generates $(p, P, \mathbb{G}, \mathbb{Z}_p^*)$ as defined in Subsect. 2.3. The EU randomly selects a number $x \in \mathbb{Z}_p^*$ and computes $P_{pub} = xP$. The EU keeps x as the secret key and publishes the public parameters and functions $(p, P, P_{pub}, \mathbb{G}, \mathbb{Z}_p^*, A_1A_1^{-1}, ..., A_lA_l^{-1}, A, \mathcal{H}, \mathcal{M}, \mathcal{M}')$.

3. Finally, the EU and all SMs construct an aggregation map. The optimal approach to construct the aggregation tree is proved in Subsect. 5.2. Each SM M_i securely communicates with its neighboring SMs by running the key establishment protocol [13]. Then, two session keys $K_{i-1,i}$ and $K_{i,i+1}$ are shared between M_i and M_{i-1} and M_i and M_{i+1} respectively.

4.2 Hop-by-hop Aggregation

In order to achieve the almost real-time usage report, SMs run the hop-by-hop aggregation protocol to aggregate the multidimensional usage data.

1. Firstly, the SM M_i compresses its multidimensional usage data $d_{1,i}, ..., d_{l,i}$ into a single dimensional one according to the Chinese remainder theorem: $D_i = d_{1,i}A_1A_1^{-1} + ... + d_{l,i}A_lA_l^{-1} \bmod A$, maps D_i into group $m_i = \mathcal{M}(D_i)$ and encrypts the element m_i. It randomly picks an integer $r_i \in \mathbb{Z}_p^*$ and computes $c_{i,1} = r_iP$, $c_{i,2} = r_iP_{pub} + m_i$.

2. Then, upon the receipt of the encrypted usage report $(\text{HMAC}_{i-1}, C_{i-1})$ from M_{i-1}, M_i checks its validity by using the session key $K_{i-1,i}$. M_i computes $\text{HMAC}_{i-1} = \mathcal{H}(K_{i-1}, C_{i-1}, t)$, and compares HMAC_{i-1} and HMAC'_{i-1}. If they are equal, M_i can confirm the usage report is from M_{i-1}.

3. After that, M_i compresses its encrypted data D_i into the usage report $C_{i,1} = c_{i,1} + C_{i-1,1}$, $C_{i,2} = c_{i,2} + C_{i-1,2}$, and reports it to its parent. It computes $\text{HMAC}_i = \mathcal{H}(C_{i,1}, C_{i,2}, t)$ and sends $(\text{HMAC}_i, C_{i,1}, C_{i,2})$ to M_{i+1}.

4. Finally, upon the receipt of a usage report $(\text{HMAC}_n, C_{n,1}, C_{n,2})$ from M_n, the EU checks its validity. If it is valid, the EU decrypts the report $(C_{n,1}, C_{n,2})$ and gets the aggregated usage data. It computes $m = C_{n,2} - xC_{n,1}$, $D = \mathcal{M}'(m)$, and extracts $d_1 = D \bmod a_1, ..., d_l = D \bmod a_l$. The multidimensional usage data D_i is also additive homomorphic, which can be implicitly expressed as $D = \sum_{i=1}^{n} D_i = \sum_{i=1}^{n} d_{1,i}A_1A_1^{-1} + ... + d_{l,i}A_lA_l^{-1}$. Therefore, $d_1 = \sum_{i=1}^{n} d_{1,i}$, ..., $d_l = \sum_{i=1}^{n} d_{l,i}$.

4.3 Failure Report

If the communication is delayed or the SM fails, its neighbors will execute the failure report protocol to inform the EU where the failure has occurred.

1. If M_{i+1} does not receive the usage report from its child M_i, it sends the report request $(R, t, \textbf{sin} (\textbf{SK}, \mathcal{H}(R, t)))$ to M_{i-1}. Next, M_{i-1} requests the usage report of M_i.
2. If M_i can receive the request, it checks whether the request $\textbf{ver}(\textbf{PK}, \mathcal{H}(R, t))$ is valid. If it's valid, it sends the report to M_{i-1}. If M_{i-1} cannot receive the usage report from M_i either, it reports the failure of M_i to EU.

4.4   Secure Response

Once the EU finds that the energy consumption is not equal to the production, it executes the secure response protocol to instruct consumers to adapt their usage behavior.

The EU first defines the consumption curtailment λ as the instruction. The EU then generates a valid signature to prove its identity using the selected public key signature scheme. It computes $f = \textbf{sin}(x, \mathcal{H}(\lambda, t))$. At last, the EU broadcasts the instructions and the signature (λ, f, t) to all SMs. Upon receiving the usage instructions, the SM checks whether the timestamp and the instruction are valid. It checks whether $\textbf{ver}(P_{pub}, \mathcal{H}(\lambda, t))$ holds. If it holds, the SM informs its consumer; otherwise, it just rejects the instruction and signature.

5   Performance Analysis

In this section, we first show that RESA satisfies the security requirements proposed in Subsect. 3.2. Then, we simulate the aggregation protocol of RESA, and compare it with existing approaches.

5.1   Security and Privacy

The security requirements can mainly be divided into trustworthiness and privacy preservation part. Trustworthiness includes the authentication and integrity of usage reports, requests and instructions in the RESA scheme. In the Initialization protocol, the public keys of SMs are predefined and auditable. Each SM shares the session key $\textbf{K}$ with its neighbors using Diffie-Hellman key exchange protocol [13]. The key exchange protocol is secure under Diffie-Hellman assumption. Therefore, the adversary cannot get the session key between the SM and its neighbors. When the SM sends the power usage report to its parent, it proves the usage report with the hash-based message authentication code. According to the security requirements of key exchange protocol and hash-based message authentication code [14], the adversary cannot forge a valid usage report or modify the legitimate usage data without authorization. If a SM finds it needs to execute the failure report protocol, it signs the request using the selected signature scheme $(\textbf{sig}, \textbf{ver})$. Therefore, the adversary cannot disturb the aggregation protocol without a SM's secret key $\textbf{SK}$, which is assumed to be protected by a tamper resistant black box [12]. During the demand response part, the EU's consumption instruction is signed by the selected public key signature $(\textbf{sin}, \textbf{ver})$. As the result, RESA can ensure integrity and authentication.

The confidentiality of RESA is based on the Engamal encryption algorithm. In RESA, M_i's usage data $d_{i1}, ..., d_{il}$ is compressed into D_i, then the ciphertext $(c_{i,1}, c_{i,2})$ is still a valid ciphertext of M_i's encryption. Elgamal encryption algorithm is semantic secure against chosen plaintext attacks. Therefore, even if an adversary eavesdrops the communication between two SMs and gets the ciphertext (C_1, C_2), he cannot get the aggregated usage data D_i. According to the analysis of the confidentiality, other parties, except the EU, cannot get the plaintext of the usage report. If an adversary intrudes into the database of the EU, he can only get the aggregated data $d_1, d_2, ..., d_l$. Therefore, the adversary cannot get the individual usage data, if the number of consumers is large enough.

5.2 Communication Analysis

During the hop-by-hop aggregation protocol, each SM compresses the multi-dimensional data, encrypts it and adds it to the aggregated usage data. Although the multi-dimension data leads to a larger message, which is inefficient in public key encryption, it is more efficient than the sum of encryption operations for all dimensions [4]. To our best knowledge, only [4,7,8] focus on the secure multi-dimensional data aggregation. [7] does not adopt additive aggregation approaches. [4,8] adopt the Paillier encryption system. The SM needs an exponentiation operation for each dimension. Moreover, the size of the base affects the security of the ciphertext. In RESA, the SM performs a multiplication operation. The whole compressed dimensional data is encrypted. The size of the parameter is not related to the security. Therefore, the computational cost is much smaller than that of [4,8] for each data dimension.

Compared with Elgamal encryption, the overhead of hash evaluations and additive operations is very small [17]. However, all SMs can perform the encryption in parallel. For one thing, the expensive encryption calculations are distributed to all SMs. For another, the highly efficient HMAC can be employed instead of public key signatures. Therefore, the computation time is $T_h + kT_a$, where k stands for the number of children, T_h stands for he homomorphic computation time, and T_a stands for authentication and addition operation time. Therefore, the more children the SM has, the more computational time it costs. At the same time, we assume that the communication time between any two neighbor SMs T_c is constant in the Smart Grid system. The height of the aggregation tree is no less than $\log_k n$, as the number of SMs n is fixed in the Smart Grid system. The lower the aggregation tree is, the less computational overhead is required. The hop-by-hop aggregation time is the sum of the computational cost and the communication overhead. Therefore, it is necessary to determine the children number k for a SM to optimize the aggregation time. We assume that the number of SMs n is fixed. The data encryption computation of all SMs can be calculated in parallel.

According to the performance analysis above, the aggregation time is $T(k) = T_h + (kT_a + T_c)\log_k n$. The differentiation of $T(k)$ is $T'(k) = -\frac{\ln n}{k(\ln k)^2 k}(kT_a + T_c) + \frac{T_a \ln n}{\ln k}$. Therefore, the aggregation time is minimal if k satisfies $k \ln k - k = \frac{T_c}{T_a}$.

Here, we set a scenario to compare the aggregation time, which includes the encryption, transmission and authentication time, of RESA and other third party free schemes [8 − 10]. We emulate the schemes on an Ubuntu 12.04 virtual machine with an Intel Core i5-4300 dual-core 2.60 GHz CPU. We only use one core 798 MHz CPU and 256 MB of RAM to simulate a SM, which is not far away from a real SM. We assume that the computational ability of EU is 100 times more than a SM. To achieve 80 bits security level, we set the length of $\mathbb{G}$ to 161 bits and p to 160 bits. The form of usage report is $\text{HMAC}_i \| C_{i,1} \| C_{i,2}$ whose size is 578 bits. The size of $\mathbf{K}$ is 128 bits. All results are obtained running 20 test repetitions for each algorithm. According to the simulation, the mean result of T_h and T_a are 21,89 ms and 0.01778 ms, which have 0.45 ms and 0.00017 ms size of 95 % confidence intervals. [19] summarizes the data rate of WIMAX in Smart Grids. Here the communication rate is set to 2 Mbps. The variation of aggregation time in terms of the number of SMs among RESA and some previous third party free schemes are compared. According to the Newton's method, the maximum number of children is 3 for each SM when communication rate is 2 Mbps. The computational costs and simulation results are depicted in Fig. 2.

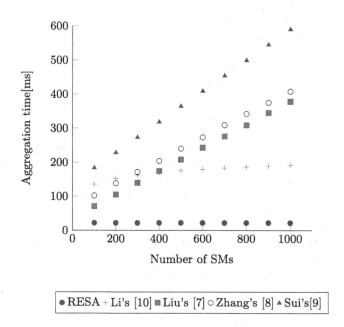

Fig. 2. Computational cost

It can be seen from Fig. 2 that the aggregation time is significantly reduced in RESA compared to other third party free aggregation schemes. According to the requirement of the IETF RFC 4594 standard [3], the signaling delay value should be no more than 240 ms. However, the aggregation time exceeds the threshold when the number of SMs reaches 1000 in [7 − 9]. One of the most important reasons is the limitation of EU's computation ability. There are usually hundreds of even thousands of SMs in a Smart Grid system. To ensure the trustworthiness, the EU should check all SMs' signatures in previous schemes. Although batch verification is popular in some systems, it cannot reduce the computation complexity to be lower than $\mathcal{O}(n)$ currently. This also can be solved by improving the computation ability at the EU's side. However, the improvement requires costly devices. In RESA and [10], the costly computation is distributed to all SMs. Each SM is responsible for checking the validity of its children's usage report. The aggregation time is $\mathcal{O}(\ln n)$. Therefore, the communication delay satisfies the requirement of IETF RFC 4594. Although [10] also employs aggregation tree models, RESA utilizes high efficient hash-based message authentication codes to reduce the computation costs, instead of public key signatures.

6 Conclusion

In this paper, a novel aggregation tree model named RESA is developed, a robust and efficient secure aggregation scheme in Smart Grids. The usage reports are aggregated according to the aggregation tree. RESA can identify and report communication failure during the aggregation time. Therefore, the robustness of the Smart Grid system is improved. Although the multi-hop communication would lead to more communication delay, we optimize the aggregation tree and build a novel model to determine the number of children in the aggregation tree. The security analysis shows that RESA satisfies the security and privacy requirements. Communication analysis proves that RESA has better communication performance than some previous works under the assumption that the computation ability is limited. Therefore, we conclude that RESA is more suitable for real time requirement than other similar approaches.

Acknowledgments. The research leading to these results was supported by the European Commission's Project No. 608090, HyRiM (Hybrid Risk Management for Utility Networks) under the 7th Framework Programme (FP7-SEC-2013-1). The first author of this work is supported by the Chinese Scholarship Council.

References

1. Iyer, S.: Cyber security for smart grid, cryptography, privacy. Int. J. Digit. Multimedia Broadcast. **2011**, 1–8 (2011)
2. Fan, Z., Kalogridis, G., Efthymiou, C., Sooriyabandara, M., Serizawa, M., McGeehan, J.: The new frontier of communications research: smart grid and smart metering. In: First International Conference on Energy-Efficient Computing and Networking, Passau, Germany, 13–15 April, pp. 115–118. ACM (2010)
3. Babizrz, J., Chan, K., Baker, F.: Configuration Guidelines for DiffServ Service Classes. IETF RFC 4594, August 2006. http://www.ietf.org/rfc/rfc4594.txt

4. Rongxing, L., Liang, X., Li, X.L., Shen, X.: Eppa: an efficient and privacy-preserving aggregation scheme for secure smart grid communications. IEEE Trans. Parallel Distrib. Syst. **23**(9), 1621–1631 (2012). IEEE

5. Paillier, P.: Public-key cryptosystems based on composite degree residuosity classes. In: Stern, J. (ed.) EUROCRYPT 1999. LNCS, vol. 1592, pp. 223–228. Springer, Heidelberg (1999)

6. Chia-Mu, Y., Chen, C.-Y., Kuo, S.-Y., Chao, H.-C.: Privacy-preserving power request in smart grid networks. IEEE Syst. J. **8**(2), 441–449 (2014). IEEE

7. Liu, X., Zhang, Y., Wang, B., Wang, H.: An anonymous data aggregation scheme for smart grid systems. Secur. Commun. Netw. **7**(3), 602–610 (2014). John Wiley & Sons

8. Zhang, J., Liu, L., Cui, Y., Chen, Z.: SP 2 DAS: self-certified PKC-based privacy-preserving data aggregation scheme in smart grid. Int. J. Distrib. Sens. Netw. **2013**, 1–11 (2013). Hindawi

9. Sui, Z., Alyousef, A., de Meer, H.: IAA: incentive-based anonymous authentication scheme in smart grids. In: Tiropanis, T., Vakali, A., Sartori, L., Burnap, P. (eds.) Internet Science. LNCS, vol. 9089, pp. 133–144. Springer, Heidelberg (2015)

10. Li, F., Luo, B.: Preserving data integrity for smart grid data aggregation. In: Third International Conference on Smart Grid Communications (SmartGridComm), Tainan, China, 5–8 November, pp. 366–371. IEEE (2012)

11. Li, F., Luo, B., Liu, P.: Secure information aggregation for smart grids using homomorphic encryption, in First IEEE International Conference on Smart Grid Communications (SmartGridComm), Gaithersburg, USA, 4–6 October, pp. 327–332. IEEE (2010)

12. Stamm, S., Sheppard, N.P., Safavi-Naini, R.: Implementing trusted terminals with a, SITDRM. Electr. Not. Theoret. Comput. Sci. **197**(1), 73–85 (2008). Elsevier

13. Diffie, W., Hellman, M.E.: New directions in cryptography. IEEE Trans. Inf. Theory **22**(6), 644–654 (1976). IEEE

14. Krawczyk, H., Canetti, R., Bellare, M.: HMAC: keyed-hashing for message authentication. Network Working Group (1997)

15. Mykletun, E., Girao, J., Westhoff, D.: Public key based cryptoschemes for data concealment in wireless sensor networks. In: IEEE International Conference on Communications, Istanbul, 11–15 June, vol. 5, pp. 2288–2295. IEEE (2006)

16. Schnorr, C.-P.: Efficient signature generation by smart cards. J. Cryptol. **4**(3), 161–174 (1991)

17. Lynn, B.: PBC library. http://crypto.stanford.edu/pbc/. last accessed January 2015

18. Multiprecision integer and rational arithmetic c/c++ library. http://www.shamus.ie/. last accessed January 2015

19. Gungor, V.C., Sahin, D., Kocak, T., Ergut, S., Buccella, C., Cecati, C., Hancke, G.P.: Smart grid technologies: communication technologies and standards. IEEE Trans. Industr. Inf. **7**(4), 529–539 (2011)

A Distributed Continuous Double Auction Framework for Resource Constrained Microgrids

Anesu M.C. Marufu[1(✉)], Anne V.D.M. Kayem[1], and Stephen D. Wolthusen[2,3]

[1] Department of Computer Science, University of Cape Town,
Rondebosch, 7701, Cape Town, South Africa
{amarufu,akayem}@cs.uct.ac.za
[2] Norwegian Information Security Laboratory,
Gjøvik University College, Gjøvik, Norway
[3] School of Mathematics and Information Security, Royal Holloway,
University of London, London, UK
stephen.wolthusen@hig.no

Abstract. Microgrids are power networks which may operate autonomously or in parallel with national grids and the ability to function in case of islanding events, allowing critical national infrastructures to be both more efficient and robust. Particularly at smaller scales and when relying on renewable energy, stability of microgrids is critical. In this paper we propose a token-based CDA algorithm variant which may be frequently run on resource-constrained devices to efficiently match loads and generator capacity. The new algorithm was proven theoretically that it satisfies the mutual exclusion properties, while yielding an acceptable time and message complexity of $\mathscr{O}(N)$ and $\mathscr{O}(\log N)$ respectively. The algorithm should generally be compatible to microgrids supported by a hierarchical network topology where households form cluster nodes around a single smart meter-cluster head (a setup similar to the one discussed in Sect. 3).

Keywords: Microgrid · Power network stability · Auction protocol

1 Introduction

Increased reliance on renewable energy in power generation results in a transition from a small number of centralised power stations to a more distributed architecture [10]. At smaller scales, *microgrids* are capable of autonomous operation such as in case of failure of national grids, or may operate independently e.g. in disadvantaged communities or remote locations. Microgrids are also of interest for critical infrastructure assets, with dependency on continuous power availability. A microgrid is an integrated energy system intelligently managing interconnected loads and distributed energy resources. This permits the construction of robust, energy-efficient systems; reduces peak operating costs; increases system-wide reliability; and reduces carbon emissions [17,18]; but also is more fragile, requiring demand management in addition to generator matching.

© Springer International Publishing Switzerland 2016
E. Rome et al. (Eds.): CRITIS 2015, LNCS 9578, pp. 183–196, 2016.
DOI: 10.1007/978-3-319-33331-1_15

Additional requirements include: pricing, end user prioritisation, and automation [17]. In this paper we concentrate on an efficient decentralised mechanism for allocating power in a resource-constrained microgrid, by relying on an auction mechanism to maximise utility. Such a mechanism must ensure: (i) coordination of distributed components performing *local decision-making based on incomplete and imperfect information* to fairly balance elastic demand and partially elastic supply; (ii) *minimal computational cost* to execute on a resource-limited information technology; and (iii) ensure *robust, reliable and fair* energy allocation. We consider "elasticity" in demand and to a lesser extent supply as users have partially predictable electricity demand which must be supported by similarly partially predictable power generation by uncontrolled sources. We understand the term "resource constrained" to imply a setting in which proper running of information technology infrastructure is impeded by factors such as low bandwidth, low computational capabilities, unreliable battery, and in some cases low technology literacy when deployed in disadvantaged environments. Fairness is important in ensuring trust among participants in the microgrid. We expect fairness of profit distribution among buyers and sellers that are attributable to the Continuous Double Auction (CDA)'s structure to incentivise more buyers and sellers to join a market governed by such a mechanism. CDA is a market institution where there are agents selling goods (sellers) and agents buying goods (buyers).

Conventional methods of energy distribution and management cannot be employed as they assume complete control over resources and requests; a steady supply of energy from more reliable sources; and finite resources for the energy distribution and control mechanism. In considering the above, and in surveying existing distributed resource allocation formulations, market based allocations mechanisms appear to be the most appropriate for microgrid resource allocation. Firstly, market-based allocation mechanisms eliminate the need for a centralised control and suit decentralised nature of the microgrid, implicitly enhancing robustness. Secondly, market-based allocation creates a competitive environment that mutually balances conflicts of interest between parties (balancing demand and supply). Moreover, pricing signals can be adjusted to achieve secondary objectives. Thirdly, such allocation provides an environment that facilitates complex combinatorial resource requests, i.e. users can freely acquire energy in a market at their convenient time, provided they pay sufficiently high prices.

Two categories of market-based allocation mechanisms are commodities market models and auction models [19]. In commodity market models, providers specify their resource price and charge users according to the amount of resources they consume, while in the auction market each provider and consumer acts independently and they agree privately on the selling price. Likewise, use of auction market mechanisms for the microgrid purpose seems appropriate; as they require little global information, support decentralisation, and are easy to implement in grid-like settings [6,11,17,18,22]. In addition, auctions are used for products that have no standard values and the prices are affected by supply and demand at specific time. Application of such auction market mechanisms has been in the heart of major road-maps for microgrid structures [1, 2, 6, 11, 18]. Among the plenitude of auction formats available, we regard the CDA as the most appropriate existing market model for distributed energy allocation. It exploits the dynamics of a free market to balance demand and supply efficiently, with only a small amount of information passing to participants at relatively low computational cost [19]. Furthermore, it offers continuous matching and clearance, which makes it flexible and fulfils the requirement for immediate allocation. Resource allocation is an emergent behaviour of the complex interactions of the individual trading agents, within the auction system with transactions corresponding to allocations [21]. The CDA addresses three main requirements which include: allowing local decision-making by users who have incomplete and imperfect information, allowing high efficiency while maintain low computational cost and ensuring fairness of resource allocation.

However, literature lacks in-depth detail on how a CDA mechanism can be implemented in a distributed manner with minimal messages passed among participants and minimal time to execute a trade. We consider high computational costs may render the envisaged CDA solution unsuitable within the resource constrained microgrid context. The *main contribution of this paper is to show that a CDA can be employed offering adequate complexity on resource-constrained devices so as to enhance the short-term balancing of load and generator capacity, also allowing for limited faults.* This allows a microgrid to operate closer to the demand and supply equilibrium, contributing to stability and robustness.

The remainder of this paper is structured as follows: Sect. 2 discusses literature review. Section 3 describes the resource constrained microgrid; while Sect. 4 details the CDA mechanism, agent strategy and the mutual exclusion problem (Subsect. 4.2). In the same section (Subsect. 4.2) we analyse the CDA algorithm through correctness, efficiency complexities and Token handling. Section 5 concludes this article and identifies on-going work and future work.

2   Related Work

A vast collection of CDA formulations have been proposed but, to the best of our knowledge do not inclusively address the main issues we are concerned with which include (i) decentralisation, (ii) robust and fair energy distribution, (iii) less computational costs. [13] made a comparative analysis of the CDA against traditional non-market based resource allocation. It was established that market based allocation had efficient resource allocation compared to simple First Come First Serve (FCFS) mechanism. [23] applied CDA for work-flow scheduling in grid resource allocation. The authors optimized execution from a user perspective neglecting the Grid-wide aspects like resource utilization or fairness. In [19] a Compulsory Bidding Adjustment Layer (CBAL) is introduced to identify an appropriate bid for a current market unlike in the traditional CDA. SCDA showed superior economic and scheduling efficiency over traditional CDA in addition to low cost, reduced price volatility and bidding complexity. In our work high price volatility is handled by the AA strategy adopted of trading agents. [19] lacks a rigorous analysis that can support implementation of their CDA in a resource constrained microgrid. [7] note that decentralised multi-lateral node interactions and the double node role as resource provider and consumer amidst resource constraints cannot be captured by single-sided auctions, even more so, by mechanisms that rely on a central controller. [20] work towards CDA structure and behaviour. Their CDA formulation contributes immensely in solving the problem of decentralised control and fair resource distribution. However, their work lacks a rigorous evaluation on robustness and computational complexity of running the CDA in a resource limited setting. [6] introduce a CDA method for grid resource allocation. [6] is aimed at management/balancing computational resources among resource owners and users through a centralised auctioneer. [5] Develop and simulate an agent-oriented double auction economic model with the aim of maximising profit for providers. Similarly to [5], we define trading agents that work autonomously on behalf of the buyers and sellers. However, CDA formulation in [5] is centralised offering no fairness as it only maximises providers profits. [18] introduce a CDA with agents using Adaptive Aggressive (AA) strategy to balance energy in a microgrid connected to a higher voltage distribution. The authors' resulting algorithm is not analysed in terms of computational complexity to support its possible implementation in resource constrained context. Overall, CDA implementations in literature are domain specific and difficult to generalise and most fail to address the issue of decentralisation as well as applicability to resource constrained contexts. Some CDA implementations adopt a decentralisation approach but to the best of our knowledge none clearly articulates how the CDA is implemented, the computational costs and robustness. Our envisaged setup describes a robust, distributed CDA implementation in a community-based resource-constrained microgrid with resource constrains.

3 Resource-Constrained Microgrid

In small microgrids it sometimes makes sense and is cost effective to empower the local population with low-cost information technology for resource management. We assume a scenario in which we have a small community microgrid where an energy sharing agreement exists to ensure fair access or distribution of electricity amongst the members. The community comprises of a number of clustered households within a particular area. Distribution of energy is facilitated by the communication network overlaying the power distribution network. To reduce cost of deploying a single smart meter at each household, close-neighbouring households share a single smart meter. Each shared smart meter is part of a wireless mesh network. Thus, we assume a hierarchically clustered network with two distinct sets of entities: a large number of mobile phones M_{mp} and relatively fewer, fixed smart meters M_{sm}, hence $M_{mp} >> M_{sm}$. Mobile phones, M_{mp}, present an affordable alternative over installing a M_{sm} at each household. We consider existence of a symmetric relationship between participants i.e. a member can behave as a seller in some instances (if he/she is generating more energy than he/she requires) or as a consumer(buying energy from other members willing to sell). We consider that a user has access to their electric energy consumption(and generation) profile allowing for significant user participation. Hence, users are able to trade energy through an agent-mediated auction market mechanism.

We understand the phrase 'resource constrained microgrid' to imply proper microgrid functioning is impeded by limitations in low-cost information technology infrastructure i.e. low-bandwidth, intermittent wireless connectivity, low computational capabilities, unreliable battery-life of some devices and low technology literacy. For instance, mobile phones hosting the trading agents are assumed to run on limited computational power, limited memory and unreliable wireless-connectivity subjected to frequent disconnections and sleep mode functions (optionally disconnecting to save battery life). Thus, an ideal auction mechanism must ensure efficient trade occurs while minimising consumption of battery and storage space. We assume intermittent, low bandwidth network is available. Fewer messages with considerable message size (afforded by the low bandwidth network) should be exchanged by the agents in all trading rounds. Low message complexity and bit size was considered priority in an ideal formulation for our context. We are aware that the envisaged algorithm should be robust enough to allow for node disconnections and link breakages but for this paper we are concerned with handling token loss and some link failures. Extensive fault tolerance is beyond the scope of this article and will be addressed in future work. Further more, the proposed solution should allow an automated, seamless transacting platform eliminating chances of technology literacy to be much of a factor. The following subsections discuss our proposed CDA formulation that supports a reliable distribution of community-shared energy over a constrained microgrid.

4   The Continuous Double Auction System

While there exist many variants of CDAs, we structure our CDA around the market protocol initially proposed in [16]. We consider that the mobile phones allow community members to participate in a CDA market through trading agents TA_n. Buyers and sellers in one CDA market trade single-type (homogeneous i.e. electricity in our case) goods. An *ask* defines the price submitted by a seller to sell a unit of goods while a *bid* is the request submitted by a buyer to buy a unit of goods. Sellers and buyers can submit their *asks* and *bids* at any time during a CDA trading day. The current lowest *ask* in the market is called the *outstandingask(oa)*. The current highest *bid* in the market is called the *outstandingbid (ob)*. We consider that our CDA protocol includes the New York Stork Exchange (NYSE) spread-improvement and the *no-order queuing rules*. NYSE spread-improvement requires that a submitted *bid* or *ask* 'improves' on the *ob* or *oa*. The *no-order queuing rule* specifies that offers are single unit, therefore are not queued in the system but are erased when a better offer is submitted as bid-spread (the difference between *ob* and *oa*) decreases. Each seller or buyer abides to an acceptable price range [*Pll, Pul*], where *Pll* is the lowest acceptable price while *Pul* is the highest acceptable price formed on the basis of the seller or buyer's experience and the trading history of the market. For a seller or buyer agent, each unit of goods has a reservation price(limit price) secret to each trader. If a seller submits an *ask* lower than the reservation price, he will lose profit. If a buyer submits a *bid* higher than the reservation price, he will also lose profit (no surplus). An individual *bid/ask* is formed through an agents' trading strategy (Sect. 4.1) and submitted into the market. Thus, the CDA mechanism continuously allows *bids* and *asks* from traders and matches the new ones with the already submitted *bids* or *asks*. A deal is made if the price of a *bid* on the market is greater or equal to price of the *ask*. There may be just one offer from one agent at a time i.e. only one trader exclusively has the right to submit a *bid/ask* (Sect. 4.2). The participant can send a new offer when their earlier offer has been cleared (if it was matched and the deal was accomplished). If the deal for energy is not accomplished the unmatched *bids* are queued in an order-book, ordered by decreasing *bid* prices such that the higher and more desirable offers -from sellers perspective, are at the top. Information about the market state is made public to all participants through the order-book, where the accepted *bids* and *asks* are listed.

We define *supply* to be the total number of units of energy that all the sellers need to sell in a trade period (run). We define *demand* to be total number of units of energy that all the buyers desire to buy in a run. Consumers and prosumers want to satisfy their need for energy while prosumers and producers aim to gain as much profit as possible from selling the energy. Hence an effective adaptive agent strategy is required to ensure the agent forms a preferable offer in the auction market.

4.1   Agent Strategy

A vast range of agent strategies for the CDA market exist which include: Zero-Intelligence (ZI); Zero Intelligence Plus (ZIP); Gjerstad-Dickhaut (GD), Adaptive Aggressive (AA). Trading agents with different strategies can operate in the same CDA market but we consider a homogeneous population with each agent using the Adaptive-Aggressive Strategy[1] (AA). In this article we focus on the AA strategy because of its performance superiority against other benchmark strategies and ability to adapt to dynamic environments that classic strategies were not explicitly designed for. The AA strategy combines estimation, modelling of aggressiveness, and short- plus long-term learning enabling trading agents to identify the abrupt price fluctuations in the market and explicitly adapt their behaviour in response to them. This strategy is discussed in [18] and a similar strategy in [9]. In order to have an in-depth understanding of AA strategy we refer the reader to [20]. Although each trading agent can participate in the auction market, only one is allowed to exclusively submit an offer. This raises the mutual exclusion problem discussed next.

---

[1] developed by Vytelingum in his PhD thesis [20] and then presented in [21].

4.2   Mutual Exclusion Problem

Our proposed distributed CDA protocol results in a mutual exclusion problem. A Mutual exclusion problem occurs when there is a collection of asynchronous processes, each alternately executing a critical and a non-critical section, that must be synchronized so that no two processes ever execute their critical sections concurrently [12]. Consider n trading agents, where $(n > 1)$ requests to submit an offer(ask/bid) in the CDA market in order to transact. Since at most, one trading agent can submit an offer in the auction market at a single instance of time, there should be a protocol for the serialization of market access and fair chances to submit an offer. The protocol must satisfy the following properties:

- **ME1:** [Mutual exclusion] At most, only one trading agent can remain in the auction market at any time. This is a safety property.
- **ME2:** [Freedom from deadlock] When the auction market is free, one of the requesting trading agents should enter the critical section. This is a liveness property.
- **ME3v:** [Freedom from Starvation] A trading agent should not be forced to wait indefinitely to execute in the auction market, while other trading agents are repeatedly executing their requests. This is a liveness property.
- **ME4:** [Fairness] requests must be executed in the order in which they are made.

Many practical solutions to the mutual exclusion problem rely on the existence of a central coordinator that acts as a manager of the critical sections [4]. We disregard centralized solutions using coordinators, and consider a decentralized algorithm, where a subset of the nodes M_{sm} have a slightly additional responsibility over M_{mp} nodes. We propose a token based approach to address the mutual exclusion problem. Our choice was inspired by low message traffic, generally associated with token based algorithms [3,4,8,14]. A token is a "permit" for entry into the auction market, passed around among requesting trading agents. A trading agent requesting to trade in the auction will have to acquire the token. Thus, at any moment, only one trading agent can exclusively hold the token. We propose an enhancement to this phenomenon in order to support the CDA market protocol. We presume that the token has a copy of the order-book to which the trading agent submits its offer once it enters the auction market (Sect. 4). Resiliency to failure is a possible weakness. If a node having the token fails or the token is lost in transit, a complex process of token regeneration and recovery has to be started. For simplicity we assume: existence of a reliable connectivity between the M_{sm} - M_{sm} links; a correct routing protocol; and a delivery of messages within a finite time. Algorithm 1 presents the distributed CDA algorithm.

At the M_{sm} the algorithm executes the following routines: *Local Token Distribution*, *GlobalTokenRequest* and *GlobalTokenTransfer*. At the M_{mp} the algorithm executes the following routines: *LocalTokenRequest*, *LocalMarket Execution* and *Local Token Transfer*. To participate in the auction market two types of request messages are passed: Req_{ms} (global token request) and Req_{mp} (local token request). Incoming Req_{sm} are enqueued in a FIFO $RQ1$ queue while

---

Algorithm 1. Proposed distributed CDA algorithm

1: **initialise** $FlagM_{sm}$, $TokenAsked$,
    $TokenReceived, TokenReturn, ob, oa, P_{ll},$
    $P_{ul}, P_t, BackupID, TokenOB, TokenID,$
    $ReqM_{sm}, ReqM_{mp}$
2:   **Global Token Request:**
3: **if** $FlagM_{sm} = FALSE$ **and** $RQ1 \neq 0$ **and**
    $TokenAsked = 0$ **then**
4:      Send $ReqM_{sm}$ to M_{sm} in POINTER
5:      Set $TokenAsked$ to TRUE
6:      $TokenReceived = $ FALSE
7:      **while** $TokenReceived = $ FALSE **do**
8:         TokenRequest($ReqM_{sm}$, $ReqM_{mp}$)
9:      **end while**
10: **end if**
11:   **Local Token Distribution:**
12: **if** TokenRecieved is TRUE **and** self
    $ReqM_{sm}$ is at head **then**
13:      Set $FlagM_{sm}$ to TRUE
14:      $GQ \leftarrow RQ2$
15:      $n \leftarrow$ number of GQ entries
16:      **while** $n \geq 1$ **do**
17:         TokenBackup ($TokenOB, TokenID$)
18:         **if** M_{mp} at head $\neq$ disconnected **then**
19:            Remove request entry in GQ
20:            Assign token to M_{mp}
21:            **if** $TokenReturn = $ TRUE **then**
22:               Move to next GQ entry
23:            **else**
24:               $TokenReturn = timed\text{-}out$
25:               Remove entry in GQ
26:               TokenRegenerate ($BackupID$)
27:            **end if**
28:         **else**
29:            Cancel request in GQ
30:            Move to next GQ entry
31:         **end if**
32:         TokenRequest($ReqM_{sm}$, $ReqM_{mp}$)
33:         $n - -$
34:      **end while**
35: **end if**
36:
37:   **Global Token Transfer:**
38: **if** $FlagMsm = TRUE$ **and** $RQ1 \neq 0$ **and**
    $ReqM_{sm}$! = 'self' **then**
39:      Set $FlagM_{sm}$ to FALSE
40:      Send token to $ReqM_{sm}$ at $RQ1$ head
41: **end if**
42:   **Local Token Request:**
43: **if** $BatteryLife > CriticalCondition$ **and**
    $FlagM_{mp}$ =FALSE **then**
44:      Send $ReqM_{mp}$ to local M_{sm}
45:      Disable doze mode
46:      Wait for token

47: **else**
48:      Do not send $ReqM_{mp}$
49: **end if**
50:   **Local Market Execution:**
51: **initialise** $Demand, Supply, bid, ask, offer$
52: **if** $TokenReceived$ at M_{mp} **then**
53:      $TokenCounter + +$
54:      Set $FlagM_{mp}$ to TRUE
55:      **if** $tradeID = buyer$ **then**
56:         FormOffer (ob, Pt, Pll, Pul)
57:         $bid \leftarrow offer$
58:         **if** $bid \leq ob$ **or** out of $[P_{ll}, P_{ul}]$ range
            then
59:            bid is invalid
60:         **else**
61:            $ob \leftarrow bid$
62:         **end if**
63:         **if** $ob >= oa$ **then**
64:            $P_t \leftarrow oa$
65:            Trade! and Obook update
66:         **end if**
67:      **else if** $tradeID = seller$ **then**
68:         FormOffer (oa, Pt, Pll, Pul)
69:         $ask \leftarrow offer$
70:         **if** $ask \geq oa$ **or** out of $[P_{ll}, P_{ul}]$ range
            then
71:            ask is invalid
72:         **else**
73:            $oa \leftarrow ask$
74:         **end if**
75:         **if** $ob \geq oa$ **then**
76:            $P_t \leftarrow ob$
77:            Trade! and Obook update
78:         **end if**
79:      **else**
80:         no new oa or ob in a pre-specified time
            period
81:         Round ended with no transaction
82:      **end if**
83:      Update $LocalOB$ from $TokenOB$
84: **end if**
85:   **Local Token Transfer:**
86: **if** Connection to $M_{sm} = ALIVE$ **then**
87:      Return Token to M_{sm}
88: **else if** Connection to M_{mp} via $M_{sm} = $
    $ALIVE$ **then**
89:      Return Token to M_{sm}
90: **else**
91:      Destroy the token
92:      Revert back changes in the $LocalOB$
93: **end if**
94: Set $FlagM_{mp}$ to FALSE

Req_{mp} are enqueued in the $RQ2$ FIFO queue at the M_{sm}. At the M_{sm} nodes is a $POINTER$ variable which stores the location of an M_{sm} in possession of the token, or next intermediate M_{sm} pointing to that token holding node (see [14]) where Req_{sm} is sent. If Req_{sm} is sent, the $TokenAsked$ boolean variable is set to $TRUE$ avoiding similar request messages to be forwarded for the same token.

On arrival of the token to M_{sm} and M_{mp} the boolean variables $FlagM_{sm}$ and $FlagM_{mp}$ are set to $TRUE$ indicating possession of the token. GQ which is a FIFO queue at M_{sm} stores a copy of requests submitted and "locked in" at the arrival of the token to the cluster head. $TokenOB$ is an online copy of the CDA order-book carried in the token. $LocalOB$ is a local copy of the CDA order-book updated each time a trading agent participates in the auction market. Each M_{mp} has a $ClusterDir$ that contains a directory of neighbouring M_{mp} nodes. A $TokenCounter$ keeps record of number of auction market rounds. When the pre-defined number of rounds is reached trading is terminated and an end of trading day message may be communicated to the rest of the participating nodes. This message may include trading-day statistical data.

Correctness of the Algorithm: We analyse how the proposed algorithm can guarantee the following properties:

- **ME1 Mutual Exclusion(Safety):** The algorithm ensures that at any instant of time, not more than one node holds the token.

- Whenever a node receives a token, it becomes exclusively privileged: (line 13) and (line 54). Similarly, when a node sends the token, it becomes unprivileged (line 39) and (line 94). Between the instants one node becomes unprivileged and another node becomes privileged, there is no privileged node. Thus, there is at most one privileged node at any point of time in the network.

Proof: Say there is a $ReqM_{sm}$ in transit on a link, then the link is not directed toward any of the two entities connected by it. More precisely, we denote by transit $(M_{sm}u, M_{sm}v)$ the set of messages in transit from u to neighbour v at time t.

Property 1: If $ReqM_{sm} \in$ transit $(M_{sm}u, M_{sm}v)[t]$, then last $(M_{sm}u)[t] \neq M_{sm}v$ and last $(M_{sm}v)[t] \neq M_{sm}u$. The property trivially holds as there are no requests in transit. More so, if a cluster node, M_{mp}, fails to return the token within prede-fined time due to link-failure, its token session is cancelled and the token is con-sidered lost. The respective cluster head will regenerate the token with all details prior its submission to the failed node. Thus, only one token can be in the system guaranteeing mutual exclusiveness.

- **ME2 (Deadlock):** When the token is free, and one or more TAs want to enter the auction market but are not able to do so, a deadlock may occur. This could happen if: the token cannot be transferred to a node because no node holds the privilege; the node in possession of the token is unaware that there are other nodes requiring the privilege; or the token does not reach the requesting unprivileged node. We are aware that the logical pattern established using $POINTER$ variables ensures a node that needs the token sends $ReqM_{sm}$ either to $M_{sm}v$ holding the token or to $M_{sm}u$ that has a path to the node holding the token. Likewise M_{mp} nodes send $ReqM_{mp}$ to their M_{sm}. Thus this can never occur. Finally we consider the orientation of tree links formed by the M_{sm} nodes, say L at time t the resulting directed graph. In all cases, there are no directed cycles.

Property 2: $L[t]$ is acyclic.

Property 3: In $L[t]$, from any non-terminal node there is a directed path to exactly one terminal entity.

Claim 1: *From* Properties 1–3, *in* $L[t]$ *any terminal path leads to either the entity holding the token.* Within finite time, we consider every message will stop travelling at a M_{sm}. Lets call target$(M_{sm}v)[t]$ the terminal node at the end of the terminal path of $M_{sm}v$ at time t; if a $ReqM_{sm}$ is travelling from $M_{sm}u$ to $M_{sm}v$ at time t, then the target of the token message is target $M_{sm}v$ $[t]$.

When a token is obtained by $M_{sm}v$, the RQ entries are migrated to the GQ. This mechanism ensures all $ReqM_{mp}$ from $M_{sm}v$ after the token is received will be considered for next token round. The token is distributed in turns according to GQ FIFO list. After GQ is empty the token is passed on to another $M_{sm}w$. We use proof by assertions on the responsible loop (line 16)

Precondition: n ← number of $ReqM_{sm}$ in GQ

Invariant: $n \neq 0$

Postcondition: all n requests receive the token after $n + 1$ iterations. This is $\mathscr{O}(n)$

Initialization: $True$ in the first iteration of the loop $n = 0$

$P(n) = n + 1$; then $P(0) = 0 + 1 = 1$ where $n \neq 0$ is $True$

Maintenance: Assume $P(k)$ is True for some k

$P(k) = k + 1$; then by induction we prove $P(k + 1)$ is $True$

$P(k + 1) = (k + 1) + 1$

$P(k + 1) = k + 2$ where $(k + 2)$ is $True$

Termination: occurs the moment the loop invariant condition does not hold $(n \neq 0)$ i.e. when GQ is empty (0 requests in queue)

Claim 2: From above proof every request will be delivered to a target M_{sm} *and* M_{mp}.

– **ME3 (Starvation):** If $M_{sm}u$ holds the token and another node $M_{sm}v$ requests for the token, the identity of $M_{sm}v$ or of proxy nodes for $M_{sm}v$ will be present in the RQ1s of various M_{sm}nodes in the path connecting the requesting node to the currently token-holding node. Thus depending on the position of the node $M_{sm}v$ requests in those $RQ1$s, $M_{sm}v$ will sooner or later receive the privilege. In addition, enqueuing $ReqM_{mp}$ requests in $RQ2$ ensures that a token gets released to the next M_{sm} at the head of the $RQ1$ once the GQ is empty, no single cluster of M_{mp} nodes continues to trade while other nodes are starved.

- **ME4 (Fairness):** Every trading agent has the same opportunity to enter into the auction market. The *FIFO* queues *RQ1* and *RQ2* are serviced in the order of arrival of the requests from nodes. A new request from an agent that acquired the token in the recent past is enqueued behind the remaining pending requests.

To maintain robustness and system stability, an ideal CDA algorithm should handle node/link failures and token loss. In this article we only address: token loss; and M_{mp} link and node failure, while assuming M_{sm} node and M_{sm}-M_{sm} link failures are handled by some protocol.

Handling Token Loss: Token handling is done independently of requests handling and is implemented using a correct routing protocol. In Sect. 4.2 we made an assumption that there is reliable connectivity between cluster nodes $M_{sm} - M_{sm}$. If a link breaks between $M_{sm} - M_{mpi}$, where M_{mpi} is in possession of the token, the token is temporarily relayed through a neighbouring M_{mpi} with better connectivity to M_{sm}. This reduces the chances of token loss due to $M_{mp}i$ node or M_{sm} -$M_{mp}i$link failure. A node in possession of the token may not disconnect or execute doze mode functions. The node can only be able to disconnect after it has released the token to the cluster head. In event that a child M_{mp} fails to pass on the token back to the network, the corresponding M_{sm} will regenerate the token; on condition M_{mp} execution time has elapsed. We introduce the aspect of a timers which start running when M_{sm} sends the token and the other when M_{mp} receives the token. Our algorithm ensures: TAs can join or leave the network without affecting functionality of the auction; invalid bids or an agent's failure to submit an offer will not affect auctioning; and no single node infinitely holds onto the token. If a trading agent takes long to complete its execution in the auction, a timer will end its execution. If the token is not sent back it is destroyed at the M_{mp} node and a copy is regenerated at cluster head.

Efficiency of Algorithm. Two metrics generally used for measuring performance of mutual exclusion algorithms are time complexity and message complexity.

Message Complexity: We assume the spanning tree and cluster forming algorithms are handled separately from our CDA algorithm, henceforth their complexities are not considered in our analysis. We employed a token based algorithm with cluster heads forming a logical spanning tree overlaying a physical hierarchically clustered network. Since the tree structure is logically imposed upon underlying network, then pathological cases (e.g. chain topology) where diameter is not $\mathscr{O}(\log N)$ can be avoided in favour of trees which approximate a radiating star topology. Thus we claim our algorithm involves the exchange of $\mathscr{O}(\log N)$ messages per market auction execution under light demand. In *Worst*

Case the token requesting M_{sm} and token holding M_{sm} will be on the farthest sides in the worst situation. In this case, the message complexity for a request is $N - 1 + N - 1 = \mathscr{O}(2N - 2)$, resulting in $\mathscr{O}(N)$. Under heavy load, we expect that as the number of nodes requesting for the privilege increases, the number of messages exchanged per access of token decreases substantially (refer to [14]). Thus, in heavy load the algorithm requires exchange of only four messages per market auction execution.

Time Complexity: We consider the input to be the number of agents participating in the CDA. Operation in *LocalMarketExecution* is dominant and will be executed n times. We expect our CDA to run in linear time complexity $\mathscr{O}(N)$.

5   Conclusions

We present a distributed CDA scheme for energy distribution within resource limited microgrids that captures: implementation simplicity; robustness through token handling; and efficiency in minimising messages exchanged; vital in critical information systems stability. Trading agents require mutually exclusive permission to submit an offer in the auction market. We cast the CDA protocol as a mutual exclusion problem in a hierarchical clustered network model. The CDA algorithm was proven theoretically that it satisfies the mutual exclusion properties, while yielding an acceptable message and time complexity of $\mathscr{O}(\log N)$ and $\mathscr{O}(N)$ respectively. Our CDA algorithm is deployable in islanded, resource-constrained microgrids operating with no centralised controller; and supported by a hierarchical network topology where households form cluster nodes around a single smart meter-cluster head (a setup similar to the one discussed in section (Sect. 3). As shown in the work of [18], satisfaction of physical restrictions that affect delivery of energy is needed in implementing such an auction mechanism. Our CDA algorithm supports decentralised control of auction trading, which creates an open question on what efficient and effective authentication mechanism would be ideal/favourable in such a decentralised resource limited context. In addition, what measures can be put in place to ensure auctioning continues seamlessly in the presence of failure or faults of components. In distant future work we seek to investigate how malware may affect fairness; thus stability of the CDA augmented microgrid.

Acknowledgements. This work is by the joint SANCOOP programme of the Norwegian Research Council and the South African National Research Foundation under NRF grant 237817; the Hasso-Plattner-Institute at UCT; and UCT postgraduate funding.

References

1. Borenstein, S., Jaske, M., Rosenfeld, A.: Dynamic pricing, advanced metering, and demand response in electricity markets. Center for the Study of Energy Markets (2002)
2. Cui, T., Wang, Y., Nazarian, S., Pedram, M.: An electricity trade model for micro-grid communities in smart grid. In: 2014 IEEE PES Innovative Smart Grid Technologies Conference (ISGT), pp. 1–5. IEEE (2014)
3. Garg, V.K.: Principles of Distributed Systems. Springer, New York (2011)
4. Ghosh, S.: Distributed Systems: An Algorithmic Approach. CRC Press, Boca Raton (2014)
5. Haque, A., Alhashmi, S.M., Parthiban, R.: Continuous double auction in grid computing: an agent based approach to maximize profit for providers. In: International Conference on Web Intelligence and Intelligent Agent Technology, vol. 2, pp. 347–351. IEEE (2010)
6. Izakian, H., Abraham, A., Ladani, B.T.: An auction method for resource allocation in computational grids. Future Gener. Comput. Syst. **26**(2), 228–235 (2010)
7. Koutsopoulos, I., Iosifidis, G.: Auction mechanisms for network resource allocation. In: 2010 Proceedings of the 8th International Symposium on Modeling and Optimization in Mobile, Ad Hoc and Wireless Networks (WiOpt), pp. 554–563. IEEE (2010)
8. Kshemkalyani, A.D., Singhal, M.: Distributed Computing: Principles, Algorithms, and Systems. Cambridge University Press, Cambridge (2008)
9. Ma, H., Leung, H.F.: An adaptive attitude bidding strategy for agents in continuous double auctions. Electron. Commer. Res. Appl. **6**(4), 383–398 (2008)
10. Marnay, C.: Microgrids and Heterogeneous Power Quality and Reliability. Lawrence Berkeley National Laboratory, Berkeley (2008)
11. Pałka, P., Radziszewska, W., Nahorski, Z.: Balancing electric power in a microgrid via programmable agents auctions. Control Cybern. **41**, 777–797 (2012)
12. Peterson, J.L.: Myths about the {Mutual}{Exclusionn} problem. Inf. Process. Lett. **12**(3), 115–116 (1981)
13. Pourebrahimi, B., Bertels, K., Kandru, G., Vassiliadis, S.: Market-based resource allocation in grids. In: e-Science, p. 80 (2006)
14. Raymond, K.: A tree-based algorithm for distributed mutual exclusion. ACM Trans. Comput. Syst. (TOCS) **7**(1), 61–77 (1989)
15. Raynal, M.: Algorithms for Mutual Exclusion. MIT Press, Cambridge (1986)
16. Smith, V.L.: An experimental study of competitive market behavior. J. Polit. Econ. **70**, 111–137 (1962)
17. Sobe, A., Elmenreich, W.: Smart microgrids: overview and outlook. In: Proceedings of the 2013 Smart Grid Workshop, Emerging Technologies (cs.ET), Braunschweig, Germany (2013)
18. Stańczak, J., Radziszewska, W., Nahorski, Z.: Dynamic pricing and balancing mechanism for a microgrid electricity market. In: Filev, D., et al. (eds.) IS 2014. AISC, vol. 323, pp. 793–806. Springer, Switzerland (2015)
19. Tan, Z., Gurd, J.R.: Market-based grid resource allocation using a stable continuous double auction. In: Proceedings of the 8th IEEE/ACM International Conference on Grid Computing, pp. 283–290. IEEE Computer Society (2007)
20. Vytelingum, P.: The structure and behaviour of the Continuous Double Auction. Ph.D. thesis, University of Southampton (2006)

21. Vytelingum, P., Cliff, D., Jennings, N.R.: Strategic bidding in continuous double auctions. Artif. Intell. **172**(14), 1700–1729 (2008)
22. Wang, C., Leung, H.F.: Anonymity and security in continuous double auctions for Internet retails market. In: 2004 Proceedings of the 37th Annual Hawaii International Conference on System Sciences, p. 10. IEEE (2004)
23. Wieczorek, M., Podlipnig, S., Prodan, R., Fahringer, T.: Applying double auctions for scheduling of workflows on the Grid. In: International Conference for High Performance Computing, Networking, Storage and Analysis, SC 2008, pp. 1–11. IEEE (2008)

CIPRNet Young CRITIS Award Candidate Papers

ARIMA-Based Modeling and Validation of Consumption Readings in Power Grids

Varun Badrinath Krishna$^{(\boxtimes)}$, Ravishankar K. Iyer, and William H. Sanders

Department of Electrical and Computer Engineering, Advanced Digital Sciences
Center, Information Trust Institute, University of Illinois at Urbana-Champaign,
1308 West Main Street, Urbana, IL 61801, USA
{varunbk,rkiyer,whs}@illinois.edu
http://iti.illinois.edu

Abstract. Smart meters are increasingly being deployed to measure electricity consumption of residential as well as non-residential consumers. The readings reported by these meters form a time series, which is stored at electric utility servers for billing purposes. Invalid readings may be reported because of malicious compromise of the smart meters themselves, or of the network infrastructure that supports their communications. Although many of these meters come equipped with encrypted communications, they may potentially be vulnerable to cyber intrusions. Therefore, there is a need for an additional layer of validation to detect these intrusion attempts. In this paper, we make three contributions. First, we show that the ARMA model proposed in the anomaly detection literature is unsuitable for electricity consumption as most consumers exhibit non-stationary consumption behavior. We use automated model fitting methods from the literature to show that first-order differencing of these non-stationary readings makes them weakly stationary. Thus, we propose the use of ARIMA forecasting methods for validating consumption readings. Second, we evaluate the effectiveness of ARIMA forecasting in the context of a specific attack model, where smart meter readings are modified to steal electricity. Third, we propose additional checks on mean and variance that can mitigate the total amount of electricity that can be stolen by an attacker by 77.46 %. Our evaluation is based on a real, open dataset of readings obtained from 450 consumer meters.

Keywords: Smart · Meter · Anomaly · Attack · Detection · Auto · Regressive · Moving · Average · Integrated · Electricity · Theft · Cyberphysical · ARIMA · ARMA · Forecasting · Critical · Infrastructure · Security · Measurements

1 Introduction

The Industrial Control Systems Cyber Emergency Response Team (ICS-CERT) within the U.S. Department of Homeland Security works to reduce risks within and across all critical infrastructure sectors. They recently published an incident

© Springer International Publishing Switzerland 2016
E. Rome et al. (Eds.): CRITIS 2015, LNCS 9578, pp. 199–210, 2016.
DOI: 10.1007/978-3-319-33331-1_16

response letter describing an unauthorized access to an electric utility's control system network [11]. Further, a network host-based forensic analysis led them to find that the utility's network was likely exposed to multiple security threats. In order to defend against these attacks, they have proposed the use of monitoring and detection methods, without making specific recommendations. In this paper, we present specific algorithms that a utility can use to verify the integrity of readings reported by smart meters that measure electricity consumption. In the U.S. alone, 50 million such smart meters had been deployed by utilities as of July 2014 [12]. Our data validation methods are envisioned to run on centralized servers in each of these utilities, where the reported measurements from all these meters are accessible.

In addition to the well-known benefits of smart meters, such as automated data collection and estimation of the state of the electric distribution grid, utilities such as BC Hydro believe that these meters would aid them in detecting electricity theft [3]. This belief was challenged in 2010, when the Cyber Intelligence Section of the FBI reported that smart meters were hijacked in Puerto Rico, causing electricity theft amounting to annual losses for the utility estimated at $400 million [7]. Given this report of the compromise of a smart meter installation, large-scale smart meter rollout efforts could potentially increase the likelihood that other smart meter installations could be compromised. In addition to electricity theft, other attacker models in the context of Advanced Metering Infrastructure (AMI) are discussed in [4]. In [20], we suggest that an attacker may destabilize a real-time electricity market system by compromising the electricity price relayed to consumers. Equivalently, it may be possible to destabilize the system by compromising smart meter consumption readings, causing suppliers to respond to the demand by modifying the electricity price.

It must be noted that smart meters, such as those manufactured by GE [5], are equipped with encrypted communication capabilities and tamper-detection features. However, as discovered by ICS-CERT, reliance on these mechanisms alone is not sufficient to ensure total defense against cyber intrusions that exploit communication vulnerabilities. The anomaly detection methods presented in this paper assume that an attacker has compromised the integrity of smart meter consumption readings, and aim to mitigate the impact of such an intrusion. How the attacker can get into a position where he is capable of modifying communication signals is not a focus of this paper and is discussed in [13,15], and [16]. Our aim is to validate the data reported to the utility by modeling the normal consumption patterns of consumers and looking for deviations from this model. We use data-driven insights on consumption characteristics, similar to our award-winning work that employs Principal Component Analysis [2]. Also, our algorithms for intrusion detection are specific, as opposed to high-level guidance for network administrators given in [4] and [11].

The Auto-Regressive Moving Average (ARMA) and Auto-Regressive Integrated Moving Average (ARIMA) models are used to predict future data points in a time series. ARIMA forecasting is used to predict annual electricity consumption in [17] and hourly electricity prices in [6]. We predict electricity consumption at a half-hour granularity using ARIMA models.

In this paper, we make three contributions. First, we show that the ARMA model proposed in the anomaly detection literature [14] is unsuitable for electricity consumption as most consumption behavior is non-stationary. We use cross-validation techniques in [10] to show that first-order differencing of the consumption data makes the data weakly stationary. Thus, the ARIMA model is a better model for capturing consumption behavior and forecasting future behaviors. Second, we evaluate the effectiveness of ARIMA forecasting in the context of a specific attack model, where smart meter measurements are modified in a way that leads to electricity theft. Third, we propose additional checks that can mitigate the total amount of electricity that can be stolen by an attacker by 77.46 %. Our evaluation is based on an open dataset of meter readings from a real deployment with 450 consumers.

2   Dataset Used in the Study

The data we used was collected by Ireland's Commission for Energy Regulation (CER) as part of a trial that aimed at studying smart meter communication technologies. This is the largest, publicly available dataset that we know of. The fact that the dataset is public makes it possible for researchers to replicate and extend this paper's results. We evaluate our models and algorithms on 450 consumers from this dataset. For each of these consumers, the smart meter readings are collected at a half-hour time resolution, for a period of up to 74 weeks. The consumers include 377 residential consumers, 18 small and medium enterprises (SMEs), and 55 unclassified by CER.

We assume that this dataset is free from maliciously compromised measurements, and use the data to understand normal consumption behavior.

3   Modeling Approach

The underlying assumption of the ARMA model is that the time series data is weakly stationary. Stationary data has three characteristics: (1) the mean is constant, (2) the variance is constant and (3) the covariance of the signal with itself at different time lags is constant. We define a weakly stationary signal as one that fails condition (1), but satisfies conditions (2) and (3). The moving average component of ARMA automatically adjusts for changing means, so condition (1) is not important for the suitability of ARMA for a given time series.

For the electricity consumption time series of a single consumer at time t, given by the value of X_t, the ARMA model is defined as follows:

$$X_t = c + \epsilon_t + \sum_{i=1}^{p} \alpha_i X_{t-i} + \sum_{j=1}^{q} \beta_j \epsilon_{t-j} \tag{1}$$

In the auto-regressive component, X_t is an affine function with intercept c of the time signal at p previous time points X_{t-i} with linear coefficients α_i.

The moving average component of ARMA handles weakly stationary signals that do not have constant means. It assumes that i.i.d Gaussian noise $\epsilon_t \sim N(0, \sigma_\epsilon^2)$ compounds over q time periods to contribute linearly to the signal X_t with coefficients β_j.

The ARMA model does not handle largely changing covariance in non-stationary signals. Figure 1(a) illustrates the Auto-Correlation Function (ACF) for a single consumer. The ACF is the correlation of the time series with itself at a specified lag. We extract the time series for a single consumer and depict the ACFs for 350 half-hour lags. There are 336 half-hours in a week, so the figure captures a little over a week. As expected, high auto-correlation was observed for this consumer at multiples of 48 half-hour (or 1 day) time periods. These high correlations persist for all lags throughout the consumption history captured in the dataset. Further, the plot demonstrates failure of the third requirement for stationarity since the ACFs change significantly over time. This lack of stationarity implies that the ARMA model would fail to provide a reliable prediction of the next point in the time series. The ACFs need to rapidly decrease to constant or insignificant values in order for the ARMA model to reliably work. The rate of ACF decrease will determine the model order.

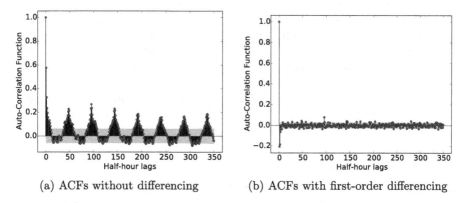

(a) ACFs without differencing   (b) ACFs with first-order differencing

Fig. 1. Auto-Correlation Function of the time series signal of a single consumer. The lag is in terms of half-hour time periods.

We propose an alternative model, the ARIMA model, which has an additional differencing term. We find that first-order differencing causes rapidly decreasing ACFs for consumers who have non-stationary consumptions. First-order differencing modifies the ARMA model in Eq. (1) as follows. Instead of predicting the next value in the time series, we predict the difference between the current and next value in the time series as a linear function of past differences.

$$X_t - X_{t-1} = c + (\epsilon_t - \epsilon_{t-1}) + \sum_{i=1}^{p} \alpha_i (X_{t-i} - X_{t-i-1}) + \sum_{j=1}^{q} \beta_j (\epsilon_{t-j} - \epsilon_{t-j-1}) \quad (2)$$

In essence, a linear model fits the gradients of the points as opposed to the points themselves. After applying first-order differencing, we observe Fig. 1(b). Clearly, the ACFs are close to zero beyond 3 time lags. Therefore, the order of the ARIMA model is finite. In addition, the order is small (p and q are around 3), which is important to ensure minimal computational costs.

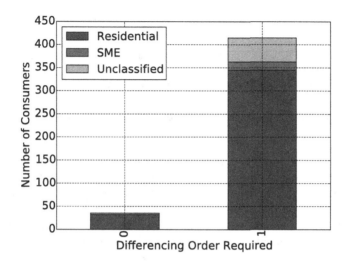

Fig. 2. Distribution of differencing order among consumers of different types.

We have applied first-order differencing and observed its benefits for one consumer, but visual inspection is impractical for our dataset of 450 consumers. Therefore, we employ the Hyndman-Khandakar algorithm [10] to estimate the model order. This method combines cross-validation techniques, unit root tests, and maximum likelihood estimation.

The results of the Hyndman-Khandakar algorithm are as follows. While the autoregressive (p) and moving average order (q) range from 0 to 5, the differencing order is either 0 or 1. A minority of consumers (35 out of 450, or 7.78 %) have stationary consumption patterns and thus the ARMA model proposed in [14] is appropriate for this minority. However, for 92.22 % of consumers, first-order differencing is required, justifying our ARIMA model proposal. The distribution of consumers, segregated by consumer type is captured in Fig. 2.

Once the ARIMA model is estimated, the next consumption point in the time series X_t is forecast. From this point forecast, a 95 % confidence interval C is constructed with the assumption of i.i.d. Gaussian errors ϵ_t as described in [1]:

$$C = X_t \pm 1.96\sigma_\epsilon \tag{3}$$

Here 1.96 comes from the fact that 95 % of the standard normal distribution lies within [-1.96,+1.96]. Recall that σ_ϵ was the standard deviation of the i.i.d. Gaussian errors ϵ_t in Eq. (1). The prediction by ARIMA and the confidence

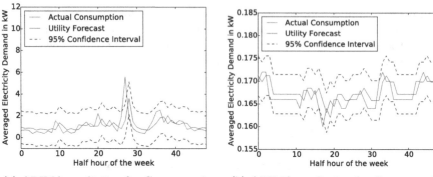

(a) ARIMA prediction for Consumer 1   (b) ARIMA prediction for Consumer 2

Fig. 3. ARIMA forecasting of points and 95 % confidence intervals.

intervals for two different consumers are illustrated in Fig. 3. In this paper, we propose the use of these confidence intervals for anomaly detection. If a smart meter reading lies outside these intervals, we say with 95 % confidence that it is anomalous. Also note that there is an order of magnitude difference between the consumptions of these two consumers and that the confidence intervals for Consumer 2 in Fig. 3(b) are relatively tighter, because of lower variance in consumption patterns. Tighter confidence intervals are preferred, as faults or attacks become easier to detect.

In our dataset, the consumers do not produce electricity and sell it back to the grid, so the consumption is never negative. Thus, the lower bound of the confidence interval is only useful if it is positive, as negative readings reported by smart meters are naturally anomalous. Note that the lower bound for Consumer 1 in Fig. 3(a) goes negative, while it stays positive for Consumer 2. The reason why the lower bound goes negative is due to the symmetry in the Gaussian error assumption that is inherent in ARIMA and ARMA models. However, in future scenarios where consumers supply to the grid, or consume a negative amount of electricity, a negative lower bound of the confidence interval will become useful.

4   Electricity Theft Attack Model

The ARIMA confidence interval provides a bound on the measurements and serves as a good detector for invalid measurements for faulty meters. However, these bounds are not sufficient to detect attacks in which the attacker has full knowledge of the system. We consider a specific attack model in which the attacker steals electricity from a neighbor for monetary gain. Let the attacker's consumption at time t be A_t and the neighbor's consumption be X_t. The attacker compromises his neighbor's smart meter and has it report a consumption of $X'_t > X_t$. At the same time, the attacker under-reports his own consumption by compromising his meter's reading to $A'_t = A_t - (X'_t - X_t)$. Therefore, he steals a positive amount from the neighbor of $(X'_t - X_t)$. He gets billed for $A'_t < A_t$

while the neighbor gets billed for $X'_t > X_t$. Note that balance checks (discussed by researchers at Mitsubishi [18]) at upstream points on the electric distribution network would find that the expected sum as reported by the smart meters $(X'_t + A'_t)$ matches the measured sum of $(A_t + X_t)$. Thus, the attacker has averted the balance check. In order to do so, he has increased his neighbor's smart meter consumption readings.

Without the ARIMA detection mechanism in place, the attacker can steal an arbitrary amount of electricity. He is only constrained by the physical limits of the electric distribution system. Specifically, electric distribution lines are rated based on the maximum current that they can carry. If the demand from the attacker increases (while the distribution voltage is kept approximately constant by reactive power compensation), the current in the distribution lines will increase. This generates heat in the form of $I^2 R$ losses, where I is the current and R is the resistance. If the current increases beyond the rated threshold, the lines will exceed their thermal limits. The ensuing damage may lead to blackouts or other equipment failures, which are an obvious indication of anomalous consumption. Therefore, we assume that the attacker would try to avoid detection by operating in a way that his own consumption is within these physical limits. A detailed study on these physical limits can be found in [21].

4.1   ARIMA Attack

In order to avoid detection in the presence of ARIMA-based detection thresholds, the attacker needs to ensure that the neighbor's consumption remains within the 95 % confidence interval. If he steals more electricity from the neighbor, the utility will find that the neighbor's consumption exceeds the upper bound of the confidence interval and is anomalous. On discovering this anomaly, the utility may dispatch a technician to manually verify the integrity of the neighbor's meter. Such investigations are already being made periodically [8]. In this section, we assume the worst-case scenario in which the attacker has full information and can estimate the 95 % confidence intervals just as well as the utility can.

The optimal value for the attacker to steal is the maximum that he can steal while averting detection. This point is reached at the 95 % confidence threshold. Thus the attacker over-reports the neighbor's consumption as the 95 % threshold point as shown in Fig. 4. Since this attacks averts the ARIMA-based detector, we refer to it as the ARIMA attack.

The ARIMA detector has bounded the attack, and the maximum electricity stolen from the neighbor is given by the difference between the ARIMA Attack curve and the Actual Consumption curve.

In order to detect the attack, the statistics of the window can be compared against statistics of previous windows. Specifically, if the observed mean μ' lies in the interval $[min(\{\mu\}), max(\{\mu\})]$ and the observed standard deviation σ' lies in the interval $[min(\{\sigma\}), max(\{\sigma\})]$, then we say the new point is not a suspected attack. Here $\{\mu\}$ and $\{\sigma\}$ are the sets of means and standard deviations observed in historic data. For the sake of standardization, we assume in our simulations that each statistic (μ and σ) is calculated on a window of a week in the historic

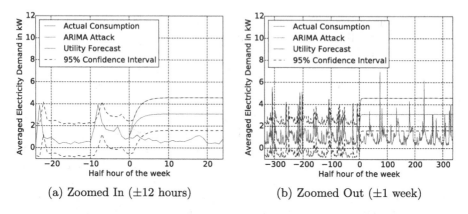

Fig. 4. Illustration of an ARIMA attack on a neighbor. The attack is launched at time 0 on the horizontal axis.

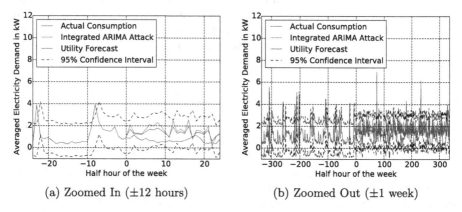

Fig. 5. Illustration of Integrated ARIMA attack on a neighbor using the Truncated Normal Distribution. The attack is launched at time 0 on the horizontal axis.

data. Therefore, the cardinality of $\{\mu\}$ and $\{\sigma\}$ is the number of weeks in the utility's smart meter data archive.

4.2 Integrated ARIMA Attack

As security researchers and practitioners, it is important for us to think about how an attacker may evade our own checks, as no check is completely foolproof. In our case, we find that, despite checks on the mean and standard deviation, it is possible for the attacker to steal electricity. He may do so by generating false consumption readings using a Truncated Normal distribution. This distribution is specified by a range, mean and standard deviation. By setting the range to the ARIMA confidence intervals, the attacker averts detection by the ARIMA detector. In addition, he can set the mean to the extreme point $max(\{\mu\})$ to avert the check on the mean. At the $max(\{\mu\})$ value, the mean quantity of electricity stolen is maximized while being undetectable. Finally, he can set the standard deviation to the extreme point $min(\{\sigma\})$ to avert the standard deviation check. We assume that he wants to minimize the standard deviation to minimize the variability that he needs to incorporate into his own consumption. If the attacker were to steal electricity from multiple consumers, the variability would add up, making it difficult for him to match with his own consumption in order to pass the balance check.

Since this attack averts all these integrated checks, we called it the *Integrated ARIMA attack* and it is illustrated in Fig. 5. It can be seen that the Integrated ARIMA attack curve has significantly higher variance as compared to the ARIMA attack curve in Fig. 4. However, its mean is lower, so we expect less electricity to be stolen under the Integrated ARIMA attack. The trade-off for the attacker is that the Integrated ARIMA attack is harder to detect.

5   Quantitative Evaluation

In this section, we present a simulation study of the ARIMA and Integrated ARIMA attacks for the set of 450 consumers in the dataset. We built the attack simulations using Python, with bridges to the R Forecast library by Hyndman and Khandakar [10]. The Integrated ARIMA attack used truncated normal random number generators, so we ran 50 simulation trajectories for each consumer in order to reduce the bias in our random samples. The massive computation requirements for this simulation occupied 70 CPU cores in our TCIPG testbed over the course of a full week.

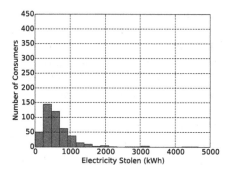 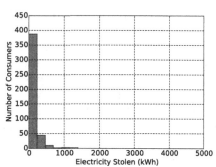

(a) Maximum electricity stolen by means of the ARIMA attack

(b) Maximum electricity stolen by means of the Integrated ARIMA attack

Fig. 6. Distribution of maximum electricity stolen from each consumer through ARIMA and Integrated ARIMA attacks.

The maximum amounts of electricity stolen for both the ARIMA attack and the Integrated ARIMA attack were calculated, and histograms of the results are given in Fig. 6. It is clear that much less electricity is stolen due to the Integrated

ARIMA attack as compared to the ARIMA attack. This serves to quantify the benefit of adding the additional checks on mean and standard deviation. The improvement seen, as a percentage for each consumer, is given in Fig. 7. Up to 99.4 % reduction in theft can be achieved with the checks on mean and variance.

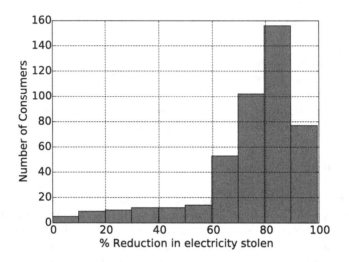

Fig. 7. The maximum electricity stolen from each consumer through an Integrated ARIMA attack is less than an ARIMA attack. The distribution of the percentage reduction is shown. For most consumers, a large reduction is seen.

The aggregated results across all 450 consumers are as follows. For a period of 1 week, the attacker managed to steal 285, 914 kWh under the ARIMA attack and 64, 447 kWh under the Integrated ARIMA attack. That is a reduction of 77.46 %. Therefore, the additional checks played a major role in mitigating the attack. We quantify the monetary benefit to the attacker by multiplying the electricity stolen with the latest $/kWh rate posted by the Pacific Gas and Electric Company (PG&E) for residential services [19]. This rate is $0.16/kWh, and the corresponding profits for the attacker under the ARIMA and Integrated ARIMA attacks are $45, 746 and $10, 311, respectively. These numbers tell us how much the attacker stands to gain under the assumption that he has full information about the system and the ability to control the meter readings reported. On the other hand, if the attacker had lesser capabilities, the attacks would be either easily detected or significantly mitigated by our proposed methods.

Note that, throughout this paper, we have spoken of an attacker in the singular. We have not, however, made any assumptions that restrict our analysis and results to a single attacker. Our sample of 450 consumers is large enough to demonstrate that it is unlikely that a single attacker will be able to steal the ARIMA attack upper bound of 285, 914 kW (averaged over an hour), due to the physical limits of distribution lines that connect his consumption facility to the nearest transformer. However, it would be possible for multiple attackers on different distribution lines to collude and steal this amount. The dynamics of collusion between multiple attackers is a subject for future work.

6   Conclusion and Future Work

In this paper, we evaluated the suitability of the ARMA and ARIMA models for forecasting electricity consumption behaviors. These forecasts produced confidence intervals using the ARIMA assumption that noise is normally distributed. The confidence intervals served as a first layer of validation for faulty smart meter measurements. In order to detect and mitigate well-crafted electricity theft attacks, additional checks needed to be put in place, and we proposed checks on mean and variance. We showed that an electricity theft attack is feasible despite these checks, but the amount of electricity that can be stolen under this attack is up to 99.4 % less than what was stolen without these checks in place. The reduction in electricity stolen, aggregated over all consumers, was 77.46 %.

In future work, we will explore ways to improve the ARIMA forecasting method by incorporating seasonalities. Since consumption patterns repeat daily or weekly, as seen by the seven daily peaks in Fig. 1(a), there is inherent seasonality that is not captured in our low-order ARIMA models. Incorporating seasonalities may not help in tightening the confidence intervals to improve detection, because the first-order differencing may flatten out seasonalities as shown in Fig. 1(b). Nevertheless, we have observed cases where the seasonalities still persist after this differencing has been done. We have not been successful in investigating these cases, because the seasonalities are at large lags of 48 half-hour periods. We have found that dealing with such high order seasonalities requires computational processing power and memory beyond the capabilities of our most powerful servers. This computational issue is well-known in the forecasting community [9], and solutions are worth exploring for future work.

Acknowledgments. This material is based upon work supported by the Department of Energy under Award Number DE-OE0000097 and the Siebel Energy Institute. The smart meter data used in this paper was accessed via the Irish Social Science Data Archive at www.ucd.ie/issda. The providers of the data, the Commission for Energy Regulation, bear no responsibility for the further analysis or interpretation of it. We thank Jenny Applequist, Jeremy Jones and Timothy Yardley for their support, and Prof. Douglas L. Jones for his feedback.

References

1. Forecasting with ARIMA Models. https://onlinecourses.science.psu.edu/stat510/node/66
2. Badrinath Krishna, V., Weaver, G.A., Sanders, W.H.: PCA-based method for detecting integrity attacks on advanced metering infrastructure. In: Campos, J., Haverkort, B.R. (eds.) Quantitative Evaluation of Systems. LNCS, vol. 9259, pp. 70–85. Springer, Heidelberg (2015)

3. BC Hydro: Smart metering program (2014). https://www.bchydro.com/energy-in-bc/projects/smart_metering_infrastructure_program.html
4. Berthier, R., Sanders, W.H., Khurana, H.: Intrusion Detection for Advanced Metering Infrastructures: Requirements and Architectural Directions. In: Proceedings of IEEE SmartGridComm 2010, pp. 350–355. IEEE, October 2010
5. ComEd: Safeguarding data through smarter technology (2014). https://www.comed.com/documents/technology/grid_mod_fact_sheet_security_2014_r2.pdf
6. Contreras, J., Espinola, R., Nogales, F.J.: ARIMA models to predict next-day electricity prices. IEEE Trans. Power Syst. 18(3), 1014–1020 (2003)
7. Cyber Intelligence Section: Smart grid electric meters altered to steal electricity, May 2010. http://krebsonsecurity.com/wp-content/uploads/2012/04/FBI-SmartMeterHack-285x305.png
8. Edison Electric Institute: Smart Meters and Smart Meter Systems : A Metering Industry Perspective, p. 35, March 2011. http://www.eei.org/issuesandpolicy/grid-enhancements/documents/smartmeters.pdf
9. Hyndman, R.J.: Forecasting with long seasonal periods, September 2010. http://robjhyndman.com/hyndsight/longseasonality/
10. Hyndman, R.J., Khandakar, Y.: Automatic time series forecasting: the forecast package for R. J.Stat. Softw. 27(3), 1–22 (2008)
11. ICS-CERT: Internet accessible control systems at risk (2014). https://ics-cert.us-cert.gov/sites/default/files/Monitors/ICS-CERT_Monitor_%20Jan-April2014.pdf
12. Institute for Electric Efficiency: Utility-Scale Smart Meter Deployments September, pp. 1–11 (2014)
13. Jiang, R., Lu, R., Wang, L., Luo, J., Changxiang, S., Xuemin, S.: Energy-theft detection issues for advanced metering infrastructure in smart grid. Tsinghua Sci. Technol. 19(2), 105–120 (2014)
14. Mashima, D., Cárdenas, A.A.: Evaluating electricity theft detectors in smart grid networks. In: Balzarotti, D., Stolfo, S.J., Cova, M. (eds.) RAID 2012. LNCS, vol. 7462, pp. 210–229. Springer, Heidelberg (2012)
15. McLaughlin, S., Holbert, B., Zonouz, S., Berthier, R.: AMIDS: A multi-sensor energy theft detection framework for advanced metering infrastructures. In: Proceedings of SmartGridComm 2012, pp. 354–359, November 2012
16. McLaughlin, S., Podkuiko, D., Miadzvezhanka, S., Delozier, A., McDaniel, P.: Multi-vendor penetration testing in the advanced metering infrastructure. In: Proceedings of ACSAC 2010, pp. 107–116. ACM, New York (2010)
17. Mohamed, Z., Bodger, P.: Forecasting electricity consumption a comparison of models for New Zealand. In: Electricity Engineers' Association of New Zealand Annual Conference, vol. 64, pp. 1–15 (2004). http://ir.canterbury.ac.nz/handle/10092/821
18. Nikovski, D.N., Wang, Z., Esenther, A., Sun, H., Sugiura, K., Muso, T., Tsuru, K.: Smart meter data analysis for power theft detection. In: Perner, P. (ed.) MLDM 2013. LNCS, vol. 7988, pp. 379–389. Springer, Heidelberg (2013)
19. PG&E: Electric schedule e-1. residntial services, February 2015. http://www.pge.com/tariffs/tm2/pdf/ELEC_SCHEDS_E-1.pdf
20. Tan, R., Badrinath Krishna, V., Yau, D.K., Kalbarczyk, Z.: Impact of integrity attacks on real-time pricing in smart grids. In: Proceedings of ACM CCS 2013, pp. 439–450. ACM, New York (2013)
21. Wan, H., McCalley, J., Vittal, V.: Increasing thermal rating by risk analysis. IEEE Trans. Power Syst. 14(3), 815–828 (1999)

The Professional Figure of the Security Liaison Officer in the Council Directive 2008/114/EC

Maria Carla De Maggio[1(✉)], Marzia Mastrapasqua[2], and Roberto Setola[1]

[1] Complex Systems and Security Lab, Università Campus Bio-Medico di Roma, Rome, Italy
{m.demaggio,r.setola}@unicampus.it
[2] Security Analysis and Business Intelligence – SNAM, Milan, Italy
m.mastrapasqua@snam.it

Abstract. The Council Directive 2008/114/EC represents a cornerstone for a common European strategy for the protection of Critical Infrastructures. Article 6 comma 2 of the Directive deals with the designation of a Security Liaison Officer for each European Critical Infrastructure. Although his designation is mandatorily stated by the Directive, his role and duties in the organization are not clearly defined. To overcome this lack of standardization across Europe, the present study aims to define and analyze the current scenario of Critical Infrastructure security, and gather opinions regarding the aspiring evolution of the regulatory framework, in order to create a "European vision" of the SLO in terms of background, competences and role.

Keywords: Security Liaison Officer · Council Directive 2008/114/EC · Critical Infrastructure Protection

1 Introduction

Advances in technology and globalization have led to a strong interconnection of the Critical Infrastructures (CIs), which are no longer separate systems, but increasingly show physical and logical interdependencies. This new configuration has positively affected the efficiency of the single infrastructures, but has exposed them to new vulnerabilities, hence the overall resilience should be accordingly updated.

In this framework, in 2005 the Justice and Home Affairs Council called on the European Commission to focus on improving the protection of Critical Infrastructures throughout the 28 European Member States (MS), characterized by different cultures, approaches and needs. The result of this standardization process was the creation of the European Programme for Critical Infrastructure Protection (EPCIP) [1, 2]: a strategy driven by an all-hazards approach to help MS increase the level of protection and resilience of their CIs, especially focused on preventing failures with potential pan-European consequences.

Tending to the enhancement of this common strategy, the Council Directive 2008/114/EC [3] aims to the identification of the European Critical Infrastructures, requiring each one of them to set-up an Operator Security Plan (OSP), and designate a Security Liaison Officer (SLO).

© Springer International Publishing Switzerland 2016
E. Rome et al. (Eds.): CRITIS 2015, LNCS 9578, pp. 211–222, 2016.
DOI: 10.1007/978-3-319-33331-1_17

Specifically, article 6 comma 2 asserts that "each Member State shall assess whether each designated ECI located on its territory possesses a Security Liaison Officer or equivalent". The objective is to allow a more effective Public-Private Partnership with the aim to share ideas/opinions/facts which can harden CI assets and help implement strategic plans.

Currently there are no specific roles, responsibilities and tasks affiliated with the SLO position in the EU, thus the Directive has been subjected to different interpretations, especially when comparing the SLO with existing figures of the security field. Although Security Manger, Chief Security Officer and Security Liaison Officer represent different positions, there are overlapping desired knowledge/skillsets in all of them. For example, if all Security Managers in Europe must not have a criminal record, thus far only Spain has mandated that the SLO be a qualified Security Manager. Further, some countries (Hungary, Romania) require agreement with the CIP authorities to appoint the SLO.

In this undetermined framework, the present study, developed within the European project "SLO – Security Liaison Officer", co-funded by the CIPS programme of the Directorate-General Home Affairs of the European Commission, aims at a clear and common approach to define the professional figure of the SLO, including duties and role, position in the organization, background and skills.

The following sections will show the methodology adopted for the study (Sect. 2) and its results (Sect. 3), presenting data regarding the approach to the security issue, the knowledge of the European regulatory framework, and the current and foreseen perspective about the SLO position.

2   Methodology

The acquisition of information describing the actual scenario and the most relevant security trends within European organizations, is the first step to understand the state of implementation of the Council Directive 2008/114/EC and its perspective in the next years. To this end, the project "SLO – Security Liaison Officer" promoted a survey via questionnaires, whose design process lasted several months. The questionnaire was created drawing on open sources and security experts' advice, in order to set up a survey able to collect the largest amount of information with an easy form to fill in.

From the early stages of the project, the idea of a single questionnaire for the broad spectrum of expertise characterizing the field of Critical Infrastructures security was considered a restriction. Thus, the questionnaire was broken down into four distinct categories of recipients:

- Public Authorities (PA)
- Chief Security Officers (CSO)
- Security Officer staff members
- Researchers/Experts

The questionnaires of each category had a specific set of questions, tailored on the recipient's peculiar field, role and position and have been provided via the web. This targeted approach provided four distinct viewpoints and helped collect a diversified set of data, more appropriate for the accurate analysis proposed by the study.

The invitation to participate in the survey has been delivered worldwide to a large mailing list (more than 3,000 players involved in Critical Infrastructure security), and disseminated during different events of the same field. In the period from October 2013 to May 2014, about 300 questionnaires from 34 different Countries (of which 19 EU Member States) were collected. The majority of data stems from EU Countries (about 70 %), but a smaller percentage participated from North America, Australia and Africa (Fig. 1).

About 37 % of feedback has been received from Chief Security Officers, a very large amount considering the questionnaires returned by their staff (only 10 %). On the other hand, the category less responsive to the survey has been the Public Authority, with 17 questionnaires coming from Germany, Italy, Romania, Sweden, The Netherlands and UK.

Fig. 1. Participation in the SLO survey per Country (a darker blue indicates a higher number of collected questionnaires). (Color figure online)

All the results obtained from the questionnaires have been integrated, analysed and discussed during three Workshop Cafés (WSC), held in three European countries in order to collect different opinions reflecting Member States' regulations and cultural business schemes in different geographical clusters.

The WSC were designed to elicit information and opinions from security experts, dividing the attendees into small groups and stimulating the discussion via open questions regarding what the SLO should be and which tasks he should perform in the European scenario.

Finally, the survey regarding the professional figure of the SLO has been completed with a series of interviews to different experts involved in the CIP, including Security Managers and Public Authorities representatives. The interviews provided the study with useful tips in order to identify the elements which discriminate the Security Liaison Officer tasks from those of the Security Manager or Chief Security Officer. These two positions are often assimilated in the field of Critical Infrastructure Protection and the EC Directive does not clarifies potential differences between these roles.

The following section will describe the results of the survey, taking into account both the findings obtained from the online questionnaires and the information collected during the Workshop Cafés.

3 Results

In this section the results of the study will be presented. Specifically, in Subsect. 3.1 a description of the overall approach towards security is emphasized; in Subsect. 3.2 the actual data describing the level of awareness regarding the European regulatory framework, perceptions and forecasts of the evolution of the professional figure of the SLO are reported.

3.1 Results on the Approach Towards Security

The first objective of the survey was to take a snapshot of the current scenario of the security management in Critical Infrastructures and how it is meant to evolve with the correct definition of the role of the SLO.

The first data to emphasize is that, according to the information collected within the survey, the interest for investments in the security field is expected to slightly increase in the next 5 years (Fig. 2). Given the current budgetary constraints within the EU and abroad, this continuing upward trend of funding is further evidence of the sizeable attention that security is garnering.

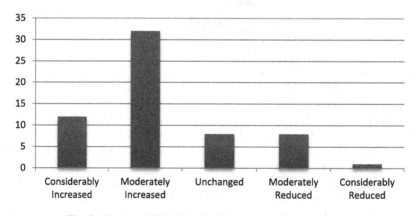

Fig. 2. Projected CI budget fluctuation over the next 5 years

The balanced approach towards security is further confirmed by the CSO category answers regarding resource allocation. From the related graph, one can notice that resources will be allocated quite uniformly on all the different aspects of the security domain. Similar indications also come from the answers provided by the other categories (Fig. 3).

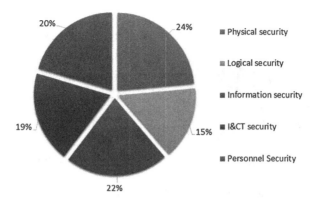

Fig. 3. Budget allocation declared by CSOs.

The data regarding the trend of the security investment is confirmed by the increase in the number of personnel of the security division in the last 5 years, in particular for CSO and security staff categories. PA register, on the other hand, no changes in the majority of cases (Fig. 4).

Fig. 4. Changes in the number of Security Personnel in the past 5 years

Aiming at understanding how to profile the SLO, the study considered important to analyze the composition of the organizations' security staff in terms of background. It allowed to understand how the security challenge is dealing with a large spectrum of issues. Indeed, even if 58 % of the CSOs have a former experience in the law enforcement, military or intelligence fields, the actual composition of a security team is more articulate, with a prevalence of competences in Computer Science, Business Administration and Engineering (Figs. 5 and 6). In fact, looking at educational experiences of the security staff, it is undeniable that the complexity of the security field imposes to complement the background of the team with technical, managerial and process-based competencies.

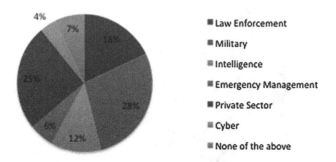

Fig. 5. Background of Chief Security Officers

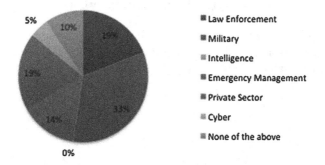

Fig. 6. Background of Security Officer Staff Members

The mentioned complexity of the field is proved, among other, by the fact that terrorist attacks, criminal behavior, and natural disasters are all elements that must be balanced into an effective protection equation. Consequently, it is becoming more and more reported a specific security education, such as minimum certifications and security

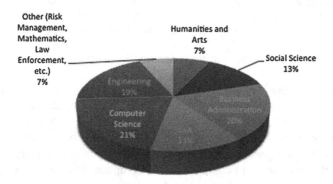

Fig. 7. Educational background of Security Team Members

awareness classes. Beyond this, the results of the survey indicate a heavy educational background in Business Management, Law, Engineering, and Computer Science, and not yet a specific security background (Fig. 7).

A final consideration useful to depict the current security scenario is the interest in different sectors of security. The data regarding the security team composition is a clue for understanding that the approach to the security is becoming more and more "all-hazards", looking at all types of threats and embedding also the safety issue. The results of the survey show that the attention paid to the different branches of security is very high for personnel, ICT, information and physical security. In particular, while personnel and physical security are almost considered important in the same percentage of responders across the different categories, it is interesting that responders coming from companies consider Information security the most important field, while PA and experts address mainly their attention to ICT security (Fig. 8).

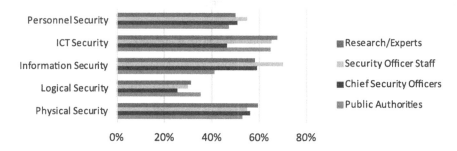

Fig. 8. Security fields requiring the most attention.

3.2 Results on Awareness of the European Regulatory Framework

The questionnaires provided by the study were also designed to understand how much organizations are aware of the European regulations and tools for Critical Infrastructure Protection.

The data collected demonstrate a moderate familiarity with the EPCIP programme [1] (less than 50 % of CSOs were aware of it, as showed in Fig. 9). The analysis regarding the CIWIN network [4] is even more resounding, being evaluated as "unknown", "not relevant" or simply unused by the majority of responders. This limited knowledge represents a partial contradiction with respect to the conclusions of the EU Commission Working Document SWD(2013)318 [2]. This discrepancy can be partially explained taking into account that the questionnaires were mainly oriented toward the private sector, while the primary customers for the EU Commission are the governments (notice that the PA involved in the questionnaire have a discrete knowledge of the programme).

Consequently, very few companies have a dedicated CIP office (Fig. 10). Notice that the Academia question was posed as *"should your organization have a dedicated CIP office"* hence it expresses a desiderata, while for the other categories it refers to an actual situation. It is interesting that there is a general sentiment which does not think it is necessary to have a dedicated CIP department inside a CI company.

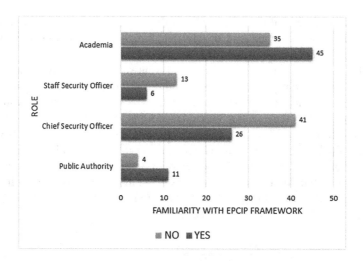

Fig. 9. Familiarity with EPCIP framework.

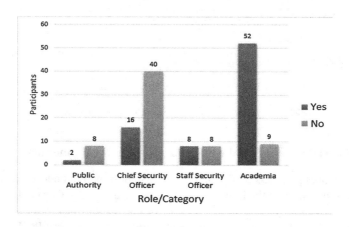

Fig. 10. Organizations having a dedicated CIP office.

It is also notably to remark what is the level of partnership initiatives between public and private sectors. Even though the transnational nature of the world today combined with an increased role of private actors has compounded the need for strong PPP, all

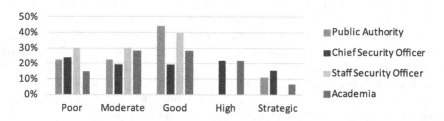

Fig. 11. Importance assigned to PPP projects regarding CIP activities

four categories demonstrate a moderate attention towards Public-Private Partnerships (PPP) within CIP (Fig. 11).

3.3   Results on the Professional Figure of the SLO

Regarding the figure of the Security Liaison Officer, and its relationship with the head of the security department, the analysis of the study emphasizes that there is still some ambiguities about the label used to describe the head of the security department, which is generally indicated as "Security Manager" or "Chief Security Officer". In Fig. 12 two responders qualified themselves as "Security Liaison Officer", from the category of Chief Security Officers and Security staff.

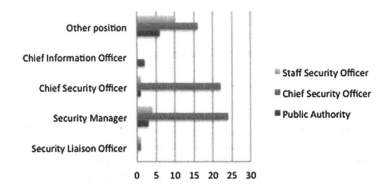

Fig. 12.   Answers to the question: *Your job description is referred to as:*

When asked directly regarding the figure of the SLO, the majority of the answers identified a good collocation inside the Security Department or as member of the Board of Directors: it is noteworthy that for the CSO these two positions have quite the same appeal, while Academia prefers the SLO to fall under a more technical level (Fig. 13).

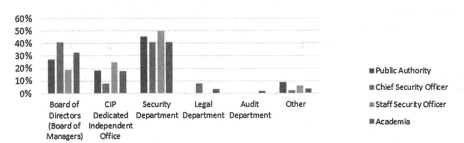

Fig. 13.   Who should the SLO belong to?

Similarly, the large majority of respondents concurred that the SLOs belong to a hierarchy where they report directly to the CEO or eventually to a CSO (Fig. 14). This conclusion was confirmed during the Workshop Cafés, whose participants overwhelmingly agreed that the SLO should have an executive level position or report directly to the CEO.

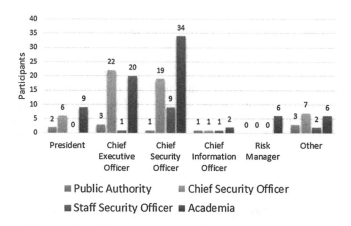

Fig. 14. Who should the SLO refer to?

WSC and interviews provided the survey with more details regarding the desiderata from the SLO profile. A great effort on this subject came from the WSC in Bucharest. Romania is the only European country where a Resolution of the Romanian Prime Minister defines the specific duties of the Security Liaison Officer [5].

According to most participants to the survey, the SLO must have the function of connecting not only structures (main reason of the "liaison" denomination), but also tasks and persons, playing a fundamental role to integrate the company activities and coordinating the personnel. The tasks attributed to the SLO figure are mainly carried out at a strategic level, thus the SLO is not appointed for an operational position. One of the most cogent opinions among the WSC attendees was that it is essential the Security Liaison Officer be aware and familiar with all the potential threats that threaten the organization and suggest solutions to the board who is entitled to make the final decision. The SLO must be able to communicate in all directions within the company and to connect all the divisions/departments. Additionally, they must also be in contact with the other Security Liaison Officers, authorities and law enforcement officers. The SLO must monitor events within their CI (with the intent to prevent incidents or crisis). Therefore the main role must be, therefore, a link between the organization and both the National and European Public Authorities and other Critical Infrastructures.

To complete these tasks, the SLO must be a person with good communication skills, able to motivate people, and in particular must have a strong commitment from the top management. In this perspective, being primarily a coordinator/facilitator able to effectively communicate inside and outside the organization, the SLO needs to be at a top management level into the company, referring preferably to the company board of directors. The SLO should in fact have experience in management, though not necessarily former experience in the law-enforcement or military field. However, the SLO should have a wide competence on his own organization and his sector, along with knowledge regarding other sectors, technologies and legislations in security matters, and a mandatory continuing training process should be aligned with context changes. During the WSC, also novel vulnerabilities stemming from the implementation of dramatically differing policies, particularly difficult for companies operating in many Member States, were analyzed [6].

Some of the participants believe that the requirement of a SLO figure must be stated by the authorities, and in this framework selected by the organization, while other opinions deal with the complete autonomy of the organization to choose a SLO. However, all the participants agreed on the need for an international standardization of the SLO professional profile that has to perform continuous learning in order to be constantly updated about technical and legislative frameworks.

4   Conclusions

The lack of regulatory references regarding the function and the characteristics of the SLO has led to the development of different dispositions in each European Member State. It is common opinion that there exists a strong motivation to establish a standard profile of the SLO figure, and to introduce a more cogent and specific regulation on the subject, in order to allow the cooperation of Security Liaison Officers of European Critical Infrastructures.

Six years after its release, Council Directive 2008/114/EC has only partially achieved its goals. It has certainly contributed to increase awareness about the intrinsic fragility of the complex system of systems and the need to identify innovative solutions and strategies capable of guaranteeing effective continuity for all-hazards approaches embracing the huge number of actual threats. However, as emphasized also by the Working Document of the European Commission, the current perception among the majority of stakeholders is that concrete improvement in European CIP as a result of the Directive 2008/114/EC has been minimal [7].

This can be explained by several reasons, starting from the complexity of the designation process, which is largely based on multi-lateral and sector-oriented criteria. Additionally, there exists a poor understanding of the effective obligations (and of the possible benefits) for the CI operators which, consequently, have generally adopted a very conservative position.

This lack of clearness is particularly evident for the figure of the Security Liaison Officer whose designation is mandatory for any European CI. The Directive does not provide any element to characterize such a professional figure. The absence of any requirement has facilitated an insecure situation where each MS, or even each CI, has adopted autonomous criteria; and this non-homogeneous situation represents a dangerous barrier for effective information sharing.

Analyzing the current EU legislative framework, it seems mandatory to supplement Council Directive 114/08 with voluntary measures to inter alia address the shortcomings of the current legal framework. All stakeholders, due to their flexibility and adaptability to special circumstances and sectorial specificities, see these enhanced voluntary measures in a positive light. However, it is highly desirable for the SLO figure to have a unified framework facilitating the definition of his role inside a company, his relationships with PA and other CIs, and to facilitate information sharing. In this way, the PA can participate in the process of designating a SLO inside CIs releasing guidelines and criteria for eligibility. Facilitating this process of standardization is the purpose of the analysis of data described in the present paper, helping understand the starting point and the desired target of a process leading to a clear definition of the professional profile of the Security Liaison Officer.

Acknowledgements. This work was partially supported by the European Commission, Directorate-General Home Affairs within the Specific Programme on "Prevention, Preparedness and Consequence Management of Terrorism and other Security-related risks" under Grant HOME/2012/CIPS/AG/4000003747 "SLO – Security Liaison Officer".

References

1. Communication from the Commission on a European Programme for Critical Infrastructure Protection (COM(2006) 786 final)
2. Commission Staff Working document on a new approach to the European Programme for Critical Infrastructure Protection Making European Critical Infrastructures more secure (SWD(2013) 318 final)
3. Council Directive 2008/114/EC of 8 December 2008 on the identification and designation of European critical infrastructures and the assessment of the need to improve their protection
4. Critical Infrastructure Warning Information Network * European Parliament legislative resolution of 22 April 2009 on the proposal for a Council decision on a Critical Infrastructure Warning Information Network (CIWIN) (COM(2008)0676 – C6-0399/2008 – 2008/0200(CNS))
5. Romanian Prime Minister Resolution N. 166 of 19 March 2013
6. SLO project Final Report. (www.coseritylab.it/News/Voci/2014/6/25_SLO_Project_Final_ Conference_files/SLO_FinalReport.pdf)
7. Study to support the preparation of the review of the council directive 2008/114/EC on the "identification and designation of European critical infrastructures (ECI) and the assessment of the need to improve their protection" contracting authority: European Commission; prepared by: Booz & Company GmbH - 05 March 2012

Identifying Critical Infrastructure Clusters via Spectral Analysis

Gabriele Oliva[1]($\boxtimes$), Stefano Panzieri[2], and Roberto Setola[1]

[1] Unit of Automatic, Department of Engineering, University Campus
Bio-Medico of Rome, Via A. del Portillo 21, 00128 Rome, Italy
{g.oliva,r.setola}@unicampus.it
[2] Department of Engineering, University Rome Tre,
Via della Vasca Navale 79, 00146 Rome, Italy
panzieri@dia.uniroma3.it

Abstract. In this paper we discuss how to identify groups composed of strictly dependent infrastructures or subsystems. To this end we suggest the use of spectral clustering methodologies, which allow to partition a set of elements in groups with strong intra-group connections and loose inter-group coupling. Moreover, the methodology allows to calculate in an automatic way a suitable number of subsets in which the network can be decomposed. The method has been applied to the Italian situation to identify, on the base of the Inoperability Input-Output model, which are the most relevant set of infrastructures. The same approach has been applied also to partition in a suitable way a network, as illustrated with respect to the IEEE 118 Bus Test Case electric grid.

Keywords: Spectral clustering · Critical-infrastructures · Laplacian matrix · Inoperability Input-Output Model

1 Introduction

In the literature a relevant effort has been spent in finding the most critical elements in a scenario composed of several tightly interconnected *Critical Infrastructures* or subsystems (see, among others, [1–3]). Traditional approaches focus on finding the single subsystems or infrastructures which are comparatively more vulnerable or critical to the whole system; however, to date, no satisfactory solution has been provided to find *critical groups* of elements or subsystems in the context of Critical Infrastructure protection. Indeed, the identification of highly clustered sets of infrastructures or elements may help understanding the complex relations that exist among the elements. Moreover, finding highly clustered groups from either a structural or functional point of view allows to identify the connections among such groups, which can be regarded as the "weak element of the chain"; such connections are often neglected or shaded by the high degree of coupling of some of the elements. In this paper, we show how to cluster groups of infrastructures or subsystems represented by a weighted graph (directed or

E. Rome et al. (Eds.): CRITIS 2015, LNCS 9578, pp. 223–235, 2016.
DOI: 10.1007/978-3-319-33331-1_18

undirected) so that the total weight of the links inside the group are large, while the weights of inter-cluster links are small; this is done by resorting to spectral clustering techniques [4,5].

We analyze two case studies with different scales and different levels of abstraction. Specifically, we apply the methodology to the Inoperability Input Output Model [6], in order to identify clusters of strongly interdependent economic sectors or infrastructures. Moreover, we investigate the structural and functional clustering of the IEEE 118 test bus case [7] and we analyze the robustness of the partitions obtained with respect to link removal.

The outline of the paper is as follows: after some preliminaries, in Sect. 2 we discuss the problem of clustering Critical Infrastructures, while in Sect. 3 we review the spectral clustering methodologies. Then, we provide our case studies in Sects. 4 and 5, while we draw some conclusions in Sect. 6.

1.1 Preliminaries

Let $diag(q_1, \ldots, q_n)$ be an $n \times n$ diagonal matrix whose diagonal entries are $q_1, \ldots, q_n$. The trace of a square matrix Q is

$$tr(Q) = \sum_{i=1}^{n} q_{ii}.$$

We denote by $|X|$ the number of elements in a set X and by $sign(x)$ the sign of $x \in \mathbb{R}$. Moreover, we denote by 1_m the vector in $\mathbb{R}^m$ whose components are all equal to 1.

Let $G = \{V, E, W\}$ be a *graph* with n nodes $V = \{v_1, v_2, \ldots, v_n\}$ and e edges $E \subseteq V \times V$, where $(v_i, v_j) \in E$ captures the existence of a link from node v_i to node v_j. The $n \times n$ matrix W is the *weighted adjacency matrix*, whose elements $w_{ij} \neq 0$ iff $(v_j, v_i) \in E$; w_{ij} is the *weight* of the edge (v_j, v_i) and can be regarded as the relative importance of the link in the graph. A weighted graph is said to be *undirected* if $(v_i, v_j) \in E$ whenever $(v_j, v_i) \in E$ and $w_{ij} = w_{ji}$, and is said to be *directed* otherwise. A *path* over a graph $G = \{V, E\}$, starting from a node $v_i \in V$ and ending in a node $v_j \in V$, is a subset of links in E that connects v_i and v_j without creating loops. A graph is *connected* if for each pair of nodes v_i, v_j there is a path over G that connects them without necessarily respecting the edge orientation, while it is *strongly connected* if the path respects the orientation of the edges. It follows that every undirected connected graph is also strongly connected. The *in-degree* d_i^{in} of a node v_i is the sum of the weight of its incoming edges, i.e., $d_i^{in} = \sum_{j=1}^{n} w_{ij}$, while the *out-degree* d_i^{out} is the number of its outgoing edges, i.e., $d_i^{out} = \sum_{j=1}^{n} w_{ji}$. For undirected graphs, it always holds that $d_i^{in} = d_i^{out}$, and in this case it is simply referred to as the *degree* d_i of node v_i. The *weighted Laplacian matrix* L of a graph G is given by

$$L = D - W,$$

where

$$D = diag(d_1^{in}, \ldots, d_n^{in}).$$

The eigenvalues of the Laplacian matrix are $0 = \lambda_1(L) \leq \lambda_2(L) \ldots \leq \lambda_n(L)$ and, in the undirected graph case, they are all real. Moreover, the multiplicity of the eigenvalue 0 coincides with the number of connected components of G, hence the multiplicity is 1 *iff* the graph G is connected. The rows of any laplacian matrix sum to zero, hence $\nu_1(L) = 1_n$ is an eigenvector associated to $\lambda_1(L) = 0$.

2   Critical Infrastructures and Clustering

As discussed in the previous section it is interesting to group infrastructures in order to create clusters characterized by a strong interrelation among elements belonging to the cluster and limited interaction with elements outside the cluster. To this end we can use the spectral clustering methodologies, whose aim is to decompose a network represented by a weighted graph into groups of nodes such that the total weight of the links inside the group is comparatively high, while the total weight of the links that connect different groups is comparatively low.

In Sect. 4 we suggest application of such methodologies to the clustering of economic sectors or infrastructures within the Inoperability Input-Output Model (IIM) [6].

The IIM is a linear model that captures the dependency and interdependency phenomena among several interdependent critical infrastructures or economic sectors. Such a dependency is considered from a high-level, holistic point of view, as each infrastructure is considered as a black box and the model focuses on the interaction among the infrastructures without inspecting their internal behavior.

For n infrastructures or sectors, the IIM model is given by

$$q = A^* q + c \Rightarrow q = (I - A^*)^{-1} c = Sc$$

where $q, c \in \mathbb{R}^n$ are the inoperability (e.g., percentage of malfunctioning) and perturbation (e.g., severity of a disaster or terroristic attack) vectors, respectively. Matrix A^* is the *first order dependency matrix*, and its elements a_{ij}^* represent the first-order (i.e., short-term) dependency of the i-th infrastructure or sector on the j-th one–the coefficient a_{ij}^* can be regarded as the fraction of inoperability of the i-th infrastructure which is transmitted to the i-th one in the immediate aftermath of a negative event.

Matrix A^* is obtained from input-output economic tables provided by several institutions such as WIOD, BEA, EUROSTAT, etc. (see [6,8] for the details on the derivation of A^*). Matrix S, conversely, is the *equilibrium interdependency matrix*, and s_{ij} represent the dependency of the i-th infrastructure on the j-th one taking into account also the domino and cascading effects that occur in the event of a perturbation.

Matrices A^* and S can be regarded, in general, as the weight matrices of (a complete) directed graph, whose nodes are the infrastructures or sectors. In this context, the spectral clustering methodology can be applied to detect groups of infrastructures/sectors that are strongly interdependent.

In Sect. 5, we identify clusters considering the topological structure of the Critical Infrastructures, e.g., the connections among equipment and subsystems. In this context, it is possible to cluster the network from a *structural* point of view, considering just the presence/absence of links, or from a *functional* point of view, taking into account also the flow of resources or goods among the elements.

Both the above applications are quite valuable, because they allows to identify which infrastructures are strongly coupled or to detect the fact that some of these groups are loosely coupled. Indeed the cut, i.e., the sum of the weights that connect two components, is a measure of the coupling among tightly dependent clusters. Such a measure can be used to complement key sector analyses [1,3], allowing to identify *key clusters*.

In the next section we provide a comprehensive review of the basic spectral clustering techniques.

3   Spectral Clustering

Let a graph $G = \{V, E, W\}$. We want to partition the nodes in the graph in K groups such that the weights of the links inside a group are large, while the weight of the links that cross the boundary of the group are small. Let us first consider the case of $K = 2$ groups A and $\overline{A}$ in the case of undirected graphs [4]. Then, we discuss the case for $K > 2$ assuming undirected graphs [5]. Finally, we show a way to extend these methodologies to the case of directed graphs [9], and we discuss a methodology for the choice of the number k of clusters [10,11].

3.1   2-Way Clustering for Undirected Graphs

The 2-*way Clustering problem* can be cast as a *Minimum-Cut* problem, where we want to minimize the *cut*

$$cut(A, \overline{A}) = \sum_{i \in A, j \in \overline{A}} w_{ij}.$$

The problem is easy to solve, and in the literature there are efficient algorithms [12,13]. However the partitions obtained in this way are typically not satisfactory, as a group might be composed of a single or few nodes.

If, further to minimizing the cut, we want to obtain balanced partitions, we need to solve the *Normalized Cut* problem [4], i.e., we need to minimize the function

$$Ncut(A, \overline{A}) = cut(A, \overline{A})\left(\frac{1}{vol(A)} + \frac{1}{vol(\overline{A})}\right)$$

where the volume $vol(A) = \sum_{i \in A} d_i$.

Let the set

$$\mathcal{X} = \{f \in \mathbb{R}^n | f_i \in \{a, b\}, a, b \in \mathbb{R}, a, b \neq 0\}.$$

In particular, if

$$f_i = \begin{cases} \frac{1}{vol(A)} & \text{if } i \in A, \\ -\frac{1}{vol(\overline{A})} & \text{if } i \in \overline{A}. \end{cases}$$

it holds

$$f^T L f = \sum_{ij} w_{ij}(f_i - f_j)^2 = \sum_{i \in A, j \in \overline{A}} w_{ij}\left(\frac{1}{vol(A)} + \frac{1}{vol(\overline{A})}\right)^2$$

and

$$f^T D f = \sum_j d_j f_j^2 = \sum_{i \in A} \frac{d_i}{vol(A)^2} + \sum_{j \in \overline{A}} \frac{d_j}{vol(\overline{A})^2} = \frac{1}{vol(A)} + \frac{1}{vol(\overline{A})}.$$

Therefore it holds

$$Ncut(A, \overline{A}) = \frac{f^T L f}{f^T D f}.$$

In [4] the normalized cut problem is shown to be equivalent to the following NP-hard optimization problem

$$\min f^T L f$$

$$\text{Subject to}$$
$$\begin{cases} f^T D f = 1 \\ f^T D 1_n = 0 \\ f \in \mathcal{X} \end{cases} \tag{1}$$

In order to provide a good approximated solution, we need to relax the constraint $f \in \mathcal{X}$, allowing f to be any nonzero vector in $\mathbb{R}^n$. Let $y = D^{1/2}f$, so that $f = D^{-1/2}y$. The relaxed problem can be formulated as

$$\min y^T L_{norm} y$$

$$\text{Subject to}$$
$$\begin{cases} y^T y = 1 \\ y^T D^{1/2} 1_n = 0 \end{cases} \tag{2}$$

where $L_{norm} = D^{-1/2} L D^{-1/2}$.

Since it holds $L 1_n = 0$, the vector $D^{1/2} 1_n$ is in the null-space of matrix L_{norm}. Notice that, by the *Rayleight-Ritz* theorem, the unconstrained problem

$$\min_{x \neq 0} \frac{x^T Q x}{x^T x}$$

is solved by choosing $x = \nu_1$ where $\nu_1(Q)$ is an eigenvector of Q with unit norm associated to the smallest eigenvalue $\lambda_1(Q)$. In the constrained case, however, since $\lambda_1(L_{norm}) = 0$ choosing a vector $y = \nu_1(L_{norm})$, for instance

$$y = \frac{D^{1/2} 1_n}{||D^{1/2} 1_n||}$$

would not satisfy the constraint $y^T D^{1/2} 1_n = 0$. According to the *Rayleight-Ritz* theorem, therefore, the optimal solution is obtained choosing $y = \nu_2(L_{norm})$. Notice that, for this choice of y the constraints are respected as $\nu_2(L_{norm})$ is orthogonal to $D^{1/2} 1_n$.

Let $\tilde{f} = D^{-1/2} \nu_2(L_{norm})$ be the solution of the relaxed problem. We need to find an admissible solution f to the original problem, given the approximated solution $\tilde{f}$. Notice that, since $\tilde{f}$ is nonzero and is orthogonal to $D^{-1/2} 1_n$, a vector with all positive entries, it must hold that $\tilde{f}$ has both positive and negative entries. A simple method to find an admissible solution for the original problem, therefore, is to select $f_i = sign(\tilde{f}_i)$ for all i, that is, to assign the nodes to the sets A and $\overline{A}$ based on the sign of the components $\tilde{f}_i$ of $\tilde{f}$.

Let us now discuss the k-way clustering for undirected graphs.

3.2 k-way Clustering for Undirected Graphs

In the k-*way Clustering* problem [5] we want to find a normalized cut for each of the k groups, i.e., we want to minimize

$$Ncut(A_1, \ldots, A_k) = \sum_{i=1}^{k} \frac{cut(A_i, \overline{A}_i)}{vol(A_i)}.$$

In this case we need to find $F = [f^1, \ldots, f^k] \in \mathbb{R}^{n \times k}$, where each $f^i \in \mathbb{R}^n$ represents the association of the nodes in V to the sets A_i and $\overline{A}_i = V - A_i$.

Notice that, for any $n \times n$ matrix Q it holds

$$\sum_{i=1}^{k} (f^i)^T Q f^i = tr(F^T Q F),$$

hence, extending the case $k = 2$ we get

$$Ncut(A_1, \ldots, A_k) = \sum_{i=1}^{k} \frac{(f^i)^T L f^i}{(f^i)^T D f^i} = \frac{tr(F^T L F)}{tr(F^T D F)}.$$

The fact that the sets $A_1, \ldots, A_k$ are pairwise disjoint can be imposed by introducing the constraint

$$(f^i)^T D f^j = 0, \quad \forall i, j = 1, \ldots, k; i \neq j,$$

or, equivalently $F^T D F = I$.

Further to that, we need to introduce the constraint that each vector f^i has at least one nonzero entry; this, combined with the above constraint, implies that each row i of F must have exactly one nonzero entry α_i. Therefore it holds

$$F^T 1_k = \left[n_1 \alpha_1, \ldots, n_k \alpha_k \right]^T$$

and

$$F^T F = diag\left(n_1 \alpha_1^2, \ldots, n_k \alpha_k^2 \right)$$

where n_i is the number of nodes in A_i. As a consequence, it holds

$$(F^T F)^{-1} F^T 1_k = \left[\frac{1}{\alpha_1}, \ldots, \frac{1}{\alpha_k}\right]^T$$

hence $F(F^T F)^{-1} F^T 1_k = 1_n$.

We can write the k-way clustering problem as

$$\min tr(F^T L F)$$

$$\text{Subject to}$$
$$\begin{cases} F^T D F = I \\ F(F^T F)^{-1} F^T 1_k = 1_n \\ F \in \mathcal{F} \end{cases} \tag{3}$$

where

$$\mathcal{F} = \left\{ [f^1, \ldots, f^k] \Big| f^i = a_i [f_1^i, \ldots f_n^i]^T, f_j^i \in \{0, 1\}, a_i \in \mathbb{R}, f^i \neq 0 \right\}.$$

Similarly to the 2-way problem we relax the problem by dropping the constraint $F \in \mathcal{F}$, and the optimal solution [5] is given by

$$\tilde{F} = D^{-1/2} [\nu_1(L_{norm}), \ldots, \nu_K(L_{norm})].$$

Differently from the case $k = 2$, however, it is not trivial to cast $\tilde{F}$ into an admissible solution for the original problem. In the literature several techniques are available. However it is common practice to consider the rows of $\tilde{F}$ as n observations $x_i \in \mathbb{R}^k$, i.e.,

$$\tilde{F} = [x_1, \ldots, x_n]^T.$$

These observations can be grouped by means of traditional data clustering algorithms such as the k-means algorithm [14].

3.3   Directed Graph

If the graph G is directed, the above techniques may fail [15]. In the literature, several methods [15–17] have been proposed to cast the laplacian matrix of a directed graph into a symmetric laplacian matrix that takes into account the original directed links.

Let us discuss the approach in [9], which results in simple computations. Such a method implicitly assumes that each node has both nonzero in-degree and nonzero out-degree.

Let us consider the *in-degree* and *out-degree* matrices D_i and D_o, defined as

$$D_i = diag(d_1^{in}, \ldots, d_n^{in}), \quad D_o = diag(d_1^{out}, \ldots, d_n^{out}).$$

In order to take into account both the in-degree and the out-degree of the nodes, in [9] the matrix $\Phi_{io} = (D_{in} D_{out})^{1/2}$ is introduced, and an undirected weight matrix is obtained as

$$W_{io} = \Phi_{io}^{-1/2}(W + W^T)\Phi_{io}^{-1/2}.$$

Then, the spectral clustering is applied to the laplacian matrix L_{io} obtained from W_{io} instead of W, i.e., $L_{io} = D_{io} - W_{io}$, where D_{io} is the diagonal matrix whose entries are equal to the sum of the row of W_{io}.

To conclude this section, let us discuss a way to chose automatically the value of k.

3.4 Automatic Choice of k

The true weak point of any clustering technique is that the number k of clusters must be specified by the user, which must have some a priori information on the structure of the graph in order to select a suitable number of clusters.

In the case of spectral clustering, however, we can use a simple, yet powerful heuristic approach to derive k automatically [10,11]. Specifically, we choose the value k that maximizes the *eigengap* of the laplacian matrix L_{norm}, i.e.,

$$k = \arg \max_{i=2...,n} \{|\lambda_k(L_{norm}) - \lambda_{k-1}(L_{norm})|\}.$$

An intuitive explanation for this choice comes from the fact that, in the ideal case of k completely disconnected clusters, the eigenvalue 0 has multiplicity k, and there is a relevant gap between the k-th and $(k+1)$-th eigenvalues of L_{norm}. Analogously, when the graph is composed of k densely clusters and the clusters are linked via links with small total weights, the eigengap is likely to reach its maximum at k.

4 Case Study 1: Inoperability Input-Output Model

The spectral clustering methodology has been used to identify the groups of most relevant infrastructures. To this end, we consider the Italian Inoperability Input-Output Model (IIM) [6] composed of 35 sectors (as listed in Table 1), based on the economic input-output data provided by WIOD for Italy in 2008 [8]; for space issues we do not report the coefficients of the matrices A^* and S (the interested reader can access the dataset at http://www.wiod.org/).

Matrices A^* and S can be seen as weight matrices of complete directed graphs (i.e., although complete, they are not symmetric, hence we resort to the approach discussed in Sect. 3.3). In this case study, therefore, we cluster the infrastructures/sectors, based on these weights, in order to capture the structure of the system of systems with respect to the first order dependencies (A^*) or with respect to higher-order dependencies at the equilibrium(S).

In both cases, the clustering yields quite few partitions ($k = 5$ partitions for the A^* case, $k = 2$ for the S matrix); also, such partitions have quite different

Table 1. Infrastructures/sectors considered in the example. Source: WIOD [8] (http://www.wiod.org/)

#	Denomination
1	Agriculture, Hunting, Forestry and Fishing
2	Mining and Quarrying
3	Food, Beverages and Tobacco
4	Textiles and Textile Products
5	Leather, Leather and Footwear
6	Wood and Products of Wood and Cork
7	Pulp, Paper, Paper, Printing and Publishing
8	Coke, Refined Petroleum and Nuclear Fuel
9	Chemicals and Chemical Products
10	Rubber and Plastics
11	Other Non-metallic Mineral
12	Basic Metals and Fabricated Metal
13	Machinery, Nec
14	Electrical and Optical Equipment
15	Transport Equipment
16	Manufacturing, Nec; Recycling
17	Electricity, Gas and Water Supply
18	Construction
19	Sale, Maintenance and Repair of Motor Vehicles and Motorcycles; Retail Sale of Fuel
20	Wholesale Trade and Commission Trade, Except of Motor Vehicles and Motorcycles
21	Retail Trade, Except of Motor Vehicles and Motorcycles; Repair of Household Goods
22	Hotels and Restaurants
23	Inland Transport
24	Water Transport
25	Air Transport
26	Other Supporting and Auxiliary Transport Activities; Activities of Travel Agencies
27	Post and Telecommunications
28	Financial Intermediation
29	Real Estate Activities
30	Renting of M&Eq and Other Business Activities
31	Public Admin and Defence; Compulsory Social Security
32	Education
33	Health and Social Work
34	Other Community, Social and Personal Services

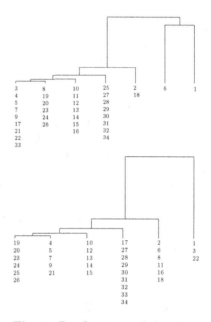

Fig. 1. Dendrograms of the clusters obtained by iterated spectral clustering over matrix A^* (upper plot) and S (lower plot).

dimensions. In the case of the A^* matrix a single partition contains 26 out of 34 elements, and the while in the case of matrix S a cluster contains 31 sectors, and the other one just 3 sectors (strictly related to food/tourism). Therefore, unless for few isolated infrastructures or small groups, in the proposed scenario the infrastructures are indeed interdependent and hard to separate, especially for the equilibrium case (Fig. 1).

In order to gain further insights on the structure of the System of Systems, we iterate the spectral clustering several times. At each iteration, we select the elements that belong to the group with smallest cardinality and remove the corresponding rows/columns from A^* or S. Iterating this procedure we obtain a hierarchical decomposition of the infrastructures/sectors, as summarized by the dendrograms depicted in Fig. 3. Specifically, the upper figure shows the results for A^*, while the lower figure shows the hierarchy obtained by considering S. For each plot, the identifiers of the sectors belonging to each cluster are reported.

Notice that, while for the A^* case we obtain in general more than 2 clusters, for matrix S we obtain $k = 2$ groups at each iteration. It can be noted that, in the first-order dependency case, the iterative decomposition yields initially (from the right to the left) clusters with very few elements (the first cluster contains just sector 1, and the second one just sector 6), implying that all other sectors are strongly interrelated. In the equilibrium case, conversely, the first clusters have higher cardinality, implying a stronger polarization in the infrastructures; again, sector 1, and sector 6, belong to the first and second cluster, respectively, but in this case other related sectors join them (the first group is composed of 3 food-related sectors, while the second group contains 6 groups somehow related to mining).

Notice that, according to the dendrogram, while there is a relevant rift between the first group and the other groups, the "distance" between the i-th group and the subsequent ones tends to reduce as the number of iterations grow.

5   Case Study 2: Power Network

In this section we consider the graph G that models the topology of the IEEE 118 Bus Test Case [7], a portion of the American Electric Power System (in the Midwestern US); specifically, we consider $n = 118$ nodes and $e = 179$ links. In this example, we consider both the network with unit weights and the network whose weights are given by the absolute value of the power flow, obtained by executing the DC Power Flow algorithm by means of the MATPOWER software package [18].

Figure 2 shows the results of the application of the k-way spectral clustering algorithm. In the upper-left plot we show the results for the k-way spectral clustering algorithm where k is the index that maximizes the eigengap, considering the network structure (i.e., using unitary weights). In the upper-right plot, instead, the links are weighted with the absolute value of the power flow. In each figure, the clusters obtained are shown by means of the convex hulls of the nodes that belong to the cluster, using different colors.

It can be of interest to analyze the robustness of the above partitions with respect to network malfunctioning. To this end in the lower plots of Fig. 2 we report the results obtained when a link is removed (the removed link is highlighted in the lower-left picture). It can be noted that in both cases there are significative changes in the clusters, due to the removal of the edge. In the unit

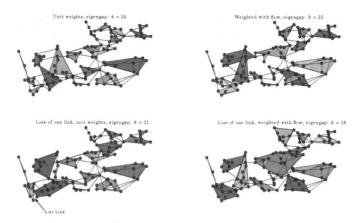

Fig. 2. Example of application of k-way spectral clustering to the IEEE 118 Bus Test Case [7].

weight case, such changes are more evident in the zone close to the removed link, but some changes occur all over the network. When we consider the power flow, instead, significative changes occur all over the graph (two partitions are merged in the zone near the removed node, and the partitions in the central and upper left zone of the figure undergo relevant changes).

To complement the above analysis, we show in Fig. 3 the distribution of the number of clusters obtained when a single link is removed. Specifically, we calculate the clustering several times, each time removing a different link, and we show the frequency in percentage of the number of clusters obtained. In the leftmost plot we show the case for unitary weights, while in the rightmost plot we show the results for the case where the links are weighted with the flow. It can be noted that, in both cases, there is a high variability of the number of clusters, although we have a clear peak at 19 clusters for the unit weights case and at 13 clusters at the flow-weighted case. These results suggest that, in both the structural (e.g., unit weights) and functional (flow) perspectives, the most tightly interconnected clusters may vary remarkably depending on the condition

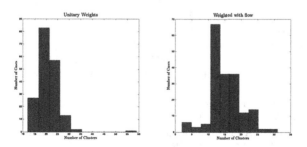

Fig. 3. Frequency of the number of clusters in the case of all possible single edge losses.

of the infrastructure. These analyses can be used as a tool to support the design of islanding zones [19] in smart grids. Moreover, the fact that removing some edges produces a large change in the eigengap (for example in the unit weight case removing a particular edge the number of clusters becomes 57) has to be further investigated to better capture the role of such edges in the network.

6   Conclusions

In this paper we discuss the applicability of spectral clustering techniques to the domain of Critical Infrastructures, considering the hierarchical clustering of infrastructure sections and the structural and functional clustering of the IEEE 118 test bus case. Future work will be devoted to define a set of indicators of the relative importance of the clusters, as well as the derivation of a metric to quantify the importance of the connections among the clusters.

References

1. Chenery, H.B., Watanabe, T.: International comparisons of the structure of production. Econom. J. Econom. Soc. **26**, 487–521 (1958)
2. Setola, R.: How to measure the degree of interdependencies among critical infrastructures. Int. J. Syst. Syst. Eng. **2**(1), 38–59 (2010)
3. Oliva, G., Setola, R., Barker, K.: Fuzzy importance measures for ranking key interdependent sectors under uncertainty. IEEE Trans. Reliab. **63**(1), 42–57 (2014)
4. Shi, J., Malik, J.: Normalized cuts and image segmentation. IEEE Trans. Pattern Anal. Mach. Intell. **22**(8), 888–905 (2000)
5. Yu, S.X., Shi, J.: Multiclass spectral clustering. In: Proceedings of Ninth IEEE International Conference on Computer Vision, pp. 313–319. IEEE (2003)
6. Haimes, Y.Y., Horowitz, B.M., Lambert, J.H., Santos, J.R., Lian, C., Crowther, K.G.: Inoperability input-output model for interdependent infrastructure sectors. i: Theory and methodology. J. Infrastruct. Syst. **11**(2), 67–79 (2005)
7. Christie, R.D.: IEEE power systems test case archive. Department of Electrical Engineering, University of Washington, Seattle, June 1999. http://ee.washington. edu/research/pstca
8. Timmer, M.P., Dietzenbacher, E., Los, B., Stehrer, R., Vries, G.J.: An illustrated user guide to the world input-output database: the case of global automotive production. Rev. Int. Econ. **23**(3), 575–605 (2015)
9. Mirzal, A., Furukawa, M.: Eigenvectors for clustering: unipartite, bipartite, and directed graph cases. In: International Conference on Electronics and Information Engineering (ICEIE), vol. 1, pp. V1-303–V1-309. IEEE (2010)
10. Chung, F.R.: Spectral Graph Theory, vol. 92. American Mathematical Society, Washington, DC (1997)
11. Mohar, B.: Some applications of Laplace eigenvalues of graphs. Graph Symmetry. Springer, The Netherlands (1997)
12. Hao, J., Orlin, J.B.: A faster algorithm for finding the minimum cut in a directed graph. J. Algorithms **17**(3), 424–446 (1994)
13. Levine, M.S.: Experimental study of minimum cut algorithms (1997)

14. MacQueen, J. et al.: Some methods for classification and analysis of multivariate observations. In: Proceedings of the Fifth Berkeley Symposium on Mathematical Statistics and Probability, vol. 1, pp. 281–297 (1967)
15. Kim, Y., Son, S.-W., Jeong, H.: Community identification in directed networks. In: Zhou, J. (ed.) Complex 2009. LNICST, vol. 5, pp. 2050–2053. Springer, Heidelberg (2009)
16. Leicht, E.A., Newman, M.E.: Community structure in directed networks. Phys. Rev. Lett. **100**(11), 118703 (2008)
17. Kim, Y., Son, S.-W., Jeong, H.: Finding communities in directed networks. Phys. Rev. E **81**(1), 016103 (2010)
18. Zimmerman, R.D., Murillo-Sánchez, C.E., Thomas, R.J.: Matpower: steady-state operations, planning, and analysis tools for power systems research and education. IEEE Trans. Power Syst. **26**(1), 12–19 (2011)
19. Bower, W., Ropp, M.: Evaluation of islanding detection methods for utility-interactive inverters in photovoltaic systems. Sandia report SAND, vol. 3591, p. 2002 (2002)

Selected Short Papers

Access Control in a Port – A GeoRBAC Approach

Eneko Olivares[1(✉)], Benjamín Molina[1], Carlos E. Palau[1], Manuel Esteve[1],
Miguel A. Portugués[2], and Alejandro García-Serrano[2]

[1] Universitat Politècnica de València, Valencia, Spain
{enolgor,benmomo,cpalau,mesteve}@upvnet.upv.es
[2] InfoPort Valencia (IPV), Valencia, Spain
{maportugues,agserrano}@infoportvalencia.es

Abstract. Access Control mechanisms are nowadays mandatory to guarantee a minimum level of security in physical or logical environments. Different attributes can be used to grant access to users. In critical infrastructures individual position of users and devices is a clear alternative or complement. GeoRBAC is an extension of the Role Based Access Control (RBAC) mechanism that considers the position as another condition when performing access control decisions. In this paper we propose a real implementation and deployment of a GeoRBAC system integrated in the ICT infrastructure of a port, using OGC Sensor Web Enablement (SWE) set of standards to allow geolocation information interoperability.

Keywords: Access control mechanisms · Location-based services · Security · Transport and logistics

1 Introduction

One of the key security aspects of any critical infrastructure (either logical or physical) to preserve security is access control, because it concerns how users can access resources in those infrastructures. It is understood as the protection of the resources of an infrastructure through a process that decides their access rights, regulated by a security policy. Different access control mechanisms have been proposed in the literature related to CIs (Critical Infrastructures) protection; however access control mechanisms considering geolocation improve security, because a user's location is correlated to the access rights he is entitled to [3].

The proposed access control system is based on the GeoRBAC model, and has been tested in the premises of a CI (i.e. the Port of Valencia).

This paper is structured as follows: Sect. 2 presents an outline of the system work. Section 3 describes the system and its main functionality. The chapter ends with the conclusions and further work.

© Springer International Publishing Switzerland 2016
E. Rome et al. (Eds.): CRITIS 2015, LNCS 9578, pp. 239–242, 2016.
DOI: 10.1007/978-3-319-33331-1_19

2 Outline of the System

The system was originally designed to fit in a specific port environment, which currently uses a Port Community System (PCS) to exchange and manage all data of the different organizations working in the port. Our system integrates with the PCS to retrieve all required data (users, roles, operations and permission sets) and store it on a separate database. The core of the system is a Complex Event Processor (CEP) that performs all different access control decisions, generating the corresponding messages and alerts of the different access control events, sending them to the management interface.

In order to retrieve real-time information about the position of the tracked users, a SOS (Sensor Observation Service) server was used as intermediary to collect and store every location device positions. The SOS is part of the Sensor Web Enablement standards and defines the web interface of a service that provides methods to perform CRUD (Create, Read, Update and Delete) actions of sensors and data provided by them [1, 2].

In the port environment the SOS collects all data regarding location of vehicles, people and tracked containers. Some of this location data comes from the PCS and some is collected directly from tracking devices.

3 Design and Development

The system has been mainly designed for outdoor environments, although it could be easily adapted for indoor cases with proper indoor positioning. The main features of GeoRBAC have been implemented (role-schemas, spatial-roles, fully OGC compliant) whereas others are missing for simplicity reasons (role hierarchies, user assignments, activation between roles and granularity) [4]. Furthermore, some features not defined as part of the GeoRBAC model were added in order to create a globally functional system (policy administration and policy integration).

3.1 Description of the GeoRBAC Implementation

The design of the system is modular, where different components can be attached to the core through adapters. In core includes the Complex Event Processor that is in charge of making access control decisions based on defined rules.

In order to determine if a particular user is inside or outside a zone the CEP uses geo-fencing algorithms. As every boundary can be modelled as a polygon, the Point In Polygon (PIP) algorithm is used, since it is independent of the units used.

Rules, users, roles, bounded areas and registered devices are fed into the core by a database. The database engine (preferably relational) is totally independent of the system, and different adapters are provided to unify the output format of the data in a common interface accessible from a Data Access Object (DAO).

The location data is received from a collector where it is possible to define different position sources (depending on the device that retrieves positioning data). The collector receives data in the same units as the defined zone boundaries for all the different sources, so an intermediate layer of conversion has to be defined if the position source feeds location data in a different unit.

There is a distinction between the user and the device that provides the position of the user (so every device can be easily replaced or reused). To achieve this, every device should have a unique identifier and be associated to a user.

The last core component is in charge of receiving and forwarding access control decisions, logging data and positioning data. Different receptors can be registered to receive all or specific types of messages so whenever any component triggers an action that generates a new message this will be forwarded to the corresponding receptor.

Every component that has to establish an outside communication (e.g. database server connector or all the position sources that are not simulated) is completely free to choose its own security layer, if any. In this way, simple components that don't need a security layer (e.g. behind a proxy inside a trusted network that handles security issues) are easier to implement and components that require specific configurations will handle its own security layer (e.g. specific SSL trusted chains).

In the following images the GeoRBAC mechanism are illustrated in the use case environment (Fig. 1), with the different building components (Fig. 2).

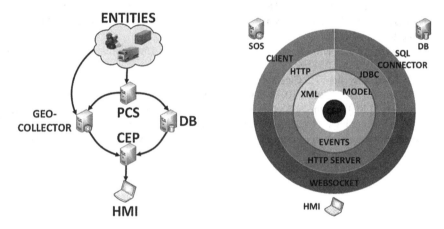

Fig. 1. General overview of the system   **Fig. 2.** Detailed GeoRBAC implementation

4   Conclusions and Future Work

The presented GeoRBAC proposal has been successfully implemented in the Valencian port system for a pilot. Although there were some features not initially implemented, in subsequent iterations this was resolved.

Some features of the Prox-RBAC model [5] were also added, such as the transmission of permissions, but only under certain circumstances.

In order to increase the interoperability with other systems, everything that had to be geometrically described such as positions (points) or zone boundaries (polygons) was defined under the OGC standards. The SWE also normalizes the interfaces for accessing sensor information and hence increases interoperability.

The system has been thoroughly tested aiming for a ready-to-use and functional service in a production environment such as a port. For this purpose, a lot of effort went into increasing the usability of the system; making a simple and clear interface to configure the server reduces the possibility of human error that could potentially lead to a security hole.

As for future work and extension points of the system, the main features that the system lacks and will be covered in future iterations are role hierarchies, multiple operations and different granularity levels.

Acknowledgment. The work in this paper has been partially funded by CELTIC ACIO: Access Control In Organizations, co-funded by the Ministry of Industry (AEESD - TSI-100201-2013-50); and H2020 DORA: Door to Door Information for Airports and Airlines (H2020-MG 635885).

References

1. Sensor Observation Service (SOS), Open Geospatial Consortium (OGC). http://www.opengeospatial.org/standards/sos. Accessed May 2013
2. Giménez, P., Molina, B., Palau, C.E., Esteve, M.: Sensor web simulation and testing for the IoT. In: IEEE International Conference on Systems, Man, and Cybernetics (IEEE SMC 2013), Manchester, October 2013
3. Ferraiolo, D.F., Kuhn, D.R.: Role-based access controls. In: 15th National Computer Security Conference, pp. 554–563 (1992)
4. Damiani, M.L., Bertino, E., Catania, B., Perlasca, P.: GeoRBAC: a spatially aware RBAC. ACM Trans. Inf. Syst. Secur. 10(1) (2007). Article 2
5. Kirkpatrick, M.S., Damiani, M.L., Bertino, E.: Prox-RBAC: a proximity-based spatially aware RBAC. In: Proceedings of the 19th ACM SIGSPATIAL International Conference on Advances in Geographic Information Systems, GIS 2011, pp. 339–348. ACM, New York (2011)

"Water, Water, Every Where": Nuances for a Water Industry Critical Infrastructure Specification Exemplar

Shamal Faily[1(✉)], George Stergiopoulos[2], Vasilios Katos[1], and Dimitris Gritzalis[2]

[1] Bournemouth University, Poole, UK
{sfaily,vkatos}@bournemouth.ac.uk
[2] Athens University of Economics and Business, Athens, Greece
dgrit@aueb.gr

Abstract. The water infrastructure is critical to human life, but little attention has been paid to the nuances of the water industry. Without such attention, evaluating security innovation in this domain without compromising the productivity goals when delivering water services is difficult. This paper proposes four nuances that need to be incorporated into a representative specification exemplar for the water industry; these provided input to the exemplar based on a fictional water company.

Keywords: Critical infrastructure · Specification exemplars

1 Introduction

The water infrastructure is one infrastructure we cannot do without. Despite the citing of water industry vulnerabilities as a motivation for critical infrastructure protection [1], there has been little work considering the nuances of this sector. As such, it is implicitly assumed that addressing security issues in one form of critical infrastructure effectively addresses the issues in all others. There are, however, many reasons why this may not be the case.

Previous work like [2] proposed security innovation in the water industry, but is premised on scenarios associated with the distribution of clean water only. However, threats in the quality of water distribution have also been identified due to loss of pressurised water, aging infrastructure, as well as vulnerabilities in interdependent infrastructure [3–5]. While case studies provide a means of disseminating nuances to the broader research and practitioner communities,it would be useful to share such insights using a format suitable for evaluating new innovation by researchers, or products and services by practitioners.

Specification exemplars are self-contained, informal descriptions of a problem in some application domain, and are designed to capture the harshness of reality [6]. They are designed to advance a single research effort, promote research and understanding among multiple researchers, and contribute to the advancement of software development practice. They should exhibit the "messy" nature

© Springer International Publishing Switzerland 2016
E. Rome et al. (Eds.): CRITIS 2015, LNCS 9578, pp. 243–246, 2016.
DOI: 10.1007/978-3-319-33331-1_20

of the real-world, but such messiness is difficult to elicit without actual case study data; commercial confidentiality concerns often impede access to such data. Specification exemplars also focus on modelling functional concerns, but many nuances related to human issues are not so easily modelled. For example, previous work has suggested that the tensions that exist between security and safety can be addressed by designing security that 'Homer Simpson' can use [7]. However, trivialising all critical infrastructure users in such a way fails to consider how their skills and expertise are brought to bear when solving difficult, but not unrealistic, operational challenges.

In this paper we propose four nuances that need to be incorporated into a representative specification exemplar for the water industry. We present these nuances in Sect. 2, and briefly summarise their implications in Sect. 3.

2   Water Industry Nuances

We examined the empirical data from two previous studies designing security for the water industry [8,9]; this data included 11 contextual interview transcripts, 4 facilitated workshop transcripts, and a variety of photographs taken during several site visits. Following this review of case study data, four types of nuances that need to be incorporated into a specification exemplar were identified.

2.1   Organisational Nuances

To many people, water companies are predominantly concerned with the supply of clean (drinking) water. However, in many cases, water companies are also concerned with the infrastructure associated with distributing and treating waste water as well. At first blush, waste water issues may not appear security critical, but there are obvious environmental implications if poorly treated water is inadvertently pumped into waterways. Similarly, accidental or deliberate harm to terminal pumping stations can pose a flooding risk to residential or commercial properties in the vicinity of waste water treatment plants, together with the health risks that this entails.

Like many other firms, water companies are also under pressure to save money and reduce energy consumption. As a result, water companies carry out internal projects to optimise equipment in order to reduce energy consumption. However, there can be tensions because the drive to save energy and money might lead to elaborate and unpredictable changes to process operations. If not carefully managed, such changes might lead to human error if changes made by technicians are complex, or violations in order to save time or achieve goals deemed more important than security. Such errors and violations can be source of latent failures which, over time, can contribute to catastrophic failures [10].

2.2   Operational Nuances

A water company depends on the skills and expertise of the people that run it. The operations and goals associated with plant operators and technicians can vary based on a variety of contextual conditions such as geographical locale, time of day, or even the season of the year; these conditions may truncate or extend activities, and practices are shaped around these different conditions. For example, plant operators may be called away to fix problems around a site depending on the availability of other staff and, depending on the site, may be required to carry out remedial activities associated with other roles, such as taking water samples to check agreed water quality criteria are met.

The use of technology for what appears to be innocuous physical artifacts is also shaped to satisfy operational requirements in such a way that they become key assets. While not normally considered a critical device, TVs in control rooms are often used to check weather reports to determine whether it was necessary to pump water from reservoirs to treatment sites. Security practices are also shaped around operational needs as well with default account logout times sometimes timed to correspond with shift hours, and information – ranging from contact phone numbers to Chlorine levels – is often written on whiteboards in control rooms; these whiteboards act as the collective memory for plant staff. Consequently, such settings can be modified without it being obvious who might have made the changes, and how warranted they might be.

2.3   Environmental Nuances

Unlike electricity, water cannot simply be turned off. A water company's infrastructure might support a large geographical region, with water pumped over 40 miles to the plant that treats it; this necessitates a large estate of supporting infrastructure to control water flow, and satisfy agreed water quality standards. After a prolonged period of hot weather, settlement can build up in the waste water distribution system; if the weather suddenly changes, this settlement can hit the treatment works at once and, if flow is obstructed, can lead to downstream flooding. The quality of water can also change in less than an hour due to weather conditions, and quality can be further exacerbated by accidents such as oil tanker spills. Automated monitoring plays an important role in monitoring clean or waste water quality, but so does human intervention and the ability to spot changes that appear unusual. As Sect. 2.1 illustrates, undertaking these processes can become error prone depending on the precise context in which any intervention takes place.

2.4   Physical Security and Safety Nuances

As important as cybersecurity is, the most pressing concern faced by many stakeholders are day-to-day physical security and safety issues. These include threats associated with the theft of metal parts for scrap. The form such attacks can take are myriad, and include theft of gates and fencing, and the damage of associated infrastructure – such as power lines – to get at copper earth connectors. Petty theft is also a concern due to externalities that might be introduced as a result. For example, the value of a stolen PC is insignificant compared to the overall impact on the infrastructure that is no longer being monitored or maintained as a result. These physical security issues also have a personal impact on stakeholders like technicians and plant operators. Plant operators working alone at night might be apprehensive about confronting scrap metal thieves, particularly if the plant is located in a remote location. This impacts how they might choose to respond to an alarm, and how they might carry out any remedial action.

3   Conclusion

This paper has presented four nuances that need to be incorporated into a representative specification exemplar for the water industry. In analysing pre-existing case study material, we have identified several classes of nuance with the potential to impact security in water companies. This impact might result from the direct loss of a physical asset, or from latent failures resulting from excessive physical and mental effort by plant operators or technicians. A limitation of this work is that these nuance classes may be specific to the water domain. We are, however, currently analysing case study data within the rail sector to see if such nuance classes are applicable there. We developed a specification exemplar for a fictional water company that encapsulates the nuances described. Further details and an evaluation of this exemplar will be described in future work.

References

1. Slay, J., Miller, M.: Lessons learned from the maroochy water breach. In: Goetz, E., Shenoi, S. (eds.) Critical Infrastructure Protection. IFIP Advances in Information and Communication Technology, vol. 253, pp. 73–82. Springer, Heidelberg (2008)
2. Eliades, D.G., Polycarpou, M.M.: Security of water infrastructure systems. In: Setola, R., Geretshuber, S. (eds.) CRITIS 2008. LNCS, vol. 5508, pp. 360–367. Springer, Heidelberg (2009)
3. Van Leuven, L.J.: Water/wastewater infrastructure security: threats and vulnerabilities. In: Clark, R.M., Hakim, S., Ostfeld, A. (eds.) Handbook of Water and Wastewater Systems Protection. Springer, Heidelberg (2011)
4. Van Eeten, M., Nieuwenhuijs, A., Luiijf, E., Klaver, M., Cruz, E.: The state and the threat of cascading failure across critical infrastructures: the implications of empirical evidence from media incident reports. Public Adm. **89**(2), 381–400 (2011)
5. Kotzanikolaou, P., Theoharidou, M., Gritzalis, D.: Assessing n-order dependencies between critical infrastructures. IJCIS **9**(1/2), 93–110 (2013)
6. Feather, M.S., Fickas, S., Finkelstein, A., van Lamsweerde, A.: Requirements and specification exemplars. Autom. Softw. Eng. **4**(4), 419–438 (1997)
7. Anderson, R., Fuloria, S.: Security economics and critical national infrastructure. In: Moore, T., Pym, D.J., Ioannidis, C. (eds.) Economics of Information Security and Privacy, pp. 55–66. Springer, Heidelbrg (2010)
8. Faily, S., Fléchais, I.: Towards tool-support for usable secure requirements engineering with CAIRIS. Int. J. Secur. Softw. Eng. **1**(3), 56–70 (2010)
9. Faily, S., Fléchais, I.: User-centered information security policy development in a post-stuxnet world. In: Proceedings of the 6th International Conference on Availability, Reliability and Security, pp. 716–721 (2011)
10. Reason, J.: Human Error. Cambridge University Press, Cambridge (1990)

On Robustness in Multilayer Interdependent Networks

Joydeep Banerjee$^{(\boxtimes)}$, Chenyang Zhou, Arun Das, and Arunabha Sen

School of Computing, Informatics and Decision System Engineering,
Arizona State University, Tempe, AZ 85287, USA
{joydeep.banerjee,czhou24,arun.das,asen}@asu.edu

Abstract. Critical Infrastructures like power and communication networks are highly interdependent on each other for their full functionality. Many significant research have been pursued to model the interdependency and failure analysis of these interdependent networks. However most of these models fail to capture the complex interdependencies that might actually exist between the infrastructures. The *Implicative Interdependency Model* that utilizes Boolean Logic to capture complex interdependencies was recently proposed which overcome the limitations of the existing models. A number of problems were studied based on this model. In this paper we study the *Robustness* problem in Interdependent Power and Communication Network. The robustness is defined with respect to two parameters $K \in I^+ \cup \{0\}$ and $\rho \in (0, 1]$. We utilized the *Implicative Interdependency Model* to capture the complex interdependencies between the two networks. The problem is solved using an Integer Linear Program and the solution is used to study the robustness of power and communication interdependent network of Maricopa County, Arizona, USA.

Keywords: Implicative Interdependency Model · Interdependent networks · Robustness

1 Introduction

Critical infrastructures (or networks) of a nation are heavily interdependent on each other for their full functionality. Two such infrastructures that engage in a heavy symbiotic dependency are the power and communication networks. For analysis of these infrastructures it is imperative to model their interdependencies. A number of such models have been proposed [2–4,6]. However, most of these models fail to account for the complex interdependencies between the networks [1]. In [5] the authors described the need to address complex interdependencies. They introduce a model (*Implicative Interdependency Model* (IIM)) that capture the interdependencies using boolean logic. We use the (IIM) model to study the *"Robustness"* problem in interdependent power and communication network. An Integer Linear Program (ILP) is provided for the problem. The ILP is used to analyze the robustness of power and communication network of Maricopa County, Arizona, USA.

© Springer International Publishing Switzerland 2016
E. Rome et al. (Eds.): CRITIS 2015, LNCS 9578, pp. 247–250, 2016.
DOI: 10.1007/978-3-319-33331-1_21

2   Problem Formulation

An Interdependent Network (IDN) is represented as $\mathcal{I}(A, B, \mathcal{F}(A, B))$ where A is the set of power entities, B is the set of communication entities and the function $\mathcal{F}(A, B)$ captures the interdependencies between the two networks. The IIM model is described by an example. Consider $A = \{a_1, a_2\}$ and $B = \{b_1, b_2, b_3\}$ and $\mathcal{F}(A, B)$ consisting of the relations $a_1 \leftarrow b_1 + b_2 b_3$, $b_1 \leftarrow a_1 a_2$ and $b_2 \leftarrow a_2$. The dependency or relation is termed as *Implicative Interdependency Relation* (IDR). In the given example, an IDR $a_1 \leftarrow b_1 + b_2 b_3$ implies that the entity a_1 is operational if entity b_1 *or* entity b_2 *and* b_3 are operational. In the IDR each conjunction term e.g. $a_1 a_2$ is referred to as *minterm*. Initial failure of a set of entities would cause the failure to cascade. The failures are assumed to happen at unit time steps denoted by t with the initial failure occurring at $t = 0$. With initial failure of entities b_1 and b_3 at $t = 0$ the entity a_1 would fail at $t = 1$ and b_2 at time step $t = 2$ signifying the cascade of failures. The entities failed after the initial failure are termed as *induced failure*.

Using the IIM model described above we define the Robustness in Interdependent Network (RIDN) problem. The RIDN problem consists of an integer $K \in I^+ \cup \{0\}$ and a real valued parameter $\rho \in \mathbb{R}$ with $0 < \rho \leq 1$. An IDN $\mathcal{I}(A, B, \mathcal{F}(A, B))$ is (K, ρ) robust if a minimum of $K + 1$ entities need to fail initially for a final failure of at least $\rho(|A| + |B|)$ entities. We formally state the optimization version of the RIDN problem as follows —.

The Robustness in Interdependent Network (RIDN) Problem

Instance— *An IDN $\mathcal{I}(A, B, \mathcal{F}(A, B))$, an integer $K \in I^+$ and a real valued parameter $\rho \in \mathbb{R}$ with $0 < \rho \leq 1$.*

Optimization Version— *Find the minimum set of entities S_I which when failed initially causes a final failure of at least $\rho(|A| + |B|)$ entities. The IDN is then referred to as $(|S_I| - 1, \rho)$ robust*

3   Integer Linear Program to the RIDN Problem

We formulate an ILP that for a given parameter $\rho \in (0, 1]$ and an IDN computes the minimum number of entities that need to fail initially for a final failure of $\rho(|A| + |B|)$ entities. Let K' be the solution to the ILP. *Then the IDN is (K, ρ) robust with $K = K' - 1$.* The ILP works with two variables x_{id} and y_{id} for each entity $x_i \in A$ and $y_i \in B$ respectively. The parameter d in the variable denotes the time step. $x_{id} = 1$ (or $y_{id} = 1$) if at time step d the entity x_i (y_i) is in a failed state and 0 otherwise. With these definitions the objective function can be formulated as follows:

$$min \sum_{i=1}^{m} x_{i0} + \sum_{j=1}^{n} y_{j0} \qquad (1)$$

In the above objective function m and n denote the size of the networks A and B respectively. The constraints of the ILP are formally described as follows:

Constraint Set 1: $x_{id} \geq x_{i(d-1)}, \forall d, 1 \leq d \leq t_f$ and $y_{id} \geq y_{i(d-1)}, \forall d, 1 \leq d \leq t_f$, where t_f denotes the final time step. The constraint satisfies the property that if the entity x_i fails at time step d it should remain to be in the failed state for all subsequent time steps [5].

Constraint Set 2: A brief overview of the constraint set to model the failure propagation through cascades is presented here. Consider an IDR of form $a_i \leftarrow b_j + b_k b_l + b_m b_n b_q$. This corresponds to the general case or Case IV as discussed earlier. The constraints created to capture the failure propagation are described in the following steps —

Step 1: We introduce new variables to represent minterms of size greater than one. In this example two new variables c_1 and c_2 are introduced to represent the minterms $b_k b_l$ and $b_m b_n b_q$ respectively. This is equivalent of adding two new IDRs $c_1 \leftarrow b_k b_l$ and $c_2 \leftarrow b_m b_n b_q$ along with the transformed IDR $a_i \leftarrow b_j + c_1 + c_2$.

Step 2: For each IDR corresponding to the c type variables and untransformed IDRs of form Case II we introduce a linear constraint to capture the failure propagation. For an IDR $c_2 \leftarrow b_m b_n b_q$ the constraint is represented as $c_{2d} \leq y_{m(d-1)} + y_{n(d-1)} + y_{q(d-1)}, \forall d, 1 \leq d \leq t_f$.

Step 3: Similarly, for each transformed IDR and untransformed IDRs of form Case III we introduce a linear constraint to capture the failure propagation. For an IDR $a_i \leftarrow b_j + c_1 + c_2$ the constraint is represented as $N \times x_{id} \leq y_{j(d-1)} + c_{1(d-1)} + c_{2(d-1)}, \forall d, 1 \leq d \leq t_f$. Here N is the number of minterms in the IDR (in this example $N = 3$).

Constraint Set 3: We must also ensure that at time step t_f at least $\rho(|A| + |B|)$ entities fail. This can be captured by introducing the constraint $\sum_{i=1}^{m} x_{i(t_f)} + \sum_{j=1}^{n} y_{j(t_f)} \geq \rho(|A| + |B|)$.

So with the objective in (1) and set of constraints the ILP finds the minimum number of entities K' which when failed initially causes at least $\rho(|A| + |B|)$ entities to fail at t_f.

4   Experimental Results

We performed experimental evaluation of the optimal solution of the RIDN problem in this section. Real world data sets were used for the experiments. The communication network data was obtained from GeoTel (www.geo-tel.com). The dataset contains 2,690 cell towers, 7,100 fiber-lit buildings and 42,723 fiber links of Maricopa County, Arizona, USA. The power network data was obtained from Platts (www.platts.com). It contains 70 power plants and 470 transmission lines of the same county. We took three non overlapping regions of the Maricopa county. It is to be noted that the union of the regions does not cover the entire space. The entities of the power and communication network for these three regions were extracted. As per notation, set A and B contain entities of the power and communication network respectively. The number of entities in set A and B are 29 and 19 for Region 1, 29 and 20 for Region 2, and 29 and 19 for Region 3. The regions were represented by an interdependent network $\mathcal{I}(A, B, \mathcal{F}(A, B))$. For these regions $\mathcal{F}(A, B)$ was generated using the IDR construction rule as defined in [5] (Fig. 1).

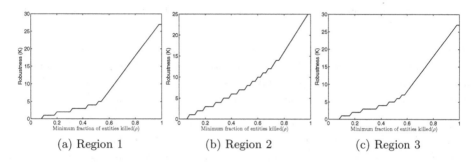

(a) Region 1   (b) Region 2   (c) Region 3

Fig. 1. Robustness parameter K returned by the optimal solution by varying parameter ρ for three regions in Maricopa County, Arizona, USA

IBM CPLEX Optimizer 12.5 is used to get the optimal solution using the ILP. For all the regions the network robustness is less than 10 for $\rho = 0.6$ with a gradual increase for higher ρ values. Hence it can be inferred that for most regions of Maricopa county the IDN is comparatively more vulnerable for lower values of ρ.

References

1. Banerjee, J., Das, A., Sen, A.: A survey of interdependency models for critical infrastructure networks. NATO Sci. Peace Secur. Ser. D Inf. Commun. Secur. **37**, 1–16 (2014)
2. Buldyrev, S.V., Parshani, R., Paul, G., Stanley, H.E., Havlin, S.: Catastrophic cascade of failures in interdependent networks. Nature **464**(7291), 1025–1028 (2010)
3. Parandehgheibi, M., Modiano, E.: Robustness of interdependent networks: The case of communication networks and the power grid (2013). arXiv preprint arXiv:1304.0356
4. Rosato, V., Issacharoff, L., Tiriticco, F., Meloni, S., Porcellinis, S., Setola, R.: Modelling interdependent infrastructures using interacting dynamical models. Int. J. Crit. Infrastruct. **4**(1), 63–79 (2008)
5. Sen, A., Mazumder, A., Banerjee, J., Das, A., Compton, R.: Identification of k most vulnerable nodes in multi-layered network using a new model of interdependency. In: 2014 IEEE Conference on Computer Communications Workshops (INFOCOM WKSHPS), pp. 831–836. IEEE (2014)
6. Zhang, P., Peeta, S., Friesz, T.: Dynamic game theoretic model of multi-layer infrastructure networks. Netw. Spat. Econ. **5**(2), 147–178 (2005)

Strategies to Improve Critical Infrastructures Robustness Against the IEMI Threat: A Review of Relevant Standards and Guidelines on the Topic

Francesca De Simio[1(✉)], Francesca De Cillis[1], Giustino Fumagalli[1],
Maria Carla De Maggio[1], Stefan van de Beek[2], John Dawson[3],
Linda Dawson[3], and Roberto Setola[1]

[1] Complex Systems and Security Lab, Università Campus Bio-Medico di Roma,
Via Álvaro del Portillo 21, 00128 Rome, Italy
{f.desimio,f.decillis,m.demaggio,r.setola}@unicampus.it,
giustinofumagalli@yahoo.it
[2] Telecommunication Engineering Group, University of Twente, 7522 NB Enschede,
The Netherlands
g.s.vandebeek@utwente.nl
[3] Department of Electronics, University of York, Heslington, York YO10 5DD, UK
{john.dawson,l.dawson}@york.ac.uk

Abstract. This paper aims to provide a brief overview of relevant standards, procedures and guidelines to standard bodies to manage the impact of the Intentional ElectroMagnetic Interference (IEMI) threat. It also provides guidelines for CI operators on how to reduce their exposure on IEMI hazards.

Keywords: IEMI · Standards · Guidelines · Critical infrastructures protection

1 Introduction

Attacks by Intentional ElectroMagnetic Interference (IEMI) on Critical Infrastructure (CI) have become a significant threat in recent years due to the availability of suitable interference sources at low cost. Intentional ElectroMagnetic Interference (IEMI), is in general defined as *the intentional malicious generation of electromagnetic energy introducing noise or signals into electrical and electronic systems, thus disrupting, confusing or damaging these systems for terrorist or criminal purposes* [1–3].

Recent years have seen the development of several international and European programs for CI Protection (CIP) such as the STRUCTURES [4] HIPOW [5], and SECRET [6] projects to raise awareness among the community on CIP and to support CI providers in the definition of specific and effective countermeasures for CIP [7,8]. This paper describes work undertaken as part of the FP7

© Springer International Publishing Switzerland 2016
E. Rome et al. (Eds.): CRITIS 2015, LNCS 9578, pp. 251–254, 2016.
DOI: 10.1007/978-3-319-33331-1_22

European project STRUCTURES (Strategies for The impRovement of critical infrastrUCTUre Resilience to Electromagnetic attackS) [9]: Sect. 2 provides a brief overview about the standards in the fields of Business Continuity Management (BCM), Risk Management (RM), Information Technology (IT) Security and Information and Communication Technology (ICT) Security related to IEMI threat. Section 3 presents the most relevant aspects to be taken into account for providing guidelines to CI operators to reduce their exposures on IEMI hazards.

2   IEMI Threats and Standardization: The State of the Art

Table 1 summarises European standards relevant to the protection of CI. As part of complex standards framework, not all relevant documents listed in Table 1 mention to the IEMI threat. In a top-down approach, higher level documents usually refer to standardized management systems (such as IT Security Management Systems - ISO27001 or BCM System - ISO22301) or define generic models to be use in a broad context or are not related to a specific threat. It is our opinion that all documents listed in Table 1 should devote specific sections to the IEMI threat topic.

For completeness we also mention that the International Electrotechnical Comission (IEC) produces a series of standards and technical reports on the effects of electromagnetic interference on electronic systems in the IEC 61000 series such as the IEC61000-1-5 technical report on "High power electromagnetic (HPEM) effects on civil systems" [10].

3   Guidelines for CI Operators

In general, BC and Information Security Management (ISM) usually rely on a cyclical process, which is arranged into several steps as described in Fig. 1. Countermeasures such as physical separation of critical electronics from possible sites for an attack, can be complemented by additional electromagnetic shielding of buildings, equipment and cables depending on the assessment of risk and evaluation of the levels of susceptibility and criticality of each sub-system. Wireless communications and navigation (e.g. GPS) systems which are becoming widely

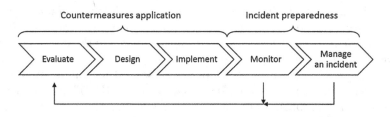

Fig. 1. The BC and ISM cyclical process

Table 1. List of relevant standards to IEMI threat for a CI.

#	Standard	Scope	Impacted by introduction of IEMI threat	Note
1	ISO/IEC 27001:2013	IT Security	×	
2	ISO/IEC 27002:2013	IT Security	√	
3	ISO/IEC 27005:2011	Risk Management	√	
4	ISO/IEC 27011:2008	IT Security	√	Specific for telecommunication
5	ISO/IEC 27019:2013	IT Security	√	Specific for Energy sector
6	ISO/IEC 27031:2011	BC Disaster Recovery	√	
7	ISO/IEC 27033:2011	ICT Security	×	
8	ISO/IEC 27035:2011	BC Disaster Recovery	×	
9	ISO 27799:2008	IT Security	√	Specific for Health sector
10	ISO/IEC 24762:2008	BC Disaster Recovery	×	
11	ISO 31000: 2009	Risk Management	×	
12	ISO/IEC 31010:2009	Risk Management	√	
13	ISO 22301:2012	BC Disaster Recovery	×	
14	ISO 22313:2012	BC Disaster Recovery	×	
15	ISO/PAS 22399:2007	BC Disaster Recovery	×	
16	ITSEC 1.2	ICT security	×	Critical equipments and applications should be certified for security characteristics against IEMI attack through these standards
17	ISO 15408: 1999	ICT security	√	Note: ITSEC has been broadly replaced by Common Criteria
18	ISO 13335-1:2004	ICT Security	×	
19	ISO 13335-4:2000	ICT Security	√	
20	BSI (Bundesamt fur Sicherheit in der Informationstechnik) Standard 100-3	Risk Management	√	DE only
21	TIA-942	IT Security	√	USA standard (ANSI) and Electronic Industries Alliance (private sector)
22	ITU-K81:2009	IT Security	√	Reference document on intentional EM threats protection

used in infrastructure systems are particularly vulnerable to IEMI and difficult to protect due to the low levels of signals at the receiver. Incident preparedness should include some means of detecting an IEMI attack [11], otherwise system failures may be incorrectly blamed on hardware failure or software errors. Detection of an attack also means that prompt action can be taken to detect the source of the attack and manage other aspects of the incident. Savage and Radasky [12,13] provide a more detailed view of the problem and possible solutions.

4 Conclusions

In this short paper we have been able to give only a brief overview of the available standards and guidelines for to improve the robustness of CI. More information and other relevant material can be found on the STRUCTURES project web site [4].

Acknowledgment. The research leading to these results has been implemented in the framework of the Project STRUCTURES co-funded by the European Union Seventh Framework Programme under grant agreement n 285257.

References

1. Sérafin, D.: Critical infrastructures are at risk under electromagnetic attacks. Eur. CIIP Newslett. **9**(i), 1 (2015)
2. The Threat of Radio Frequency Weapons to Critical Infrastructures Facilities, TSWG & DETO Publication, August 2015
3. Parfenov, Y.V., Zdoukhov, L.N., Radasky, W.A., Ianoz, M.: Conducted IEMI threats for commercial buildings. IEEE Trans. Electromagn. Compat. **46**(3), 404–411 (2004)
4. STRUCTURES Strategies for The impRovement of critical infrastrUCTUre Resilience to Electromagnetic attackS. http://www.structures-project.eu/. Accessed 4 May 2015
5. HIPOW Protection of Critical Infrastructure against High Power Microwave Threats. http://www.hipow-project.eu/hipow/. Accessed 8 Sep. 2015
6. SECRET - SECurity of the Railway network against ElectromagneticATtacks. http://www.secret-project.eu/. Accessed 8, Sep. 2015
7. European Commission. http://ec.europa.eu/dgs/home-affairs/what-we-do/policies/crisis-and-terrorism/critical-infrastructure/index_en.htm. Accessed 4 May 2015
8. Flammini, F., Setola, R., Franceschetti, G. (eds.): Effective Surveillance for Homeland Security: Balancing Technology and Social Issues. CRC Press (2013)
9. van de Beek, S., Dawson, J., Flintoft, I., Leferink, F., Mora, N., Rachidi, F., Righero, M.: Overview of the European project STRUCTURES. Electromagn. Compat. Mag. IEEE **3**(4), 70–79 (2014)
10. International Electrotechnical Commission, IEC Technical Report, 61000-1-5, Electromagnetic compatibility (EMC) - Part 1–5: General - High power electromagnetic (HPEM) effects on civil systems, IEC (2004)
11. Dawson, J.F., Flintoft, I.D., Kortoci, P., Dawson, L., Marvin, A.C., Robinson, M.P., Stojilovic, M., Rubinstein, M., Menssen, B., Garbe, H., Hirschi, W., Rouiller, L.: A cost-efficient system for detecting an intentional electromagnetic interference (IEMI) attack. In: 2014 International Symposium on Electromagnetic Compatibility (EMC Europe), pp. 1252–1256 (2014)
12. Savage, E., Radasky, W.: Overview of the threat of IEMI (intentional electromagnetic interference). In: 2012 IEEE International Symposium on Electromagnetic Compatibility (EMC), pp. 317–322, August 2012
13. Radasky, W.: Fear of frying electromagnetic weapons threaten our data networks. Here's how to stop them, Spectrum IEEE **51**(9), 46–51 (2014)

The Challenge of Critical Infrastructure Dependency Modelling and Simulation for Emergency Management and Decision Making by the Civil Security Authorities

Grangeat Amélie[1](✉), Bony Aurélia[2], Lapebie Emmanuel[1],
Eid Mohamed[3], and Dusserre Gilles[2]

[1] CEA, DAM, GRAMAT, 46500 Gramat, France
{amelie.grangeat,emmanuel.lapebie}@cea.fr
[2] Laboratoire de Génie de l'Environnement Industriel et des Risques,
Ecole Nationale Supérieure des Mines d'Alès, 30100 Alès, France
{aurelia.bony-dandrieux,gilles.dusserre}@mines-ales.fr
[3] DANS/DM2S/SERMA, CEA Saclay, 91191 Gif-sur-Yvette Cedex, France
mohamed.eid@cea.fr

Abstract. Large Geographically-distributed and Hardware-based Networks (GHN) act as lifeline systems in providing energy, transportation, telecommunication, drinking water supply and sewage water treatment in any society. From the Civil Security (CS) point of view, it may also be a vector of failure propagation (cascade effects). Numerous disasters highlight the fact that GHN's service disruption extends the crisis duration (their restoration takes time) and the geographical area of the impacts because of dependencies between GHN. Several tools have been created to simulate dependencies between GHN. This article is a short illustrative catalog for CS Managers, providing various solutions, for modelling and simulating dependencies for/between different critical infrastructures.

Keywords: Critical infrastructure · Dependencies · Crisis management · Emergency action plan · Civil security · Decision support systems

1 Introduction

Societies' functioning relies on flows of goods and services between Critical Infrastructures (CI) through Geographically-distributed and Hardware-based Networks (GHN). Emergency Action Plans (EAP) - prepared by the Civil Security (CS) for mitigating the effects of a crisis- are based on the comprehension of the concerned territory and on the crisis stakeholders' interactions. Knowing each EAP, the CS Manager (CSM) has to coordinate the actions prescribed. However, the disruption of a GHN during a crisis complicates the realization of the EAP and extends the crisis impacts in duration and location. For helping the CSM to guarantee the coherence between EAP and to assess consequences of GHN failures on society during crisis, several tools have been created that simulate dependencies between GHN. This work presents some Decision Support

© Springer International Publishing Switzerland 2016
E. Rome et al. (Eds.): CRITIS 2015, LNCS 9578, pp. 255–258, 2016.
DOI: 10.1007/978-3-319-33331-1_23

Systems (DSS) already applied on a real territory at least equal to a city and lists models included in these tools. It is an illustrative catalog that aims proving for CSMs that off-the-shelf solutions already exist.

2   Tools Already Using Real Data that Deal with GHN Dependencies

GHN dependencies analyses aim at identifying the emergent behavior of a complex system under a disruption. Several research teams manage to deal with real data, at least at a city scale, with precision at the infrastructure granularity, using tools presented in Table 1. The studied criteria for the DSS are: 1. Coupling with threat simulators or models (flood scenarios, seismic simulation) 2. Models: ABM (Agent-Based Model), DS: Dynamic System, IIM (Input-output Inoperability Model), RDBM (Relational Data Based Model), FS (Federated Simulators) 3. Help for the decision making: presence of strategies assessment or optimization algorithm for the response. "Y" means Yes, "N" means No. Authors refer to the work of Ouyang [9] or Yusta [15] for comparing advantages of modelling techniques. Each tool is coupled with a Geographical Information System. Each one is shortly described by the model used, the critical sectors of activities modelled and the application context of the tools.

Table 1. Summary of tools' particularities

Criteria tools	Threat models' coupling	Models	Strategies assessment	References
CIPMA	Y	DS	Y	[7, 10, 12]
CISIA	Y	IIM for inter-domains links, FS for intra-domain dependencies	N	[2, 6]
DIESIS	Y	FS	N	[5, 13]
DOMINO	N	RDBM	N	[3, 11]
I2SIM	Y	IIM extended + FS	Y	[8, 14]

CI Program for Modelling and Analysis (CIPMA) is a public private approach in Australia that aims at: Identifying and evaluating the CI risks, Advising on investment prioritization and Evaluating mitigation strategies or business continuity plans. It covers communication, energy, water and transport sectors. It has been used to study large scale scenarios like a cyclone event in Queensland, a gas supply disruption on the North West Shelf or a submarine cable disruption [1, 7, 10, 12].

CISIA, CI Simulation by Interdependent Agents is an Italian platform that manages heterogeneous level: Each GHN is a macro-element characterized by its operative level (ability to perform its job), its operational requirements and its failure modes (level of failure) and its inter-domain links. Behind each GHN, a specific simulator runs according to the internal dynamic of a set of interconnected specific components of the GHN and reports results to the macro-level. CISIA models uncertainty thanks to the use of fuzzy numbers. It has been applied to simulate the effect of a solar wind on the CI of a Rome area. Sectors covered were: power distribution grid, telecommunication network, transportation network, railroads and airports [2, 6].

DIESIS is the tool of the European project "Design of an Interoperable European federated Simulation network for critical InfraStructures". It is a federated simulation tool, which couples laterally four specific sectorial simulators: power transmission, telecommunication network, railway and flooding simulator. It aims at providing real-time training and operational support through "what-if" analysis. It has been applied on a district of Rome [5, 13].

DOMINO is a secured web-based DSS implemented in the Montreal (Canada) civil security services. Each CI manager fulfills himself and updates questionnaires on his structure autonomy in case of lack of resources and on their alternative resources. CIs are black boxes and CI operators are motivated by the idea of assuring their business continuity in case of events through a kind of early warning system. Based on this updated database, DOMINO provides potential cascading effects in a temporal and spatial manner for training scenarios [3, 11].

Infrastructure Interdependency Simulator (I2Sim, Canada) includes engineering and human systems in the same mathematical framework, resulting in nonlinear relationships. I2Sim is based on four types of objects: tokens (resources exchanged like ambulances), cells (production or storage; a hospital is a cell!), channels (that carry the tokens) and control units for distributing resources. Cells are evaluated through "physical damages" and the state of their available resources (for instance operability of doctors in hospital will decrease with their fatigue if mobilized a too long time). I2Sim can calculate the best allocation of available resources as a function of the given objective. It is coupled with a seismic simulation model, a power and a telecommunications system simulator. I2Sim has been applied several times, especially for emergency action planning during the Olympic Games of Vancouver in 2010 [8, 14]. It is currently used in the CIPRNet tool for the impacts assessment phase [4].

3 Conclusion

Geographically-distributed and Hardware-based Networks are lifeline systems. However, they may also be vectors of failure propagation during a crisis. Civil Security Managers are often aware of the utility of decision support systems in critical infrastructure dependency analyses. Nevertheless, it is not easy to define the approach the most suitable to their needs. This article presents a short list of existing tools, their models and their applications. It could help CSM to grasp the diversity of the solutions. Other approaches are currently under development and will increase our capabilities in CI dependencies analyses. The authors think for instance in CIPRNet (Project Number: 312450) and PREDICT (Project Number: 607697) projects.

Acknowledgements. The work presented in this paper has been partially funded by the CIPRNet and the PREDICT European projects. The French project DEMOCRITE helps the authors to understand the operational needs of CSM.

References

1. Australian Government, Attorney-General's Department: CIPMA: Critical Infrastructure Program for Modelling and Analysis, 20 April 2015. http://www.ag.gov.au/NationalSecurity/InfrastructureResilience/Pages/CriticalInfrastructureProgramforModellingandAnalysisCIPMA.aspx
2. Casalicchio, E., Setola, R., Bologna, S.: A two-stage approach to simulate interdependent critical infrastructures. In: Complexity in Engineering, COMPENG 2010, pp. 76–78 (2010)
3. CENTRE RISQUE & PERFORMANCE, École Polytechnique de Montréal: Un nouveau projet pour le CRP en lien avec le développement et le transfert technologique de l'outil Domino, Actualités, 7 May 2015. www.polymtl.ca/crp/nouvelle/index.php#nouv2
4. EU FP7 Project CIPRNet, Di Pietro A., La Porta L., Lavalle, L., Pollino M., Rosato V., Tofani A.: D7.4 Implementation of the DSS with consequence analysis, p. 50. Version 1, Submitted the 30 June 2015
5. EU FP7 Project DIESIS, RI212830 - Final Report: Design of an Interoperable European federated Simulation network for critical InfraStructures. Version 3, p. 23 (2010)
6. Gaetano, F., Oliva, G., Panzieri, S., Romani, C., Setola, R.: Analysis of severe space weather on critical infrastructures. In: Luiijf, E., Hartel, P. (eds.) CRITIS 2013. LNCS, vol. 8328, pp. 62–73. Springer, Heidelberg (2013)
7. Lew, H.: CIPMA: Critical Infrastructure Protection Modelling and Analysis, Australian Government, Attorney-General's Department National Critical Infrastructure Capability Branch National Security Capability Development Division, 1 September 2011. PowerPoint Presentation
8. Marti, J.: Hybrid Engineering/Phenomenological Approach to Simulate a System of Systems. Modelling, Simulation and Analysis of Critical Infrastructures Master Class, edn. 1, UIC Headquarters – Paris, France, 24–25 April 2014. PowerPoint Presentation
9. Ouyang, M.: Review on modeling and simulation of interdependent critical infrastructure systems. Reliab. Eng. Syst. Saf. **121**, 43–60 (2014)
10. Pederson, P., Dudenhoeffer, D., Hartley, S., Permann, M.: Critical Infrastructure Interdependency Modeling: A Survey of U.S. and International Research. Idaho National Laboratory, p. 116 (2006)
11. Robert, B., Morabito, L., Debernard, C.: Simulation and anticipation of domino effects among critical infrastructures. Int. J. Crit. Infrastruct. **9**(4), 275–303 (2013)
12. Rothery, M.: Barriers to Effective Climate Change Adaptation. Productivity Commission Issues Paper. Submission by Attorney-General's Department, 11/28763, December 2011
13. Usov, A.: Modelling and Simulation Techniques for Critical Infrastructure Protection. Modelling, Simulation and Analysis of Critical Infrastructures Master Class, edn. 1, UIC Headquarters – Paris, France, 24–25 April 2014
14. Wang, J.: Vulnerability and Risk Analysis of the Guadeloupe Island for Disaster Scenario using the Modified I2SIM Toolbox, The University of British Columbia, p. 91 (2013)
15. Yusta, J., Correa, G., Lacal-Arantegui, R.: Methodologies and applications for critical infrastructure protection: state-of-the-art. Energy Policy **39**, 19 (2011)

A Mean Field Model of Coupled Cascades in Flow Networks

Antonio Scala[1,2,3(✉)], Stefano Sebastio[1], Pier Giorgio De Sanctis Lucentini[4], and Gregorio D'Agostino[1,5]

[1] London Institute of Mathematical Sciences,
22 South Audley St Mayfair, London W1K 2NY, UK
stefano.sebastio@alumni.imtlucca.it
[2] ISC-CNR Physics Department, University "La Sapienza",
Piazzale Moro 5, 00185 Roma, Italy
antonio.scala@phys.uniroma1.it
[3] IMT Alti Studi Lucca, Piazza S. Ponziano 6, 55100 Lucca, Italy
[4] Gubkin Russian State University of Oil and Gas,
65, Leninsky Prospekt, Moskow, Russia
desanctislucentini.pg@gubkin.ru
[5] ENEA: Italian National Agency for New Technologies,
Energy and Sustainable Economic Development, Rome, Italy
gregorio.dagostino@enea.it

Abstract. We introduce an analytical model of cascading behavior of interdependent networks under stressing conditions and find evidence of abrupt breakdown phenomena. Our results indicate that coupling several infrastructures can diminish the impact of small cascades at the cost of increasing system wide ones. As a consequence, the enhancement of the systemic risk failures with increasing network size, represents an effect to be accounted while planning projects aiming to integrate national networks into "super-networks".

Keywords: Mean field theory · Interdependent networks · Cascading failures · Interacting networks

1 Introduction

Cascading failures are characterized by the propagation and amplification of a small number of initial failures that, due to non-linearity of the system, assume system-wide magnitudes. In particular, since most infrastructures can be considered to be aggregations of a large number of simple units, we must take into account the possibility that most networked infrastructure can exhibit emergent behavior, i.e. they show as a whole additional complexity beyond what is dictated by the simple sum of its parts [1].

We introduce a model of interacting network inspired by the possible configuration for future power systems where network nodes are the so-called energy

© Springer International Publishing Switzerland 2016
E. Rome et al. (Eds.): CRITIS 2015, LNCS 9578, pp. 259–263, 2016.
DOI: 10.1007/978-3-319-33331-1_24

hubs [4], i.e. points where several energy vectors[1] converge and where energy demand/supply can be satisfied converting one kind of energy into another. Hubs condition, transform and deliver energy in order to cover consumer needs [3]; in this configuration, it would be possible to mitigate the stress on the network of an energy vector by using other energy vectors.

In Sect. 2, we develop our simplified model of overload cascades in isolated and coupled systems, first by introducing the mean field model for the cascade failures and then extending it to the case of several interacting systems. Finally, in Sect. 3 we discuss and summarize our results.

2   Model

We consider network where a single commodity (typically an energy source) is distributed as a flow. To understand the qualitative behavior of such networks we resort to a mean field model where one assumes that when a link fails, its flow is re-distributed equally among all other links. Subsequently, the lines above their threshold capacity would fail again, their flow would be re-distributed (acting like a *stress* on the other lines) and so on, up to convergence. Such model resembles the democratic fiber-bundle model [2,7] and has been introduced to describe electric power cascades in [6] and studied in more details in [8,11]. Such mean field model can be reduced to a single equation by considering a situation where the system is composed by a large number M of elements with capacity c described by a probability function $p(c)$. Let L be the overall load of the system, f^t the fraction of links survived at the tth stage of a cascade and $l^t = L/Mf^t$ the flow per link; then the system is described by the equation:

$$f^{t+1} = P\left(\frac{l}{1 - f^t}\right)$$ (1)

where $P(x)$ is the cumulative distribution function associated with $p(c)$. The fix-point $f^* = P\left(\frac{l}{1-f^*}\right)$ represents the total fraction of links broken by the failure cascade upon reaching equilibrium [6]. The behavior of f^* depends on the functional form of $p(c)$ and is known to present a first order transition for a wide family of curves [9].

We can extend the model described by Eq. (1) by considering several coupled systems that transport substitutable commodities: as an example, take the networks corresponding to the several energy vectors connected at the energy hubs [4].

Consider now n coupled systems assuming that when a system a is subject to some failures, it sheds a fraction $T_{a \to b}$ of such failures on system b, i.e. it increases the load of system b by $l_a f_a T_{a \to b}$ and decreases loads in a by the same quantity. Then Eq.(1) becomes a set of n equations

$$f_a^{t+1} = \pi_a\left(\frac{\tilde{l}_a^t}{1 - f_a^t}\right)$$ (2)

---

[1] Man-made forms of energy that enable energy to be carried and can then be converted back into any other form of energy.

where the system coupling is reflected in the fact that

$$\tilde{l}_a^t = l_a(1 - f_a^t \sum_b T_{a \to b}) + \sum_b T_{b \to a} \, l_b \, f_b^t = l_a + \sum_b \mathcal{L}_{ab} \, l_b \, f_b^t \qquad (3)$$

where $\mathcal{L}_{ab}$ has the form of a Laplacian operator:

$$\mathcal{L}_{ab} = (1 - \delta_{ab})T_{b \to a} + \delta_{ab} \sum_b T_{a \to b} \qquad (4)$$

We solve Eq. (3) by finding the fix-point via Newton-Raphson iterations; in particular, we consider for simplicity the case of two coupled systems.

In Fig. 1 we show the phase diagram in the symmetric case of two systems with same parameters: according to the initial loads, we can distinguish three separate cascade regimes: B_1 and B_2, where either system 1 or 2 has failed, and B_{12} where both systems have failed. We notice that, by increasing the coupling among the systems, both the area where the two systems are safe and the area where they are together in a failed state grow.

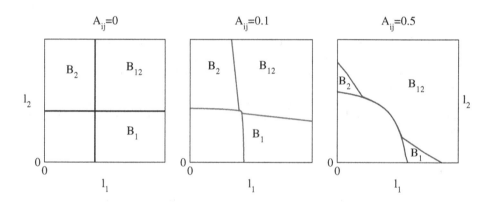

Fig. 1. Phase diagrams of two identical coupled systems with symmetric interactions $(A_{1 \to 2} = A_{2 \to 1})$. The plane of initial loads l_1 and l_2 is separated in different regions by the transition lines. The labels B_i mark the areas where only system i suffers systemic cascades; label B_{12} marks the area where both system suffer system wide cascades. The unlabeled area near the origin is the region where no systemic cascades occur. The leftmost case $(A_{ij} = 0)$ corresponds to two uncoupled systems: thus, each system suffers systemic failure at $l_i > l^C$ (where l^C is the critical load for an isolated system); both systems are failed in the B_{12} area corresponding to the quadrant $(l_1 > l^C, l_2 > l^C)$. We notice that when couplings are introduced, each system is able to discharge stress on the other one and the area where both systems are safe increases. On the other hand, the area B_{12} where *both* systems are failed increases.

3   Discussion

We have discussed the mapping of one possible mechanism of failures (i.e. over-load of link capacity) to a simplified model of mean-field failures for networks distributing a commodity under the form of a flow. We have then extended such mean-field model to the case of several interacting networks. By analyzing the case of two coupled systems and by varying the strength of the interactions among them, we have shown that, while there is a beneficial effect at low stresses since some of the loads are shed to the other systems, there is an increase of the probability that when a system fail it will more likely cause the failure of all the other systems.

It is worth noting that while fault propagation models do predict a general lowering of the threshold for coupled systems [10], in the present model a beneficial effect due to the existence of the interdependent networks is observed for small enough overloads, while the expected cascading effects take place only for large initial disturbances. This picture is consistent with the observed phenomena for interdependent Electric Systems. Moreover the existence of interlinks among different networks may increase their synchronization capabilities [5].

Acknowledgements. AS, SB and GD acknowledge the support from EU HOME/2013/CIPS/AG/4000005013 project CI2C. AS acknowledges the support from CNR-PNR National Project Crisis-Lab, EU FET project DOLFINS nr 640772 and EU FET project MULTIPLEX nr.317532. GD acknowledges the support from FP7 project n.261788 AFTER.

Any opinion, findings and conclusions or recommendations expressed in this material are those of the author(s) and do not necessary reflect the views of the funding parties.

References

1. Anderson, P.W.: More is different. Science **177**(4047), 393–396 (1972). http://www.sciencemag.org/content/177/4047/393.short
2. Daniels, H.E.: The statistical theory of the strength of bundles of threads. I. In: Proceedings of the Royal Society of London. Series A. Mathematical and Physical Sciences, vol. 183, no. 995, pp. 405–435 (1945)
3. Favre-Perrod, P.: A vision of future energy networks. In: Power Engineering Society Inaugural Conference and Exposition in Africa, pp. 13–17. IEEE July 2005
4. Geidl, M., Koeppel, G., Favre-Perrod, P., Klockl, B., Andersson, G., Frohlich, K.: Energy hubs for the future. IEEE Power Energ. Mag. **5**(1), 24–30 (2007)
5. Martin-Hernandez, J., Wang, H., Mieghem, P.V., D'Agostino, G.: Algebraic connectivity of interdependent networks. Physica A: Stat. Mech. Appl. **404**, 92–105 (2014). http://www.sciencedirect.com/science/article/pii/S0378437114001526
6. Pahwa, S., Scoglio, C., Scala, A.: Abruptness of cascade failures in power grids. Sci. Rep., vol. 4, January 2014. http://dx.doi.org/10.1038/srep03694
7. Peirce, F.: Tensile tests for cotton yarns, part "v": the weakest link theorems on strength of long and composite specimens. J. Text. Inst. **17**, T355–T368 (1926)

8. Scala, A., De Sanctis Lucentini, P.G.: The equal load-sharing model of cascade failures in power grids. ArXiv e-prints, June 2015
9. da Silveira, R.: Comment on "tricritical behavior in rupture induced by disorder". Phys. Rev. Lett. **80**, 3157–3157 (1998)
10. Wang, H., Li, Q., D'Agostino, G., Havlin, S., Stanley, H.E., Van Mieghem, P.: Effect of the interconnected network structure on the epidemic threshold. Phys. Rev. E **88**, 022801 (2013). http://link.aps.org/doi/10.1103/PhysRevE.88.022801
11. Yagan, O.: Robustness of power systems under a democratic-fiber-bundle-like model. Phys. Rev. E **91**, 062811 (2015). http://link.aps.org/doi/10.1103/PhysRevE.91.062811

Author Index

Printed in the United States
By Bookmasters